MUSIC HO!

All: The music ho!
                  [*Enter Mardian the Eunuch*
Cleopatra: Let it alone; let's to billiards.
                        WILLIAM SHAKESPEARE

CONSTANT LAMBERT

MUSIC HO!

A Study of Music in Decline

by

CONSTANT LAMBERT

With an introduction by
ARTHUR HUTCHINGS

OCTOBER HOUSE INC.
NEW YORK

First published in the United States of America, 1967 by
October House Inc.
134 East 22nd Street
New York, N.Y. 10010

Copyright © Introduction by Arthur Hutchings 1966
All rights reserved
Library of Congress catalogue card no. 67-10606
Manufactured in Great Britain

TO
MY MOTHER

MY MOTHER

CONTENTS

7

Contents

INTRODUCTION

Lambert was not the man to don a seer's mantle except in mockery, yet many of us who were his contemporaries, now wise after events since his death, are less surprised that we often disagree with verdicts in *Music Ho!* than that the passage of thirty years has turned many of our own verdicts towards reluctant concurrence with Lambert's. This experience is remarkable because thirty years measures approximately the full growth of those reactions of taste in artistic expression and style which affect the least sheepish, least vogue-following of listeners.

By 1934 a taste for Hindemith and Stravinsky was belatedly ascendant in London, and so was a more rapidly ascendant and sooner exhausted taste for Sibelius. Most British listeners were thus ill equipped to weigh comments upon non-British music made by a British musician who, like Burney, had minimized in himself the proverbial time-lag between continental and insular connoisseurship. Lambert's first readers included many who were annoyed by his unmaliciously limited admiration for the English 'nationalist' school, then at its zenith of popularity. Most of them knew so little continental music that they swallowed much nonsense about it from writers who knew only a little more than they. I recall angry doubts of Lambert's assertion that 'Nothing approaching a folk song' was found in Sibelius's symphonies, which were 'not Finnish symphonies but symphonies by a Finn'; the sting lay in an implied

9

comparison with English symphonists in some contiguous phrases about 'that particular form of provinciality that has degraded nationalism to the level of the exotic' with the 'essential falsehood of assuming a dialect'. Lambert wrote more harshly of Hindemith, Stravinsky, Schönberg and the French composers (by whom he was plainly influenced and fascinated) than he did of his countrymen.

He did not rile us by disparagement of any man's artistic competence but by an obviously sincere belief that, with a few exceptions such as Debussy, Bartók, Sibelius and certain minor composers, most twentieth-century composers perpetrated artistic falsehoods—not because individually they were cheats (he did not scourge avowedly commercial musicians) but because they could not represent their potential twentieth-century listeners without reflecting the false values of twentieth-century society. At heart a Spenglerian, Lambert saw no difference between the falsehood of English or Scots servicemen singing songs of cockney provenance with a Texan pronunciation or a Negro crooner's mannerisms and the falsehood of 'an empty and wilful pastiche' of old music, or 'an equally fruitless concentration on the purely mechanical and objective sides of their arts'. Of course, such words as 'empty' and 'fruitless' may be challenged, along with whole passages of tendentious writing, e.g. 'Since the Shropshire Lad himself published his last poems some ten years ago it may without impertinence be suggested that it is high time his musical followers published their last songs.' 'To be honest' the artist must accept 'a work like Eliot's *Waste Land* as symbolizing the essentially negative and bleak spirit of post-war intellectual England'. (Alas! since Lambert's time only too many artists accept no other kind of symbol; but the fact does not negate the trenchancy of Lambert's survey of his times.)

Has there been since *Music Ho!* a single piece of musico-

graphy in our language which offers so many statements or questions worth discussion by people for whom the craft of music is fascinating yet its vividness as human expression more fascinating? Does the passage that follows readily suggest the authorship of a hard-driven conductor and composer, writing in 1934 for publication the following year?—
'One does not so much bemoan the passing of picturesque old London as deplore the absence of anything stimulating in the newly built London. One would not mind the Dickens streets disappearing to give way to the Babylonian beauty of the New York skyscrapers, but one does object to their giving way to such appalling examples of modern degeneracy as ... Regent Street.' And how many less trenchant minds have dwelt at great length upon the observations made, without any feeling of compression, in the following:

'The more intelligent composer is forced in on himself and made to overconcentrate on his own musical personality.' [We shall see that Lambert was ready to apply this and other strictures to other artists than musicians.] 'The premature senility of so many modern composers can mainly be ascribed to this concentration on purely personal mannerisms. Most of the great figures of the past have been content to leave their personal imprint on the *materia musica* of their day without remodelling it entirely. It is only the minor figure whose every bar is recognizable, just as it is only the minor painter, like Marie Laurencin, whose handiwork can be detected at a hundred yards. ... What we require from the composer is neither a contemplation of his own navel, nor a frenzied dashing about in sports cars, but an expression of musical personality free from deliberate pastiche—which is escape— or from mechanical revolution—which is submission. The composers ... who ... represent this spiritual freedom rarely, if ever, form a school and are not usually the most outwardly advanced in style. They are free from the vulgarity of the

Introduction

label, above all the official "revolutionary" label, with which so great a figure as Schönberg has unfortunately been associated.'

Surely that is thought worth opposition or examination. It is expressed a little aggressively, and Lambert's was an aggressive personality even among friends. He was readily companionable but he disliked that deceit which one may call commercial mateyness, by which a broadcaster unnecessarily using first names or nicknames claims familiarity with his interlocutor. I heard Lambert interpolate suddenly: 'Don't do that!' when Cecil Gray, who was among his closest friends, took him by the coat-lapel. When asked: 'Why so sensitive?' his reply included 'false'—the only thoroughly damning word he applied to music and the arts. It was not that his pride was offended, that the gesture presumed what he did not concede or was a sign of patronage and 'one-upmanship', but that it was false.

And it would be false to pretend that Lambert's conviviality and brilliant conversation came from a genial nature. When he was musing and thought himself unobserved the chin was still upturned, as when addressing one; the mouth was still scornful and the eyes unblinking as if held by a distant event, and their sudden focus when one took his attention could be disarming, despite the immediate change from pout to smile. His walk was resolute, but as ungainly as that of an older man defying the onset of sclerosis. I do not know whether this malady, or some malformation or injury, caused the backward thrust of his head and his somewhat Churchillian carriage, but these traits were not noticeable on that first occasion of my seeing him. When I went towards him his stare was so piercing and his movement away so swift that I forbore to address him without introduction. (I must unfortunately write about myself in order to illuminate the personality of Lambert.)

Introduction

My motives in seeking his acquaintance were neither snobbish nor self-advancing. Young English musicians in the 1920's and early 1930's, lacking a 'Third' or 'Music' programme and recordings of *avant-garde* music, had almost no chance of hearing any. It would be unforgiveable to minimize the enterprise shown by Henry Wood before and after (which is more remarkable!) receiving his knighthood; as far as I know there is no other English conductor who can claim his distinction of performing Schönberg's Op. 16, *Five Orchestral Pieces*, actually before the first war. Wood was the conductor most willing to let the younger musicians hear music of their own century, but programmes of the Promenade Concerts for the years following the first war reveal little that was strikingly contemporary, let alone *avant-garde*. Yet Wood did at least help the young *British* performer, composer or conductor, and he set aside each Thursday night for a 'British Composers' Concert'.

It is easy to be understood by the young of today as I relate how my young companions deserted the promenade for the coffee bar during a Rachmaninoff concerto or Elgar symphony, and gave rapt attention to any trifle by Berners, Milhaud or Stravinsky; it is less easy to be understood for suddenly regarding Lambert as the champion of their generation, since as a composer he is now remembered by only a few works—*The Rio Grande*, *Aubade héroique* and some of the music from *Horoscope*. Those who had known him at Christ's Hospital (the school magazines show that he was formidable in debate) or at the R.C.M. already respected him as a leader; the rest of us did so because we associated Diaghilev with talent-spotting and enterprise—chiefly because of his patronage and indulgence of Stravinsky and his French camp-followers—and the first Englishman from whom Diaghilev commissioned a work was this twenty-year-old R.C.M. student. Lambert's father was an A.R.A. and his brother a sculptor; through them he knew the painter Dulac who introduced him to Diaghilev. His fulfilment of this commission exploited the time-honoured situation of a rehearsal but, being a ballet, it was set in a dancing school, and finished in twentyish fashion with an elopement by aeroplane. Lambert's jazzed baroqueries are precisely the kind of music which he savagely called sterile in *Music Ho!* Early in 1927 his *Pomona* (produced in Buenos Aires) shed the silly mannerisms of the previous work in a pastoral but athletic score containing well-spun textures and stretches of melody that showed English authorship.

The prospectus of the Promenade Concerts for that year mentioned few first London performances and few new works that were specially attractive to those of us who hoped for music by composers aged less than forty. We fondly thought ourselves anti-romantic, though in fact we were victims of that decadence which romanticises a cultural mirage, 'classicism' or 'a classical revival'. Though none of us had heard *Pomona* we looked forward to one particular Thursday night because the very title of a new Lambert work was thrilling; it was no tone-poem, overture or genre piece, nothing intended to convey the atmosphere of a legend or place; it was simply *Music for Orchestra*. We should probably have received it with pointed applause even if it had been frivolous and unsubstantial. I myself could hardly refrain from applauding the opening stretch of 'clean' unharmonized non-vibrato melody. Although I still think the piece to be worth more frequent airing, the chief effect of the occasion was to show Lambert as a first-rate conductor.

On that evening I first spoke to him. I merely congratulated him on *Music for Orchestra* and was thanked. A few months later, when he had taken a flat in Ridinghouse Street, between the Queen's Hall and All Souls, Langham

Place, I met him in the pub still called 'The Glue Pot' by employees and artists from the nearby BBC building, few of whom may know who first gave *The George* this unofficial name. It was Sir Henry Wood—'I call it "The Glue Pot". You bandsmen go in there and get stuck there!' I waited to push into the conversation and found opportunity when Cecil Gray had finished dilating on Berlioz. I retailed the trite information that Berlioz achieved melody without the conventional two-bar or four-bar punctuation. Lambert turned to face me: 'Any fool can write an odd-bar phrase. You simply let a four-bar one dither to a late death instead of finishing it honestly as you conceived it'. I was too inexperienced in verbal punching to retort: 'Any fool can *write* a melody. All he needs is a stave and a pencil'. Instead I played the role of gratuitous teacher, mentioning admirable melodies by Berlioz but, patronizing and encouraging the unenlightened, confessing that certain Berlioz pieces which Gray admired left me cold, and I could not say why. This elicited from Lambert: 'Because, my dear sir, you have an essentially vulgar mind.' Despite this second punch my guardian angel prompted me to say: 'Don't bully me: I hadn't finished,' and I was rewarded with a smile and 'I'm sorry. Please go on.' Nobody present could have supposed this to be merely a polite apology or willingness to tolerate a bore for a few minutes longer. Nor do I flatter myself that it was a deliberate compliment. It was the spontaneous revelation of such generosity and friendliness as is not sleeve-worn by creatures as urbane as Lambert.

Others can testify better than I can to this saving grace in a pessimist whose value and duty included consistent verbal pugilism—on committees, in articles, and with entrenched conservatism at the R.C.M., the B.B.C., Sadler's Wells or wherever he secured an ear. I did not enjoy his company on more than five occasions for I was not allowed to return from

Bengal immediately the war was over. It was pleasant to find him still friendly when we did happen to meet. We became aggressively opposed in argument because we were diametrically opposed in temperament. The literary heroes of my adolescence were Richard Jefferies, W. H. Hudson, Ernest Thompson Seton, Wordsworth of the *Prelude* and *Excursion* and Thomas Hardy. In due course I was told: 'My dear sir, you are essentially naïve', and was unkind enough to ask irritably the difference between his habit of saying 'My dear sir' and the buttonholing habit which he had so swiftly rebuked. Once more the unexpected humility: 'None. I'm sorry. It becomes a mechanical defence during the bloodiest days of one's life. Are there any viler affectations than those of schoolboys from about fourteen to sixteen?' But he continued with the frequent 'My dear sir' and his readers will notice 'essentially' as a mannerism.

'But, my dear sir, there is all the difference in the world between Fauré or Ravel wilfully indulging in sentiment and a German making a religion of it and regarding it as essential to what he calls profundity. The Frenchman says: "Now we'll enjoy a little slop"—and that hurts your Anglo-Saxon feelings. You love slop as much as I do, but you are ashamed to recognize it for what it is—inessential. You are musical enough to see that Fauré does his slop more subtly than Strauss, but the deliberate indulgence hits your belief in it . . . no, don't answer until I remind you of the last time we met here. On that occasion you told Bernard Stevens that you got no kick out of High Mass at some church or other in Paris because they went through the ceremonial and the music "as a formality"—those were your words. If you are religious it is your Protestantism, or if you aren't perhaps it's your British Way of Life that prevents understanding a faith which needs no exhibition of fervour.' One enjoyed scorn from lips that were quick to defend what others scorned, even when one was the victim and when the scorn was so fiercely pronounced that it seemed no longer playful. The old gramophone records of the Sitwell-Walton *Façade* in which Lambert is the speaker (surely they should be reissued on L.P.) recapture the splendid tones of his scorn. His speech seemed innocent of conscious grooming and, though slightly less 'fruity', it was quite as rich as Dylan Thomas's. I imitated some of his *Façade* recitations in his presence. I collapsed incompetently during the prestissimo of 'Thetis wrote a treatise' etc. and declared, still imitating, that I failed 'Because, my dear sir, I have an essentially vulgar mind'. At least that made *him* blush, but he brilliantly forestalled further blows by 'No parody can be less vulgar than the original!' The company was delighted; before Lambert's arrival we had all been practising his perfect pronunciation of 'vulgar'.

Only once did I enjoy his conversation without other company. We became sentimental about the past. From my own boyhood I seemed to remember only the splendours and few of the miseries. Lambert asked what music first gave me the irretrievable thrill denied when shades of the prison-house begin to close. As a boy soloist I received much physical thrill from 'Let the bright seraphim' and the finale of Bach's *Jauchzet Gott* cantata, but I had to confess that the music I first wished I could claim to have composed was called 'Lucy Moore'—or so I thought when I heard it as a violin solo at Ilfracombe and tried to order it from the local music shop. I later recognized it as an arrangement of Elgar's *Salut d'amour;* it was ousted in my experience by Chopin's *Marche funèbre*, played after Sunday church service, as was then the custom, to mark some notable person's demise. Lambert said nothing except: 'Many first compositions are attempts at dirges or funeral marches', until I defended my hankering love of some of the Victorian popular music, played and sung at our family reunions, and some of the hymn tunes we sang in church. Quite unexpectedly Lambert waxed enthusiastic about Dr. Dykes's harmonies. Then and there he played a tune from 'A. and M.' which I did *not* happen to know. 'But you should, my dear sir; go and look at it. No. 204—*O quickly come!*' I forget what part of what French ballet or opera he cited as using similar progressions, but I know that I found myself high in Lambert's favour for praising *Faust* and being able to sing one or two of Gounod's songs.

After my return from war service I often saw Lambert from an auditorium but only once again spoke to him. He looked ill, prematurely old and puffy, and he was somewhat cantankerous. I admired each of Rubbra's later symphonies and wished they were more often played. 'Oh don't worry about Rubbra. He has nothing to grouse about. He's quite sure of himself. Weren't you fond of Brahms, too?' 'I don't see why that should make me like Rubbra's stuff.' 'I didn't say it should.' 'I still do like most of Brahms, especially the chamber music, now that everybody raves only about his songs.' 'I haven't met everybody so I hadn't noticed the trend. As for the quartets and things, I like most of the tunes and tolerate the conscientious development between them.' 'Oh, I like that too; Brahms gives you value for your money.' 'For *your* money, my dear sir, and good luck to you. At least you know what you like. I get wild with the student-herds of today who only know what are supposed to be the right things to like. They now have the impudence to talk of our generation as "the silly twenties". My God! We did at least believe in what we wanted . . . and we called for it till we got it.' The rest of his conversation was a threnody for the political and social condition of almost every western nation, the 'sterility' of its artists, the persistent philistinism of educators who supposed themselves the apostles of aesthetic enlightenment. In America and England we had belatedly followed Germany in taking the history of music seriously, and the prelude to adult education in the fine arts was 'appreciation' in the schools. The word made him savagely bitter. Music and the arts in universities, colleges and schools seemed chiefly to produce a limited connoisseurship of what was correct to admire. I recall his unexpectedly harsh remarks on Corbusier's flats in Marseilles. He did not blame people for being unwilling to live in this much-photographed block of cement.

This last meeting with Lambert was about four years before his death, long after *Music Ho!* had come to be regarded as a minor classic. Until well after the war there had been so much verve and wit in the man, such delight in securing opportunity to put into rehearsal either new works or nineteenth-century ones which he thought unduly neglected, such enthusiasm for any enterprise in opera, ballet or music-giving, that few of his contemporaries took the subtitle 'A Study of Music in Decline' as expressing more than dissatisfaction with a *temporary* artistic depression, impatience with an insular *provision* of music. After the war, however, we were increasingly aware that Lambert shared the pessimism of others whose prophetic creations were published in the same decade as *Music Ho!*, such as *The Shape of Things to Come* and *Brave New World*, the latter appearing exactly a year before Lambert's book.

There was a striking similiarity of temperament between Constant Lambert and Aldous Huxley, including a taste for Latin rather than Teutonic art. Both were compassionate towards the individual within the herd but both felt towards herd-brutality and philistinism that aristocratic contempt which is nowadays miscalled snobbery. Snobs, like all fools, think and act by false valuation, seeking or praising others for their position, pedigree or money, their diplomas or status-measured intellect as distinct from their intelligence, their qualifications instead of their quality. If a conductor is a snob the fact is spread so quickly by bandsmen and theatre workers that it crosses the footlights. Great ability and artistry have not prevented at least two contemporary musicians of deserved eminence from being the subject of tap-room and after-dinner stories about their snobbery. Lambert could quickly have become the subject of such stories, for he did not rise from the ranks of orchestral players. His advent as a conductor was dangerously sudden and his voice and manner that of the young pup bossing the experienced. I have never heard a single green-room story about him that suggested the antagonism of players and collaborators, though I could fill pages with unexamined stories of his scornful wit *against* pretentious snobbery. I have limited my own anecdotal material to conversation which I myself heard because I was the very sort of person who might have elicited snobbery, if snob he were. As a young man I was almost psychotically suspicious of snobbery. (As late as 1940, let it not be forgotten, 'Establishment' social snobbery was a stronger rung on Young Ambition's ladder than is our modern snobbery of a 'meritocracy'.)

Nor was there about Lambert any taint of the inverted snobbery that is now associated with the pretentious and indolent products of 'welfare'. Unwilling to wash, shave, earn or undertake any personal discipline, they disguise a pathetic feeling of inferiority to their talented and disciplined contemporaries under a false bohemianism. Let Lambert's remarks on jazz and popular music be read particularly carefully. Throughout history perceptive artists have been willing to learn from popular and 'light' expression. Beethoven, with his increasing recourse to variation-form in his last and greatest music, testifies to a great artist's wish to speak to and for the untrained and sincere as distinct from the insensitive herd. Jazz idiom, writes Lambert, 'is a more plastic basis than the folk song or the pre-jazz popular songs', depending much upon 'rhythmic and melodic inflections'; yet his comments on most attempts at highbrow jazz are contemptuous. He had no more time for the patronizing artist who 'plays down' than for the preacher who falsely affects a street vocabulary or intonation. Beethoven's scherzos developed from minuets 'as rhythmically effete as commercial jazz' and *Portsmouth Point* produced 'an atmosphere as far removed from Harlem as Beethoven's minuets did from the atmosphere of the dancing room'.

'The jazz composer is now stagnating, bound to a narrow circle of rhythmic and harmonic devices and neglecting the possibilities of form. It is for the highbrow composer to take the next step ... Jazz ... is not raw ... but half-finished material in which European sophistication has been imposed over coloured crudity. There is always the danger that the highbrow composer may . . . leave only the sophisticated trappings.' He castigated 'synthetic vitality' in a jazz idiom as much as in a neo-classical or serial one. We can surely understand his almost obsessive love of certain Russian and French composers—Glinka, Borodin, Bizet, Chabrier— though this enthusiasm made naïve creatures like myself misunderstand him. Why did he not share our interest in the Bach or the Mozart 'revival'? Why was he so angry because the R.C.M. wanted him to rehearse a Beethoven overture instead of that to Sullivan's *Tempest*, a Brandenburg concerto instead of Borodin's little-known first symphony or the music he had rescued from Chabrier's *Le Roi malgré lui*?

I was foolish to suppose that Lambert failed to recognize the towering genius of Bach or Mozart, and equally foolish to read without pondering his assertion that most art is 'produced at a lower level of concentration' than that of the sublime classics. Our century was conspicuously lacking in genial music such as he admired in those Russian and French masters.

'The presence of so many renowned impersonations of great music is no consolation. . . . The dreary spate of classical titles and classical subject . . . is the symbol not of a classical austerity to be admired but of an antique-fancying aridity to be despised.'

A little thought will show that I do not commit a *non sequitur* by immediately quoting *Music Ho!* on the subject of jazz:

'I see no reason . . . why a composer should not . . . rid himself . . . from the night-club element in jazz as Haydn did from the ballroom element in the minuet, and produce the modern equivalent of those dance suites of Bach which we treat with as much seriousness as the sonatas of Beethoven. . . . The man who plays jazz all day is no more a music lover than the man who drinks "hooch" all day is a connoisseur of wines.'

The Rio Grande cannot be repeated because it is not mere 'symphonic jazz'. Not even the appropriate 'blues' element in 'The noisy streets are empty' gives us decadent, devitalized popular music, and the scoring is as far from that of commercial jazz or swing as the best Haydn minuet from a Vauxhall or Ranelagh dance. Do not let it be supposed that I regard *The Rio Grande* as a work of major importance: I merely praise Lambert for putting his advice into practice and adding to the store of 'genial' rather than sublime pieces. Versatility, intellect, wide knowledge of music and the arts—these cannot give a man the highly personal style which is rightly or wrongly the hallmark by which we acclaim a composer. Unlike Walton, with whom he was often coupled in commentaries, Lambert cultivated no immediately recognizable style of composition, despite a quality miscalled 'distinction' but meaning inventive and self-critical skill, or perhaps a refined taste. I can now understand his 'Don't worry about Rubbra.' The artist who can do one thing very well, such as compose or play an instrument, pursuing a personal vein of expression with faith in himself (however much he longs for the confidence of a wide audience) is surely a more happy creature than the highly talented polymath who lacks the faith and therefore the egocentricity. (By that last word I refer to an artistic not a moral trait.) Even beneath the debonair Lambert of the twenties was the pessimist who could claim only courage and dedicate himself to a strugggle instead of a faith.

One critic, Rutland Boughton, with his strong faith in 'left' politics and sociology, was quick to single out this paragraph in *Music Ho!*:

'The recent invention . . . of a hitherto unknown art described as "pure music" has resulted in the criticism of music becoming more and more detached from any form of life, composers being treated as though they produced patterns of notes in a spiritual vacuum, uninfluenced by landscape, social life, and political situations surrounding them. For every technical argument against a method of composing there is at least one social argument, and the social argument is often the more far reaching and convincing.'

Boughton naturally complained that Lambert had failed to apply the social argument as Boughton himself naïvely did, as even Vaughan Williams occasionally did in such crude phrases as 'Bach the great bourgeois'. Lambert was honest not to pretend to a faith, and sensible not to stray too far from the musician's intuitive response to music into sociological analysis. He could sometimes make shrewd diagnoses: he knew few cures. Bernard Shaw, forty years before Lambert, had asked serious musicians to study the idiom of the music-hall.

Today, as when *Music Ho!* first appeared, Lambert is enigmatic. We can still enjoy this malice:

Introduction

'Milhaud's earlier works, which jump sharply from the most academic euphony to the most startling cacophony, remind one of a host who having forgotten to put gin in the first round of cocktails puts methylated spirit in the second round to make up for it.'

Yet was not Lambert himself always fond of the 'cocktail' schools in all the arts? Was this simply the part of him which would not admit to having grown up and also grown pessimistic while our arts were dominated by smug officials and educators, an establishment less easy to attack than the central Ministry of Fine Arts in France? To describe gentlemen of this regiment he coined the unforgettable word 'po-faced', and in conversation he applied it to any element of pedantry in a composer—Stravinsky, Schönberg, Hindemith—however much he admired him. He was brilliantly aware of the puritanism which infects the artist with no kind of faith, and he even recognized Stravinsky's religious nature before Stravinsky had published liturgical work. His quest for genial if not sublime art, his delight in musical cocktails, in skilled confections for ballet or light opera—these surely were a reaction against a teutonic bias in English musicography which lasted long into our century. Unless one oddly supposes that no music before Schönberg's is to be called 'modern' (i.e., not owing most of its shape to the Viennese classics) then modern music does not begin in Germany. Its patriarchs are Liszt, Mussorgsky and Debussy, and Lambert's bias is excusable in the first brilliant writer on music of the twentieth century. The most surprising feature of *Music Ho!* is the final panegyric of Sibelius; but I believe it is explained by what I have called the enigmatic conflict of Lambert's ideals.

We do not read Lambert to agree but to enjoy. The *belles-lettres* are normally the most ephemeral and, to me, boring articles in musical periodicals, and their erection into a book should not entice the good musician even for reading in bed. A *Music Ho!* by a less profound and perceptive author would deserve a po-faced reception. No doubt sections of *Music Ho!* deserve it. 'There is no demand for a new concerto as such irrespective of quality': no, and Hindemith never said that there was! (Moreover there was no demand for a new cocktail' ballet-score as such.) Of course Lambert did not know *Mathis der Maler* at the time of writing. Lambert probably dips to his destructive lowest when he dubs most post-war composers as 'cinema producers manqués. . . . Instead of producing null and void concertos, Hindemith should be the camera man, Honegger should be in charge of the sound effects and Stravinsky, with his genius for pastiche, should be entrusted with the cutting.' Yet the same pen writes almost on the same page: 'There is nothing in music which has really lost its meaning, no device of rhythm, no harmonic combination which the composer of vision cannot reanimate.' A trimmed *Music Ho!* is as unthinkable as an 'improved' composition by Berlioz or some other genius with glaring faults which we take as part of his whole artistic personality. To remove the weeds is to snap the plants.

Music Ho! still fascinates us, first because it is the artistic autobiography of an outstandingly sensitive young man, secondly because it is one of the best documentary revelations of a short but interesting era, thirdly because it is a projection (to borrow a geometrical term) rather than a prediction. Seers with sensitive minds valiant for truth, though unafraid of the call to declare this road right and that one wrong, do not compete with the Sibyl. We can admire their visionary power even when it bespeaks their limitations, when the vision is largely a projection of ideas 'in the air' at the time of writing, painting or composing. It is still uneconomic to send coal or iron-ore across the world by air, yet we enjoy the delighted vision of total air traffic in novels which no doubt Blériot enjoyed. So also in *Brave New World* and *Music*

Introduction

Ho! we can enjoy the illusory fears and hopes of the 1920's and 1930's while we also marvel that so much prophecy within their covers is true—not 'has come true'. The best things in *Music Ho!* apply to the whole history of artistic endeavour and thus transcend a Study of Music in Decline.

ARTHUR HUTCHINGS

Durham, 1965

PREFACE
TO THE SECOND EDITION

W hen this book first appeared more than one critic commented on the gloomy nature of the views it expounded. It would have been pleasant had I been able to make this preface to the new edition the occasion for a recantation or at least a slight softening down of these views. But unfortunately, I can see no cause to do so.

Naturally, there are some things one would not say now (notably some of the political comments which have inevitably become dated) and others that one might modify, but apart from these minor details, the situation still seems to me precisely the same and the book as a whole is regrettably undated.

Compared to the vertiginous 'twenties' the 'thirties' are curiously static and even Stravinsky seems to have stopped reacting. London has woken up to surrealism just as Paris was forgetting about it, Vaughan Williams and William Walton have written symphonies, the latter marking yet a further stage in this composer's return to consonance, Igor Markevitch, a curious, unsympathetic but decided talent, has emerged as the leading figure of the Franco-Russian school, but otherwise things, particularly in the world of popular music, are very much as they were.

This book was never intended to be an exhaustive study

Preface to the Second Edition

of individual figures, so there would be little point in a detailed examination of the composers who have come into prominence since the 'twenties'. In any case there does not appear to be among them any figure of dominating force, capable of wielding the influence of a Schönberg or a Hindemith.

Of the older composers, Sibelius has remained silent, and Schönberg has produced nothing of importance. When we come to the next generation it is distressing to have to record the deaths of two of the greatest musicians of our day, Alban Berg and Bernard van Dieren. Their loss is doubly felt, for not only were they great artists but they belonged to that intermediate generation to which the younger composer naturally looks for spiritual guidance. Van Dieren was too crippled by ill health to add anything of importance to his musical output, but Berg left behind him an elegiac Violin Concerto of astonishing mastery and haunting beauty. Let us hope that it is only a personal elegy and not the elegy of modern music.

C.L.

October 1936

PREFACE
TO THE FIRST EDITION

T his book makes no attempt to be an ordnance survey of modern music or a study of modern composers as individual artists. Many composers of merit are not mentioned in it at all, and in the case of others attention has unfortunately been focused upon their lesser works. The task of docketing the outstanding figures of modern music has been ably done by other writers, and as for the purely technical questions raised by unusual combinations of sound I am of the opinion that craft-analysis like craftsmanship itself is of interest mainly as a preliminary. Avoiding both the pigeon-hole and the blackboard I have tried to trace a connecting line between the apparently diverse and contradictory manifestations of contemporary music.

The theme of the book is modern music in relation to the other arts and in relation to the social and mechanical background of modern life. It is a study of movements rather than musicians and individual works are cited not so much on their own account as for being examples of a particular tendency. When absolutely necessary technical arguments are introduced, but there are few technical terms and no music-type illustrations. The book as a whole is meant to be a non-technical presentation of the position the composer (and, for that matter, the listener) finds himself in today, though in order to establish this position clearly it is occasionally necessary to hark back a bit, as in the section devoted to nationalism.

I hope that this brief study, though inevitably one-sided and incomplete, may lead the way to a broader and more 'humane' critical attitude towards an art which, though the most instinctive and physical of all the arts, tends more and more to be treated as the intellectual preserve of the specialist.

My thanks are due to Lord Berners, Mr. Cecil Gray and Messrs. J. and W. Chester for the loan of music.

C.L.

December 1933

PART ONE

PRE-WAR PIONEERS

(a) The Revolutionary Situation

Revolutionaries themselves are the last people to realize when, through force of time and circumstance, they have gradually become conservatives. It is scarcely to be wondered at if the public is very nearly as slow in the uptake. To the public a red flag remains a red rag even when so battered by wind and weather that it could almost be used as a pink coat. Nothing is so common as to see a political upheaval pass practically unnoticed merely because the names of the leaders and their parties remain the same. Similarly in the world of music, the fact that some of the key-names in modern music, such as Stravinsky and Schönberg, are the same as before the war has blinded us to the real nature of the present-day musical revolution. We go on using the words 'revolutionary composer' just as we go on using the words 'Liberal' and 'Bolshevik'; but between the modern music of pre-war days and that of today lies as much difference as that between the jolly old Gilbertian 'Liberal or Conservat*ive*' situation and the present mingled state of the parties, or that between the clear anarchical issues of the October revolution and the present situation in Russian politics with Stalin at the head of a frustrated Five Year Plan and Trotsky fuming in exile.

31

Pre-war Pioneers

To the seeker after the new, or the sensational, to those who expect a sinister *frisson* from modern music, it is my melancholy duty to point out that all the bomb throwing and guillotining has already taken place. If by the word 'advanced' we mean art that departs as far as possible from the classical and conventional norm, then we must admit that pre-war music was considerably more advanced (if that is any recommendation) than the music of our own days. Schönberg's *Erwartung*, for example, still the most sensational essay in modern music from the point of view of pure strangeness of sound, was actually finished in 1909. If your ear can assimilate and tolerate the music written in 1913 and earlier, then there is nothing in post-war music that can conceivably give you an aural shock, though the illogicality of some of the present-day pastiches may give you 'a rare turn' comparable to the sudden stopping of a lift in transit.

We are most of us sensationalists at heart, and there is something rather sad about the modern composer's relapse into good behaviour. There is a wistful look about the more elderly 'emancipated' critics when they listen to a concert of contemporary music; they seem to remember the barricades of the old Russian Ballet and sniff plaintively for blood. The years that succeed a revolution have an inevitable air of anticlimax, and it is noticeable that popular interest in the Russian Soviet films has considerably waned since the directors turned from the joys of destruction to the more sober delights of construction. With the best will in the world we cannot get as excited about *The General Line* as we did about *Potemkin*, and it is doubtful if any of the works written since the war will become a popular date in musical history, like those old revolutionary war-horses *Le Sacre du Printemps* and *Pierrot Lunaire*.

But it is only the more elderly emancipated critics who have lived through both campaigns, so to speak, and who

32

realize the subtle difference between the two. There is a large mass of the public that has only become modern-music conscious since the war, and they are hardly to be blamed if they lump the two periods together as 'all this modern music'.

During the war people had sterner things to think of than Schönberg, and a concert of his works would have been not only impracticable, but unpatriotic. The general cessation of musical activities during the war resulted in many pre-war works only becoming known a considerable number of years after they were written. This may seem platitudinous, but it should be remembered that it would not necessarily be true of literature. If Joyce, for example, had written and published *Anna Livia Plurabelle* in 1913, there would have been nothing, theoretically speaking, to prevent it from becoming familiar to every schoolboy by about 1919; but the number of people who can read a modern score is fewer even than the number who claim that they can, and the more extreme examples of modern music cannot be grasped without several actual hearings. Moreover, the printing of literature is not the same as the playing of music. Any printer can print *Ulysses* (if the law lets him), but not every orchestra can play *Erwartung*. It is regrettable, but hardly surprising, that this work had to wait sixteen years for its first performance.

Purely practical and circumstantial difficulties of war, finance, patriotism and musical inefficiency having kept back the actual hearing of contemporary music, the wave of enthusiasm for this music that carried away the intellectual world shortly after the war was, though the intellectuals hardly realized it, mainly retrospective in character. It could not be compared for example to the contemporary interest in Brancusi's sculpture or Edith Sitwell's poetry. It was a 'hangover' from a previous period, and the famous series of concerts given by Eugène Goossens n London in 1920 were historical in more ways than one. They apparently announced the dawn of a new era, but curiously enough their most potent arguments were drawn from the era which we all imagined to be closed. The *clou* of the concerts was Stravinsky's *Le Sacre du Printemps*—a work which was merely the logical outcome of a barbaric outlook applied to the technique of impressionism.

Impressionism is a loose and easily misapplied term, but one can think of no other that sums up so conveniently the undeniable connecting link between the various revolutionary composers of before the war. The connecting link may not be obvious, but it is there nevertheless, and it is something for which we may search in vain at the present time.

To put the problem in its most naïve form, a representative pre-war concert of modern works would have struck the man in the street—if we may conjure up a figure somewhere between Strube's 'Little Man' and Ernest Newman's 'Plain Man'—as definitely queer. He would have found great difficulty in relating it to his previous musical experiences and, giving up all attempt to follow it as form, would probably have relapsed into a purely passive state in which the strange colours and rhythms were allowed to make a direct appeal to his nerves. His experiences would be unusual, but would assume a certain uniformity and logic through the very consistency of their strangeness.

Let us suppose the same admittedly naïve character at a representative concert of contemporary music. What conceivable connecting link would he find between, for example, Von Webern and Sauguet, between a cold and mathematical reversal of previous tradition and a deliberate return to its most sentimental and least valuable elements? He would find less difficulty in relating this music to his previous experiences, for so much of it would be but a pale reflection of the spirit of former ages; but the only connecting link he would find would be that of indecision and lack of logic.

Experiments may take many forms, but only one general direction, whereas the spirit of pastiche has no guiding impulse. Once invoked it becomes like the magic broom of the sorcerer's apprentice, to whom indeed the average modern composer, with his fluent technique, but lack of co-ordinative sense, may well be compared. It is the element of deliberate pastiche in modern music that chiefly distinguishes it from the experimental period of before the war. The landmarks of pre-war music, such as *Le Sacre du Printemps*, *Pierrot Lunaire* and Debussy's *Iberia*, are all definitely antitraditional; but they are curiously linked to tradition by the continuous curve of their break-away, comparable to the parabola traced in the air by a shell. But this shell has reached no objective, like a rocket in mid air it has exploded into a thousand multicoloured stars, scattering in as many different directions, and sharing only a common brilliance and evanescence.

It may be said in defence of the present age that the elements of decay are already to be found in the period that immediately preceded it, that the experiments of the pre-war period were of a type to lead inevitably to the present cul-de-sac. Whether this be so or not, it is impossible clearly to grasp the difference between post-war and pre-war modern music, or fully to understand the present situation without a brief review of the impressionist, or disruptive period which may conveniently be placed in time as stretching from the beginning of the century until 1914.

(b) Impressionism and Disruption

The development of music has not shown the same logical

growth that we find in painting. Impressionism in music came later than in painting, and music has made up for loss of time by leaving out the post-impressionist period. There has been no Cézanne in music—it is as though one went straight from Monet to Picabia.

Impressionism, as I have said, is a term easily misused, and one may doubt the logic of its use as a musical term at all; but its association with the work of Debussy and his followers is so widespread that one may conveniently use it as a generic label for that period of disruption in music of which Debussy was the dominating figure. The word impressionism is used illogically enough to cover a picture of a cathedral by Monet that bears remarkably little resemblance to the original, and a piece by Debussy that stretches the musical medium to the utmost, in order to conjure up as strong a visual image as possible. The contradiction is nevertheless more apparent than real. The academic picture being realistic, and the academic piece of music being abstract and formal, any departure from the norm results in their losing their respective conventional qualities until eventually they meet in a sort of *terrain vague* of the arts.

Roughly speaking, impressionist music provides a parallel to impressionist painting in its emphasis on atmosphere and colour, and its comparative neglect of construction and formal balance. More technically speaking, the methods of the pointillist painters have something in common with the use of the orchestra as displayed in Debussy's works. While from the general and literary point of view both impressionist painters and composers display a liking for a sort of Nordic vagueness, which is sharply at variance with the clear-cut logicality of the French tradition to which they are for some reason supposed to belong. Monet, in search of suitable material, went to the fogs of London, and Debussy went to the poetic prose of Maeterlinck.

Impressionism and Disruption

Although in his abandonment of linear continuity and symmetrical design Debussy is linked to the impressionist painters, the famous 'harmonic revolution', for which he was supposed to be responsible, has more in common with the Symbolist movement in poetry. The Symbolist poets did not invent new words, nor did Debussy—contrary to general belief—invent new chords. There are very few actual harmonic combinations in Debussy that cannot be found in Liszt; the novelty of Debussy's harmonic method consists in his using a chord as such, and not as a unit in a form of emotional and musical argument.

For ninths and elevenths and whole-tone chords that form the stock-in-trade of Debussy's early mannered style are also to be found in Liszt's *Années de Pèlerinage*, but in Liszt they form a definite point of stress in a continuous line of thought, a point of stress that demands a resolution. For that reason we are apt to pass over their actual quality as pure sound. But Debussy takes a certain chord and, by leaving it unresolved, or by putting it under every note of a phrase (in a manner that dates back to Hucbald in the eleventh century), he draws our attention to this harmony as an entity in itself, with its own powers of evocation. We do not take it in our stride as we do any word in a sentence like 'the ultimate interests of the electors' or a figure in a photographic group, 'reading from left to right'. We examine it separately as we might an Egyptian hieroglyphic or Chinese ideograph.

It is not my intention in a non-technical study such as this to trace back the origins of Debussy's harmonic vocabulary to Mussorgsky, Liszt, Chabrier or Satie, to the exotic influences of the gipsy music he heard in Russia or of the Indo-Chinese music he heard at the Paris Colonial Exhibition. I merely wish to point out that Debussy's real revolution in harmony consists far more in the way he uses chords, than in the chords he uses. It is a development in harmony more far reaching than any of Liszt's or Wagner's developments of harmonic vocabulary.

By suspending a chord in space, as it were, Debussy recalls the methods of the literary Symbolists. There is nothing particularly Symbolist about a greenhouse attached to a vegetable garden with a gardener working near it; but when this greenhouse occurs, deserted and unexpected, in the middle of a forest (as in Maeterlinck's poems) it immediately arouses a different and more instinctive set of feelings, even though we might be hard put to it to analyse their precise nature.

The difficulty many people experienced on first hearing Debussy's work was not due so much as they thought to any strangeness in the sound. It was created far more by the lack of rhetorical and emotional reasoning in his music. His use of successions of the same chord, of the pentatonic and whole-tone scales and the harmonies based on them, is entirely lacking in the thrust and counterthrust methods of the German Romantics. By his overthrow of the old principles of contrasted discord and concord, of suspension and resolution, by his destruction of the key-system, Debussy puts an end to the somewhat mechanical eloquence into which the German Romantics had degenerated and which is based on these premises. The old principles of logic no longer obtain, and we are forced to listen less with our minds and more with our nerves.

The essential difference between Debussy and Wagner is summed up in the contrast between the sailors' chorus at the end of the first act of *Tristan* and the sailors' chorus in the third scene of *Pelléas and Mélisande*. We cannot listen to the chorus in *Tristan* with our ears alone. We do not allow its effect to sink in as pure sound. We realize all its emotional and intellectual implications, we take it in relation to the

38

emotional climax we have just experienced and we recognize that it announces the setting of the next phase in the tragedy. The sailors' chorus in *Pelléas and Mélisande* has no such force as an emotional argument. The departure of this shadowy boat has no direct bearing on the emotional situation and there is strictly speaking no reason why it should come into the opera at all. The sound does not provoke an intellectual reaction like a bell calling us to church or a hooter calling us to work. It impinges on our sense like an image in a dream or some half-recognized sound in nature and evokes a vague nostalgia like a perfume whose previous associations we cannot quite recall.

The emotional reaction we get from Wagner may be compared to the direct and almost cinematic emotional appeal of a ship with the hero's sweetheart on board leaving the quay, or the departure of a troop train in time of war. The emotional reaction we get from Debussy is of the less personal and more subtle order that we get from the mere sight of an unknown ship in sail.

The complete contrast of both method and aim between Debussy's work and that of the German Romantics may be seen again if we compare the maddening repetitions in Wagner's operas with the equally maddening repetitions in *Pelléas and Mélisande*. The Wagnerian repetitions are a mounting and rhetorical series reminiscent of a lawyer's speech—an oratorical device whose aim is to emphasize the meaning of the argument until not even the dullest member of the jury remains unconvinced. Debussy's static repetitions do not quicken the pulse—they slacken it. Like the repetitions of an oriental priest their aim is to destroy the superficial connotations of the phrase until it appeals to the deeper instinct rather than to the reason.

I have drawn my examples from *Pelléas*, not because I consider it Debussy at his best—it is on the contrary one of his weakest and most mannered works—but because it is a convenient textbook of his technical reactions. *Pelléas* represents a phase which it was necessary for Debussy to go through before he could completely rid himself of the oppressive weight of the Teutonic romantic tradition; and it is to the force of this tradition that the excessively stylized manner of *Pelléas* is negatively due.

It is legitimate to suppose that Debussy's technical esperiments were a means—not an end. That is to say, it is more probable that the static style and harmonic mannerisms of *Pelléas* are due to his attempt to create a world of half-lights and dimly realized emotions, than that he chose this subject because he felt himself unable to achieve music in another style. At the same time we can see that by his treatment of harmony as an entity in itself Debussy prepares the way for the latter-day unmotivated experiments that have been described by a sympathetic critic as 'objective investigation of aural phenomena', while in his rejection of emotional rhetoric he unconsciously prepares the way for those who would reject emotion itself and throw out the baby with the bath water.

It need hardly be said that the coldness of much of Debussy's earlier music has nothing to do with the abstraction aimed at by certain present-day composers; it is a coldness of the natural world, not of the mechanical. This coldness is the most remarkable feature of the orchestral *Nocturnes*, a transitional work half-way between the static and symbolist manner of *Pelléas* and the more fully developed impressionism of *La Mer*. These *Nocturnes*, as Mr. Edwin Evans has rightly pointed out, recall Whistler rather than Chopin. They are like an exquisitely wrought Mohammedan decoration in which no human form is allowed to appear. The majestic procession of clouds in *Nuages* is a procession of clouds—not a symbol of evanescence; the wild exhilaration

40

of *Fêtes* is the exhilarating bustle of wind and rain, with nothing in it of human gaiety. The icy waves that lap the sirens' rock are disturbed by no Ulysses and his seamen.

This detached and objective attitude towards nature is even more marked in the symphonic sketches *La Mer*. Whereas in most works of art inspired by the sea, Vaughan Williams' *Sea Symphony*, for example, we are given the sea as a highly picturesque background to human endeavour and human emotion, a suitable setting for introspective skippers, heroic herring fishers and intrepid explorers, *La Mer* is actually a picture of the sea itself, a landscape without figures, or rather a seascape without ships. There was little of Walt Whitman about Debussy, and it is significant that he chose for the cover design of this work Hokusai's famous print of the Great Wave.

This cold and detached pictorialism is by now so familiar to us as an element in music that it is worth while recalling its novelty at the time these works were written. There is no trace of it in Wagner, to whom natural phenomena were, in the main, useful adjuncts to his own emotions as expressed in his characters. The sun rises to greet Brünnhilde, the forest murmurs to soothe Siegfried, and the wind rises to bring Waltraute in its wake. A tempestuous sky merely reflects the cruder melodrama of the composer's soul.

In *Pelléas* Debussy overthrew, as far as possible, the old romantic rhetoric, but even so the human element was at times too strong for him, and he was forced back into the traditional methods of expression by the operatic quality of some of the situations. In *La Mer* even this half-human element has disappeared, and from the purist's point of view it is the most finished and typical of Debussy's works—though, as I have pointed out, this lack of rhetorical emotion is by no means the same thing as abstraction. A picture does not become an abstract design because it has banished all purely literary interest. In its abandonment of formal principles, its lack of continuous melodic line, counterpoint, or development, in the accepted sense of the word, and in the pointillism of its scoring, *La Mer* represents the apex of Debussy's impressionist manner. Colour and atmosphere have taken the place of design and eloquence, and sounds succeed each other neither in definite continuity nor in deliberate contrast, but with the arbitrary caprice of nature itself. There is no further development possible purely on these lines, and Debussy's many short impressionist piano pieces—notably the two books of preludes—are a splitting up of the pictorialism of *La Mer* into its various facets. They are charming exploitations of an already established formula.

Had Debussy died after writing *La Mer* he would have remained a great historical figure who had revolutionized the technique of music in a way that no one man had ever done before; but he would hardly have been remembered as an intrinsically great composer. Many of the works written after the *Nocturnes* and *La Mer* are definitely inferior in quality, and there is no doubt that the somewhat precious enthusiasm of the 'Debussyistes' and the unaccustomed demand for his work caused him to publish in his later years certain pieces that his acute critical sense would previously have rejected; but it is the best works of his later period—notably the orchestral *Images*—that show Debussy's real strength as an artist.

A lesser man, having reached the technical apex represented by *La Mer*, would either have gone on contentedly exploiting this vein, or would have completely changed his external style. Debussy was far too sincere and too intelligent an artist to recklessly change his style, for to him musical style was not a matter of good taste and objective selection but part of his very being. He had revolted against academic technique not in a wilful and deliberate search for novelty

42

but in an attempt to find a sincere and personal expression. The comparatively conventional lyricism of the 'juicy' middle section in the *Prélude à l'Après-midi d'un Faune* disappears in the *Nocturnes* and *La Mer*, not because Debussy despised lyricism but because he preferred not to be lyrical at all rather than to express anything at second hand. By throwing over the whole paraphernalia of traditional musical romanticism he undoubtedly handicapped himself for a number of years and confined himself to a somewhat narrow range of expression, but his rigid self-control was rewarded by the eventual freedom and richness of style that he achieved in the orchestral *Images*.

In these works, and notably in *Iberia*, the most extended of the three, Debussy enters into a new emotional world. It is neither the old emotional world of the artist as hero that we find in the nineteenth-century Romantics, nor is it the aesthetic and purely decorative world of Debussy's earlier works. The personality of the artist is there, but is part of its surroundings, and intrudes no more than in a work of Mozart. It is an emotional world so peculiar to music that it is difficult in any way to define it in words, though Aldous Huxley perhaps hinted at it when he wrote: 'Occasionally in certain states which may vaguely be described as mystical we have an immediate perception of an external unity embracing and embraced by our own internal unity. We feel the whole universe as a single individual mysteriously fused with ourselves.'

Such a revelation is not necessarily encouraging, and there is a curious note of nostalgia and melancholy in these three pieces, though of a completely unsentimental nature. The original title of *Gigues* was *Gigue Triste*, and *Rondes de Printemps* belies the lighthearted quotation that heads the score, much as *Iberia* belies its apparently superficial atmosphere of southern gaiety. Through his capacity for investing an

43

apparently insignificant and light-hearted tune with an almost tragic significance, Debussy stands very close to Mozart. We find the same quality in, for example, the Siciliana that forms the finale of the D Minor quartet—a simple dance tune into which and its variations Mozart seems to have compressed the emotional experience of a lifetime.

The scraps of popular melody that occur in all three *Images* are not merely evocative and picturesque, they have a more profound significance. They recall the often quoted lines from Sir Thomas Browne: 'For even that vulgar and tavern musick which makes one man merry another mad strikes in me a deep fit of devotion and a profound contemplation of the First Composer. There is something in it of Divinity more than the ear discovers; it is a hieroglyphical and shadowed lesson of the whole world.' This passage, I feel, gives a clue to the signficance of Debussy's best works. The world they conjure up is not a Barriesque dream world, a soothing and comforting escape from reality. It is the world around us, but seen with an intense and unique vision, and the melancholy that pervades this music is no personal complaining but the underlying melancholy of human life itself.

Technically speaking these *Images* display a far greater liveliness and variety of texture than the early works of Debussy. His harmonic gift has lost none of its richness but here it is subordinated to the main scheme and not developed merely for its own sake. There is nothing approaching counterpoint in the academic sense of the word, but the skilful weaving together of innumerable threads of sound represents Debussy's own solution of the contrapuntal problem, and is far removed from the mainly static and vertical quality of the *Nocturnes*. Similarly, in the melodic line we find that Debussy has achieved at first hand the lyricism which in his early works appears only at second hand; and although his melodies may be a little short-winded, improvisatory, and lacking in the *grande envergure* of the nineteenth-century composers, they have a flexibility and force that is not to be found in the plaintive wisps of melody that float dimly through the overshadowing trees of *Pelléas and Mélisande*.

The orchestral *Images* represent, in fact, a synthesis of the various elements in music that Debussy had, in his earlier days, examined and developed separately in the interests of technical experiment. They show conclusively that Debussy's technical experiments were not the detached and empirical jugglings with sounds that they were at one time held to be, but a logical development towards complete self-realization. Though more advanced in the true sense of the word than his earlier works, they are less disruptive and revolutionary from the technical point of view. Just as Debussy ruthlessly rejected the clichés of the romantic school, so he rid himself of his own marked mannerisms when they had served his purpose (I am referring now to the major works of his latter period and not to his lesser piano pieces). The mechanical use of the whole-tone scale, and the many other devices which must have been considered so modern at the beginning of the century, find little or no place in these later orchestral works. In the best of the later piano *Études*, in the pieces for two pianos *En Blanc et Noir*, the ballet *Jeux* and the *Trio* for flute, viola and harp, Debussy maintained the high standard of the orchestral *Images;* but he never surpassed it, and we may take these works then as the culmination of Debussy's style and the most important contribution of impressionism towards music.

Although the present study is primarily an examination of post-war musical problems, this brief sketch of Debussy's outstanding works has been necessary not only because he was intrinsically the most important artist of the pre-war period but because he is undeniably the guiding principle and unifying link behind its apparently disparate experiments. It is easy enough to recognize the influence of Debussy's impressionism on his own countrymen, whose response to his music takes the form of a fairly direct imitation of its superficial characteristics, but Debussy's real influence is infinitely more far reaching than that. Once we realize that his impressionism was not only a manner, but a method, we can see the workings of this method in music that at first sight might seem totally opposed in general atmosphere. The direct, or indirect, influence of Debussy is to be found in such outwardly differentiated works as the ballets of Stravinsky and the operas of Schönberg, the *London Symphony* of Vaughan Williams and the *Chinese Symphony* of Van Dieren, the mystical poems of Scriabin and the vivid picture postcards of Albeniz, the *Bluebeard* of Béla Bartók and the *Bluebeard* of Paul Dukas, the *North Country Sketches* of Delius and *The Oceanides* of Sibelius.

Unfortunately the influence has been not so much that of Debussy the artist as of Debussy the experimenter. Viewing his work in retrospect we can see that his experiments were a necessary and integral part of his own artistic development, an example to be followed, but not a method to be imitated. To his contemporaries, however, Debussy's experiments assumed an almost political quality as a revolt against the tradition of German romanticism, and became a convenient handbook of revolution. The scaffolding which Debussy had used in the course of building his solitary tower was admired for its own sake, seized on, broken up, and made to serve as principal prop in many a jerry-built house.

(c) Debussy as Key-figure

When we consider the stuffy and faded academicism of

Stravinsky's and Schönberg's first works, it is impossible not to draw the conclusion that the disruptive element in Debussy's impressionism provided the liberating force that led these composers to their own revolutionary style.

It is strange to think that Stravinsky's ballets were at one time considered to be a healthy and vigorous reaction against the impression of Debussy, comparable in force to the reaction of Cézanne against Monet. Novelty of colour alone can be held to explain this confusion of thought. The garish and overloaded orchestration, barbaric rhythms and savagely applied discords of Stravinsky's ballets temporarily numb the critical faculties, and prevent one from realizing that however different the texture may be Stravinsky is using sound in the same way as Debussy. Barbaric impressionism has taken the place of super-civilized impressionism—that is all.

The difficulty of estimating Debussy's influence on Stravinsky is complicated by their common derivation from the Russian nationalists. A famous instance of this derivation is to be found in the similarity between the opening of Debussy's *Nuages* and the opening of Stravinsky's *Le Rossignol*. Both passages bear an extraordinary resemblance to one of the songs in Mussorgsky's *Without Sunlight* cycle. It is almost impossible to decide whether Stravinsky, the last of the three, is reacting to Russian nationalism, or to that side of Debussy that reacted to Russian nationalism; and we are faced with the same difficulty when we try to decide whether the oriental arabesques that occur from time to time in Stravinsky's melodic writing are a latter-day continuation of the oriental tradition started by Glinka in *Russlan and Ludmilla*, or whether they are a reflection of the undoubtedly oriental quality in many of Debussy's themes.

We must remember that Russian nationalism is by no means a continuous tradition. The death of Borodin was succeeded by a period of conservatism and academic reaction, in comparison with which the works of Brahms take on an almost Offenbachian quality. It is not too much to say that the vividly picturesque tradition of the Russian nationalists emigrated to France somewhere in the early 'nineties to return home dressed in the latest Paris models, just in time to join in the Diaghileff balllet. In *L'Oiseau de Feu* Stravinsky applied the rejuvenating influence of Debussy's impressionism to the by now somewhat faded Russian fairy tale tradition in much the way that one pours a glass of port into a Stilton, thereby hastening the already present element of decomposition. The resultant effect is rich and *faisandé*, but a little overripe, with a suggestion of maggots in the offing. The exhilarating and wintry gaiety of the fair in *Petrushka* with its buxom nurses, dancing bears, drunkards, gipsies and barrelorgans, seems at first sight far removed from the ruined temples in the moonlight, the reflections in the water, of Debussy's pictorial world, but the difference between *Petrushka* and the fair scenes in the early Russian operas lies precisely in the application of Debussy's pictorial methods to a cruder and more vivid tradition.

In *Le Sacre du Printemps*, considered at one time as the outstanding reaction against the invertebrate qualities of the Impressionist school, the influence of Debussy's technical methods is even more marked, though the self-consciously barbaric colour of the ballet may make this influence a little hard to recognize at first sight. The two finest sections in the work, the preludes to either part, are in the direct Impressionist tradition, although one may notice in passing that Stravinsky manages his orchestral texture less skilfully than Debussy; the various threads of *La Nuit Païenne* are less clearly presented than those of *Les Parfums de la Nuit;* the whole effect, in its lack of definition and its reliance on colour alone, being more impressionist than Debussy—*plus royaliste que le roi*, in fact.

Debussy as Key-figure

It is true that the outstanding feature in *Le Sacre* is its rhythmic experiment, an element which on the whole is lacking in the French school, mainly for national reasons. The French folk song has almost as little rhythmic interest and variety as the German, and the rhythmic tradition of French music lies more in the popular music of a later day, square-cut marches, can-cans, and gallops, material that is obviously unsuited to the fin-de-siècle aestheticism of Debussy's more mannered works. The French as a race have a remarkably poor sense of rhythm as compared with the Russians, and it is only to be expected that the rhythmic element should play a greater part in Stravinsky's make-up than in Debussy's.

I shall discuss in another place the barbaric and exotic elements in Stravinsky's rhythm. All that concerns us at the moment is the fact that, unlike earlier experiments in changing and varied rhythm, such as those of Borodin or Ladmirault, Stravinsky's rhythmic experiments are concerned not with the rhythm of melody, but with rhythm alone. They are rhythms suspended in space, arbitrary patterns in time, forming a parallel to Debussy's impressionist use of harmonies detached from melodic reasoning. Stravinsky carries one stage further the process of disruption and the dissection of the different elements in music that was started by Debussy. Debussy gives us harmony for its own sake, and Stravinsky gives us rhythm for its own sake, but by divorcing these functions of the musical mind from their normal surroundings they actually restrict the development of the specific element on which they are concentrating. Debussy's *Danse Sacrée et Danse Profane* cannot be compared for variety of harmony with a motet by Vittoria any more than Stravinsky's ballets can be compared for genuine rhythmic interest with the pavans and galliards of John Dowland.

Stravinsky's rhythm is not rhythm in the true sense of the

term, but rather 'metre' or 'measure'. In many sections of *Le Sacre du Printemps* the notes are merely pegs on which to hang the rhythm, and the orchestration and harmony are designed as far as possible to convert melodic instruments into the equivalent of percussion instruments. The essential effect of *Augures Printanières*—a passage in which the regular pulse of an unchanging chord is accented with irregular beats—could be obtained equally well on a single drum, and, in a more elaborate passage such as the *Glorification de l'Élue*, we feel that an upwards skirl or flam on the flute is merely a more elaborate notation for a high percussive instrument like the tambourine, that an arbitrary discord in the bass is merely a more emphatic kettledrum. The essential thought could be expressed on a large number of varied percussive instruments, though admittedly without the heightening of the nervous effect obtained by Stravinsky's pointillist scoring.

Whether rhythm or metre divorced from the other elements in music can be said to have any musical value is a problem older than the present century. It is discussed with great good sense by Roger North in his *Musicall Gramarian* (circa 1728) and his passage on the subject is so much to the point—even more so in our own days than when it was written—that it is worth quoting in full:

'Therefore in order to find a criterium of Good musick wee must (as I sayd) look into nature it Self, and ye truth of things. Musick hath 2 ends, first to please the sence, & that is done by the pure Dulcor of Harmony, which is found chiefly in ye elder musick, of wch much hath bin sayd, & more is to come, & secondly to move ye affections or excite passion. And that is done by measures of time joyned with the former. And it must be granted that pure Impuls artificially acted, and continued, hath Great power to excite men to act, but not to think. And this distinction resolves the enigma of Vossius de viribus Rithmi; wch pretends that the efficacy of musick is derived wholly from the measure. Sounds may have effect as symptomes of passion; but wch way he can by any possibility make out, that any pure measure Inclines to thinking, and without thinking there is no passion or affection, I cannot fathom, he instances In ye beats of a Drum, and also the Cooper at work as In the rediculer with his phrigian or Lydian dubbs. Nay condiscends to make a man comb'd Into a passion by ye barbers Lyricks upon his nodle. And it is true enough that the force of such violent Impulses, may excite actions, If any may be conformable. As in ye musick of dances the time is chiefly materiall, and who doth not keep active time to a jigg? The melody is only to add to the diversion, but (as hath bin noted) is not necessary to ye porpose, for many nations dannce onely to a tambour. Therefore I must sever the vertue of time in musick, from the musick itself, as having another scope and effect. And may be sayd to stir up comformable actions but not to excite thinking or pleas the sense.'

Stravinsky certainly succeeds in stirring up conformable action on the stage—and even, as some will remember, in the audience—but the melody is only to add to the diversion and his main object is to excite passion by rhythm or 'measure'. *Le Sacre du Printemps* foreshadows that modern craving —essentially a product of oversophistication—for the dark and instinctive that we find in D. H. Lawrence, and whose psychological bases have been so well summed up in Wyndham Lewis's *Paleface*. The immense prestige that this work enjoys with a certain type of intellectual is due to the fact that it is barbaric music for the supercivilized, an aphrodisiac for the jaded and surfeited. Whether we like Stravinsky's use of rhythm in *Le Sacre* or not, we must realize that unlike his later rhythmic experiments it is far from being purely detached and objective. It is experiment directed towards a

85374

more intense form of expression and a greater heightening of the nervous effect.

The music of Schönberg, the other great revolutionary figure in pre-war music, does not lend itself so easily to analysis as does that of Stravinsky. In rejecting the Teutonic romantic tradition Debussy and Stravinsky were rejecting something essentially alien; the issue was a clear one and though the struggle may have been hard there was no element in it of civil war. Schönberg is that anomalous figure, an anarchist with blue blood in his veins. He is historically and racially attached to those whom he seeks to destroy, and the spiritual conflict in his works is obvious, even though he may cry '*A la lanterne*' with more fervour than the most bloodthirsty of sansculottes. Like a priest of Diana he is forced to take up the role of the predecessor whom he has slain, and behind his most revolutionary passages lurks the highly respectable shade of Mendelssohn.

Schönberg's music as a whole will be discussed elsewhere in this volume, and for the moment we are concerned with him not so much as an individual figure as in relation to the Impressionist movement. There is little direct influence of Debussy in Schönberg's works, and his overthrowal of the Romantic tradition takes the form of a reversal or distortion of previously established formulae. But though there may be no direct influence there is a certain parallelism between the results they achieve by apparently opposed means.

There are two ways of destroying the significance of the House of Lords—you can either abolish it or you can make everyone a member. We have no sense of modulation in Debussy's music for the simple reason that he doesn't modulate, and we have no sense of modulation in Schönberg's music because the work itself has become one vast modulation. Debussy destroys the old diatonic scale, with its class distinctions between tones and semitones, by restricting it to

Debussy as Key-figure

whole tones and pentatonic intervals; Schönberg by extending equal importance to all twelve semitones. Debussy destroys one's sense of harmonic progression by eliminating all contrapuntal feeling; Schönberg by the sheer multiplicity and mechanical application of his contrapuntal devices. The method of approach may be different, but the disruption effect is the same. Schönberg dissects counterpoint in the way that Debussy dissected harmony and Stravinsky dissected rhythm; and devices such as the *canon cankrisans*, whose somewhat shaky *raison d'être* rests entirely on the meticulous observance of academic harmonic rules, are introduced without restriction and for their own sake. Unlike his harmonic and melodic experiments, which are there to give expression to his peculiar vein of tortured romanticism, these contrapuntal devices foreshadow the abstract investigations of the post-war period.

The one element in Schönberg's music which relates him directly to Debussy is the elaborate pointillism of his scoring, a pointillism that obscures the theoretical formalism of his works just as an efficient camouflage destroys the outline of a boat. This pointillist orchestration gives to many of Schönberg's works an impressionist effect in performance that an inspection of the score with the eye along would hardly lead one to expect, but after all it is the ear that is the final judge. It is no use claiming formal unity for a work on the theoretical grounds of its contrapuntal construction when this construction cannot possibly be observed by a listener who has not been primed, or supplied by the composer with a crib. The element in Schönberg's pre-war music— as for example the *Five Orchestral Pieces, Erwartung*, and *Pierrot Lunaire*—that most strikes the listener is their impressionist use of colour and their appeal to the musical nerves rather than to the musical reason. It is this that justifies our linking them with the impressionism of Debussy and Stravin-

53

sky in spite of the many technical and national differences between the three composers.

The present study being concerned with musical movements more than with individual composers and separate works, I need hardly detail the many minor writers who group themselves round the three key-figures we have been examining. Debussy, if only through sheer precedence of date, is the main influence of the period, and the general trend of development is therefore more harmonic than rhythmic, while both melody and form—the two elements that might have bound the disruptive experiments of the period together—are sacrificed in the interests of orchestral colour and atmosphere. Although he had an exquisite feeling for the turn of some half-improvisatory phrase, Debussy as a melodist was shortwinded and unforceful and, in spite of the subtle and impersonal form of his best works, his worst —which, as I have pointed out, had a regrettably stronger influence—are formless to a degree.

These invertebrate qualities are to be observed in a heightened form in the innumerable works of his followers, and are indeed the outstanding weaknesses of the Impressionist school as a whole. That they are part of a general trend and not only the result of one man's influence is shown, I think, by the common lack of formal and melodic interests to be found in the work or two such widely differentiated writers as Stravinsky and Delius. His greatest admirer could hardly describe Delius as a master of form, and even Mr. Cecil Gray, in the course of a highly laudatory essay, has admitted that many passages in Delius's music would retain the major element of their charm if all trace of melodic line were removed.

Stravinsky's ballets depend almost entirely on traditional themes or close imitations of the folk-song style for what melodic interest they possess, and they can hardly be considered as possessing any formal qualities that are not dictated by their dramatic interest. *L'Oiseau de Feu* is a pleasant pantomine, but its harmonic *idée fixe*—to which Mr. Edwin Evans has drawn attention in an interesting pamphlet—gives it no more formal continuity than we find in the Rimsky-Korsakoff operas which are similarly obsessed with a particular progression.

In *Petrushka* we find the composer playing—albeit with consummate brilliance—the role of effects man in music, and a concert performance of the work is intolerable to those unacquainted with every detail of stage action. A few years ago it might have been necessary to discuss the statement made by some of Stravinsky's followers that *Le Sacre du Printemps* was an abstract symphony in all but name; fortunately there are a few things that Time spares the critic, and we can see now that this work is merely a string of ballet movements lacking even in the formal cohesion of an opera ballet like the Polovtsian dances in Borodin's *Prince Igor*. We need not consider Stravinsky as formalist or melodist until we come to the post-war period of pastiche.

Quite apart, however, from any technical similarity in the methods of the pre-war revolutionaries, there is a common spiritual quality that can be recognized by any listener susceptible to the literary and evocative elements in music, whether he is interested in the historical and technical side or not. I refer to the aesthetic and neurasthenic qualities of the Impressionist period in music which, spiritually speaking, is a parallel to the naughty 'nineties in literature.

(d) Music and the Naughty 'Nineties

Modern music, as I have said, has not developed logically, as did the other arts. Technically speaking, the Impressionist period in music anticipates the most daring experiments in *Transition*, but the spirit it expresses is that of *The Yellow Book*, while the whole is set against the incongruous background of Edwardian prosperity, progress, and Utopianism.

The 'nineties themselves had no music properly speaking, and the writers of that period were consequently driven to desperate similes when trying to add appropriate musical touches. Poor Wilde in his search for the 'curiously coloured, scarlet music' that his soul desired could find nothing better than the piano pieces of Dvořák, and Beardsley was forced to read his own subtle perversity into the ponderous arguments and Victorian scene painting of *Das Rheingold*. The comparative lack of neurasthenia in the music of the nineteenth century is strikingly illustrated by the essentially heroic, 'hearty', and normal atmosphere of *The Ring;* the somewhat peculiar sexual relationships of the characters are in no way reflected in the score and it is not until we reach *Parsifal* with its erotic religiosity, its Oedipus and other complexes, that we get a foretaste of the suddenly released nerves of twentieth-century music. But the literary 'nineties did not know their *Parsifal* and so were forced to fall back on their fecund imagination for music of a sufficiently decadent type. Enoch Soames's famous lines:

> *Pale tunes irresolute,*
> *And traceries of old sounds*
> *Blown from a rotted flute,*
> *Mingle with noise of cymbals rouged with rust,*

are really a very good description of Debussy at his worst—though the wretched author was not destined to be consoled by this sympathetic world of sound. However much one admires Debussy there is no denying the vaguely aesthetic and 'arty' quality of much of his music—a quality that has even more in common with the English than with the

French decadents. The note first struck in his early setting of Rossetti's 'Blessed Damozel' permeates his work to a greater or less degree to the end of his career.

Pelléas is the ne plus ultra of the relaxed vitality and dimly realized emotions of the aesthetic movement. The *Nocturnes* recall Whistler, and the innumerable pictorial pieces such as *Poissons d'Or, Des Pas sur la Neige, Jardins sous la Pluie*, etc., are the musical equivalent of the Japanese prints whose vogue in England owed much to Whistler's guidance. The Greek evocations of some of the *Préludes* and the *Epigraphes Antiques* belong, not to the masculine world of the Greek philosphers and tragedians, but to the feminine world of the antique-fanciers like Pierre Louÿs and Maurice de Guérin. *Le Martyre de Saint Sébastien* is the swan song of the 'nineties, recalling *La Demoiselle Élue* in much the way that Beardsley recalls Rossetti. The later ballet *Jeux* may seem a foretaste of the slap-you-on-the-back, hiking spirit of the post-war composers and of their obsession with topicality, but the dim tennis players who flit inconsequently through the garden are no more genuinely *sportifs* than croquet players in a fan by Conder, and it is clear that Debussy's real interest is in the atmospheric background where 'Les sons et les parfums tournent dans l'air du soir'. Debussy harps back to Baudelaire, not forward to Borotra.[1]

The magnificent orchestral *Images* are free from any superficial 'artiness', but we do not require to be told that Debussy was an ill man when he wrote them to realize that they represent not the extrovert's enjoyment of present activity, but the introvert's half-recollected, half-imagined fantasia round action. Chabrier's valses are like Chabrier himself valsing with the utmost gusto, but Debussy's *Gigues* is like a

---

[1] We must remember, too, the years that Debussy spent on the unfinished *La Chute de la maison Usher* and the profound admiration he had for Poe, the patron saint of French decadence.

Proustian synthesis of the emotion drawn from some jig danced on the Breton coast, a jig in which he himself could never genuinely take part.

The crude force of the Russian peasant tradition gives to Stravinsky's ballets a superficial vigour that seems at first sight far removed from the nervous sensibility of Debussy's stage works. But the Russian ballet itself, exquisite entertainment though it was, belonged essentially to the 'nineties. Its most fanatical adherents were usually those who, though priding themselves on their modishness, were actually fin-de-siècle characters born out of their time. The change in style observable between the pre-war and post-war Diaghileff ballets reflects the purely fashionable change in the tastes of the concentration camp of intellectuals to whom Diaghileff played up, and whom the plain or comparatively plain man meekly followed. The sailor replaced the sex appeal of the oriental slave; factories, dungarees and talc provided the glamour once sought for in fairy palaces and fastuous costumes; but the essential channel of attraction remained the same. The knowing and Firbankian *Les Biches* was only a natural successor to the lavish and Wildean *Scheherezade*.

Stravinsky's ballets, then, belong as much to the aesthetic movement as do Debussy's piano pieces. *L'Oiseau de Feu* and *Petrushka* are more entertaining to see than Wilde's fairy-tales are to read because they make that direct physical appeal that Wilde could only get at second hand in his particular medium, but they cannot be said to carry us any further spiritually than *The Fisherman and his Soul* or *The Birthday of the Infanta*. *Le Sacre du Printemps* with its sophisticated and deliberate brutality had more in common, perhaps, with post-war fashions in literature, but its sadism is the natural counterpart of the masochism of *Le Martyre de Saint Sébastien*. The opera *Le Rossignol*, an overloaded piece of chinoiserie and preciosity, plunges us back again into the aesthetic and decadent world of art which found its strongest expression in the music of a later generation. There is nothing of Andersen left under the rich arabesques of the chinoiserie any more than there is any Malory left in Beardsley's illustrations to *La Morte d'Arthur*. Mr. Cecil Gray has rightly described this work as a monstrous Beardsleyesque afterbirth of the 'nineties, and together with *Le Martyre de Saint Sébastien* of Debussy and the *Pierrot Lunaire* of Schönberg it forms the culmination of the neurasthenia and preciosity of the impressionist or disruptive period.

The apparently coldblooded and mathematical music of Schönberg provides an even stronger and more avowed link with the 'nineties than any we get in Debussy, for while Debussy's choice of texts can be explained by the fact that they are not merely 'ninetyish in feeling, but also among the finest poems in his own language, Schönberg's choice of the watered-down decadence of Albert Giraud's verses can only be attributed to the fact that he found this Dowsonish atmosphere essentially sympathetic.

In *Pierrot Lunaire* the ghost of the German *Lied* meets the ghost of French decadence. The old faded characters from Bergamo take on new meanings in a sinister half-light:

> *Till Pierrot moon steals slyly in,*
> *His face more white than sin,*
> *Black-masked, and with cool touch lays bare*
> *Each cherry, plum, and pear.*

> *Then underneath the veiléd eyes*
> *of houses, darkness lies—*
> *Tall houses; like a hopeless prayer*
> *They cleave the sly dumb air.*

Pre-war Pioneers

Blind are those houses, paper-thin;
Old shadows hid therein,
With sly and crazy movements creep
Like marionettes, and weep.

The quotation is not from a poet of the 'nineties, but from
a poem of Edith Sitwell's which, taking up the 'nineties
where they left off, so to speak, expresses perfectly the nervous appeal of the last work in which those stock figures of
the fancy-dress ball have for us any meaning.

Pierrot Lunaire, morever, cannot be considered an isolated
example of the fin-de-siècle quality in Schönberg's music.
Die Glückliche Hand, with its great black cat crouching like
an incubus or succubus on the hero, and its green-faced
chorus peering through dark violet hangings, is in the purest
Edgar Allan Poe tradition, while *Erwartung*, with its vague
hints of necrophily, brings in the Krafft-Ebing touch (Jung
at the prow and Freud at the helm) which is the twentieth
century's only gift to the 'nineties. I am not suggesting for a
moment that Schönberg rises no higher than the weak decadence of Giraud. There is in his music a fierce despair, an
almost flamelike disgust which recalls the mood of Baudelaire's *La Charogne* and places it far above the watercolour
morbidities of his chosen text. But at the moment I am not
trying to determine the purely musical value of Schönberg's
various works—I merely wish to indicate the undoubted
neurasthenic strain that is symptomatic of his period, and
which can be found in works like Strauss's *Salome* and
Elektra which, musically speaking, are widely differentiated
from Schönberg's in technique.

I realize that nothing fades so quickly as the average
musical 'thriller', and it may seem that in accusing the
Impressionist composers of neurasthenia and decadence I
am taking a shortsighted view based mainly on present-day

insensibility to the efforts of nineteenth-century composers to horrify and startle; but we have only to consider nineteenth-century music as a whole to realize that the occasional diabolism of Berlioz and Liszt is a comparatively isolated phenomenon. A certain ghoulishness is a natural part of the German Romantic tradition, and Liszt's Mephistophelean studies, though brilliantly convincing, are more than counterbalanced by his sentimental feelings for Gretchen. Berlioz had more of the authentic Messe Noire feeling, but the finale of the *Symphonie Fantastique* is, after all, in the nature of a genre piece, and although it has lost none of its uncanny power it is by no means so typical of Berlioz's work as might be supposed.

One is in no way straining facts, or distorting history to suit one's own ends, by placing the musical 'nineties in the rather incongruous background of the opening years of the present century. The only problem is why this neurasthenic period should so suddenly appear in this particular art at this particular time. Some may put it down to the 'time-lag' which, until the present period, music has always shown (as for example in the seventeenth century in England, when the Elizabethan tradition extended into the Caroline period): others, wise after the event, may see in the disintegrating brutality of *Elektra, Le Sacre du Printemps,* and other works, a Dunne-like reflection of the brutality of the succeeding war years, similar to the moral laxity, failure to keep up appearances before the servants, and general disintegration of behaviour that invariably precedes revolutions.

There is something to be said for both these points of view, but the fundamental reason I believe to be both more simple and more technical. Horror and neurasthenia are absent from pre-Impressionist music for the simple reason that composers lacked the technical means to give as much expression to this side of their nature as was accomplished by the poets and novelists. Horror and neurasthenia in literature can be expressed without resorting to extremes of technique. They can be expressed not by style, but by statement, and even, as in Defoe, by a sort of cool ironic understatement. Poe can chill our nerves by a mere description of a situation without resorting to any eccentricity of vocabulary or distortion of language. He can convince us, for example, that Roderick Usher's personal variations on Weber's last waltz were strange and morbid by merely telling us so. But a composer treating the same subject could only convince us by making the waltz actually sound strange and morbid, an effect which would demand a greater break with musical tradition than was possible in Poe's day.

Classical music has little sense of horror about it, not because classical composers despised such an appeal to the nerves, but because they were unable to achieve it. Dido's lament remains as deeply moving today as when it was written—we have to make no mental adjustments to the period in order to appreciate its emotional appeal; but *The Echo Dance of Furies* in the same opera can only be appreciated as a hieroglyphic of the sinister—it makes no direct nervous physical appeal as does the other music in the opera. On certain occasions Purcell, the most picturesque of the pre-Romantic composers, could obtain an effect of strangeness and awe as in the amazing passage which accompanies the words 'From your sleepy mansion rise' in *The Indian Queen;* but for the most part his flexible technique enabled him to express anything but the outré. The same may be said of Mozart, whose music for the statue in *Don Giovanni* owes its effect more to dramatic situation and contrast of colour than to anything essentially strange in the music itself.

The early nineteenth century, to which we naturally look for technical advance in this respect, presents a curious contrast between the romantic and magical subjects chosen by composers and the musical material employed in their illustration. The dawn of the Tale of Terror in literature coincides with the growth of the musical style least suited to the expression of the strange, the unearthly, and the sinister. In spite of the romantic orchestration introduced by Weber, the solid hymn-tune harmonies, the *Ländler* rhythms, the firm basis of tonic and dominant that lie at the root of the German nineteenth-century tradition are, on the face of it, a little difficult to invest with macabre qualities. Composers like Marschner were forced to resort to a monotonous and despairing use of the chord of the diminished seventh in a vain effort to provide a suitable musical background for their dastardly English lords.

The Russian school, unhampered by the essential normality of Teutonic technique, were more successful in their depiction of the magical, though it is noticeable that both Glinka and Dargomizhky, the one in portraying the wizard Chernomor in *Russlan*, the other in portraying the Commendador in the *Stone Guest*, make use of the whole-tone scale, a device which must at the time have seemed the most extreme in the vocabulary of music. It was only by such an overthrowal of traditional practice that they were able to convey an impression of strangeness and horror. Their experiments, however, were isolated and without successors,[1] and it was not until the coming of the harmonic and orchestral revolution that centres round Debussy that the composer found himself with a vocabulary capable of expressing the fin-de-siècle spirit that was already a commonplace in literature.

The complete break-up of the traditional Teutonic technique released a new world of sound and a new world of sensation. Like a repressed character who, having at last

---

[1] Liszt's tentative experiments with the whole-tone scale can hardly be said to supply a link between Glinka and Debussy.

lost his inhibition, flings himself into a debauch with a hardihood and gusto that would astonish the accustomed pagan, so the composer, suddenly conscious of his nerves, almost lost consciousness of any other faculties and concentrated in one single generation the neurasthenia of fifty years of literature. It is a little difficult, perhaps, to decide whether the impressionist composers turned to neurasthenic expression because at last a suitable technique was at hand, or whether they forged this suitable technique in an effort to express this side of their nature—ultimately it does not matter. One can say to a man: 'That egg is only cooked because the water round it was boiling', or one can say: 'You are only boiling that water in order to cook the egg', without altering the fact that a boiled egg is eventually put before you.

There is no doubt that revolutionary technique and neurasthenic expression acted as a mutual stimulus, and that the composer, led by his newly-won technical freedom to the expression of the less commonplace and recognized emotions, was led thence to even more esoteric subjects requiring an even greater departure from academic uses. Moreover, the composer was drawn on at increasing speed by the fact that nothing dates so quickly as musical sensationalism. The whole-tone scale, which must have caused such a fluttering of breasts when first exploited by Debussy, is by now the merest stock-in-trade of the hack composer of the cinema. Once embarked on a course of sensationalism, the composer is forced into a descending spiral spin from which only the most experienced pilot can flatten out in time.

This extraordinary speeding up in technical experiment gives a pleasantly vertiginous quality to the Impressionist period, which distinguishes it from all other experimental periods in music; and in spite of the fact that much of their experiment leads us to a blind alley there is an exhilaration of the barricades about the Impressionist composers that imposes a certain gratitude. 'Pioneers, O Pioneers!' we feel as we listen to *Iberia*, *Pierrot Lunaire*, and *Le Sacre du Printemps*. To be a pioneer is not necessarily the proudest of boasts for a composer—but it is at least something to boast about. We cannot turn to the present generation and sing: 'Pasticheurs, O Pasticheurs!' with the same grateful enthusiasm.

PART TWO

POST-WAR PASTICHEURS

(a) The Age of Pastiche

To describe the present age in music as one of pastiche may seem a sweeping generalization but, like the description of the Impressionist period as one of disruption, it is a generalization with a strong basis in fact. There are many contemporary composers of note who stand to some extent outside this classification, just as there were many composers who stood outside the Impressionism of the pre-war period, but the dominant characteristic of post-war music is either pastiche or an attempted consolidation that achieves only pastiche.

Pastiche has existed in music for many years, but it is only since the war that it has taken the place of development and experiment. In the nineteenth century a number of minor composers turned out their suites in the olden style, but these mild pièces d'occasion no more affected the main course of music than an Olde Worlde Bunne Shoppe affects the architectural experiments of Corbusier and Mallet-Stevens. Apart from these studio pieces, pastiche has always existed in the form of stage decoration as, for example, the Mozartean divertissement in Tchaikovsky's *Queen of Spades*, or the music off stage in the second act of Puccini's *Tosca*. It need hardly be pointed out, though, that these touches of dramatic

66

colour indicated no change of heart on the part of the com-
poser. Tchaikovsky did not write symphonies modelled on
Haydn any more than Puccini set out to imitate Rossini or
Mercadante.

The deliberate and serious use of pastiche, not as a
curiosity or as a pièce d'occasion but as a chosen medium for
self-expression, is the property of the post-war period alone.

The idea that music of an earlier age can be better than
the music of one's own is an essentially modern attitude.
The Elizabethans did not tire of their conceits and go back
to the sweet simplicity of Hucbald, any more than the late
Caroline composers deserted the new and airy Italian style
for the grave fantasias of Dowland. Burney's *History of
Music* is an astonishing example of the complete satisfaction
with its own period so typical of the eighteenth century. To
him the earlier composers were only of interest as stepping-
stones to the glorious and unassailable music of his own day.
Passages in the earlier music which do not display the
smoothness of texture that the eighteenth century looked on
as technical perfection were dismissed as crudities due to
lack of taste and skill.

The nineteenth century was to carry this smug attitude
one stage further. The eighteenth-century masters were
admired not so much for their own sake as for being pre-
cursors of the romantic school which through its sheer position in time was naturally an improvement. Once Beethoven's Symphonies were accepted they were considered as
being superior to Mozart's in the way that a six-cylinder car
is preferred to a four-cylinder car, or a talking to a silent
film. Schumann, it is true, admired Scarlatti, but with a
touch of the patronage displayed by a Lady Bountiful
visiting the village, and Clara Schumann simply could not
understand how Brahms could take any interest in composers earlier than Bach. Wagner's followers did not look

upon *The Ring* as a way of writing operas that was different from Bellini's, but as a way that clearly was a much better one.

Even in the early twentieth century, when the attitude towards music of a past age was broader and more cultured, showing at times a certain humility, the direction taken, not only by composers but by the public and critics, was progressive in the mechanical sense of the word. Those who were swept off their feet by Strauss and, later, by Scriabin—and they included some of our most levelheaded critics—thought nothing of referring to Mozart as a snuffbox composer in comparison with these cosmic masters; and it is clear that the more fervent admirers of Debussy and Stravinsky regarded their music as not only a reaction against Wagner, but as the death of Wagner.

That is not to say that music until the present has proceeded in a mechanical series of reactions. It is not until Stravinsky that a new movement in music is held to have automatically wiped out all traces of the preceding one (of which the wretched followers, like Babylonian courtiers, are forcibly immolated on the tomb of their master). The new music from Italy undoubtedly changed the course of Purcell's musical thought, but the Elizabethan spirit and technique displayed in his early string fantasias is not entirely banished from his later work, which, though experimental to a degree, and in no way reactionary, yet has a distinct connection with the work of previous generations.

Revolutionary, in fact, is an unsuitable word with which to describe the experimental periods of past ages. The revolutionaries of the seventeenth century were hardy pioneers who struck out boldly across undiscovered plains and cultivated the virgin soil. The revolutionaries of today are no more hardy than the man who takes a ticket on the Inner Circle, and is at liberty to travel in either direction, knowing that eventually he will arrive at the station which the fashion of the day has decreed to be the centre of the town. The modern musical revolutions are revolutions in the meanest sense of the word—the mere turning of a stationary wheel.

A great deal of pre-war music may have sounded, to use a dear old phrase, 'like nothing on earth', but that at least is a negative merit from the revolutionaries' point of view. Most music of today sounds only too reminiscent of something that has previously been in existence.

Comparison to an earlier composer, at one time a well-known form of musician-baiting, is now come to be a delicate compliment. If you had told Wagner that you admired his operas because they were 'like' Cimarosa he would probably have kicked you out of the house, and I doubt if Liszt would have been pleased if you had said that his *Études transcendentales* were charming because they were 'like' Couperin.

But today every composer's overcoat has its corresponding hook in the cloakroom of the past. Stravinsky's concertos (we have it on the composer's own authority) are 'like' Bach and Mozart; Sauguet's music is admired because 'c'est dans le vrai tradition de Gounod'; another composer's score is praised because in it 'se retrouvent les graces étincellantes de Scarlatti'. The composer can no longer pride himself on being true to himself—he can only receive the pale reflected glory of being true to whichever past composer is credited at the moment with having possessed the Elixir of Life.

It would be a mistake, I think, to put this attitude down to a spiritual humility comparable to the quite natural inferiority complex a modern sculptor might feel in the presence of some early Chinese carving. It is more in the nature of a last refuge, comparable to the maudlin religiosity of a satiated rake. After the debauches of the Impressionist period nothing is left to the modern composer in the way of a new *frisson* save a fashionable repentance.

Unlike the experimental period of the seventeenth century the pre-war period has led to a psychological cul-de-sac. There are many explanations of this, of which the most convincing is a simple and practical one. By 1913 music had already reached the absolute limit of complication allowed by the capacity of composers, players, listeners and instrument makers. With very few exceptions in detail—such as the piano writing of Sorabji, the polytonal choral writing of Milhaud and the quarter-tone writing of Aloys Haba—there is nothing in present-day music more complicated from any point of view than what we find in the music of twenty years ago. The composer is now faced, not with further experiment but with the more difficult task of consolidating the experiments of this vertiginous period. He is like a man in a high-powered motor-car that has got out of control. He must either steer it away from the cliff's edge back to the road or leap out of it altogether. Most modern composers have chosen the latter plan, remarking, as they dexterously save their precious lives: 'I think motor-cars are a little *vieux jeu*—don't you?'

There is an obvious end to the amount of purely physical experiment in music, just as there is an obvious end to geographical exploration. Wyndham Lewis has pointed out that when speed and familiarity have reduced travelling in space to the level of the humdrum those in search of the exotic will have to travel in time, and this is what has already happened in music. The Impressionist composers vastly speeded up the facilities for space travel in music, exploring the remotest jungles and treating uncharted seas as though they were the Serpentine. Stravinsky, at one time the globe trotter par excellence, can no longer thrill us with his traveller's tales of the primitive steppe and has, quite logically, taken to time travelling instead. He reminds one of the character in a play by Evreinoff who lives half in the eighteenth century, half in the present.

The advantages of time travelling are obvious. The pioneer work has been done for you already and, owing to the increased facilites for moving from one century or decade to another, you can always be in the right decade at the right time, whereas in space travelling you may be delayed by a month or two, or even find that the intellectual world has gone on to the next port.

(b) Diaghileff and Stravinsky as Time Travellers

The most successful time traveller of our days was undoubtedly Serge Diaghileff, though it might be more accurate to describe him as a ubiquitous and highly efficient Cook's man to the time travellers, rather than a bona fide voyager. Though he had to the end a congenital, but carefully disguised, dislike of time travelling, he was the first to realize the artistic and commercial possibilities of the new device. In his palmy days before the war he was, of course, a space traveller, bringing to the Western world a picturesque oriental caravan laden with the rich tapestries and carpets so suited to the taste of an age that was able to combine material prosperity and spiritual preciosity in such nice proportions. He was not only giving the intellectual public what it wanted, he was giving them what he liked himself. In music his genuine taste was for the luscious, and in décor for the opulent. In spite of all his very successful and convincing toying with post-war intellectuality, his favourite ballet was probably *Scheherezade*.

But an impresario however gifted cannot remain fixed in any particular world of taste whether he find it sympathetic or no. He depends on surprise and novelty for his *réclame*, and Diaghileff, by appealing to a more intelligent audience than that sought by the ordinary commercial impressario, was, like the composers of the Impressionist period, forced into a policy of novelty and sensationalism that gathered speed as it went. By the time the audience has just caught up with his last creation he must be ready with the cards of the next trick up his sleeve. He thus found himself in something of a dilemma after the war, for although the audiences were fully prepared to go on applauding the old ballets, and to find all the old glamour in an entertainment that now had the added glamour of being 'White Russian', he himself knew that this enthusiasm was in the nature of a 'hangover' from the pre-war period, and that unless he could find a new avenue of taste for exploration he would be as dated as the older dancers whom he had ruthlessly left by the way. But he could never again achieve his earlier triumphs of the exotic period. He could not bring to the delighted eyes of Western Europe the then unrealized glories of Eastern Europe. He was now part of Western Europe himself—a little déraciné and a little old. He was no longer one of a group of young enthusiastic artists imposing on the world their particular dernier cri, for the dernier cri was now in the hands of the Paris intellectuals.

A lesser man than Diaghileff might have found the situation beyond him, but Diaghileff, with that genius for production that was in many ways so much more impressive than the talent of those he produced, executed a series of rapid and perplexing manœuvres with a view to establishing a mastery over a patch of intellectual ground, which, it must be remembered, was not his by racial heredity or by right of youth. Still a little uncertain of his ground he relied to some extent on typical Parisians, like Jean Cocteau, who occupied much the same place in the Paris intellectual world of their day as he himself had at one time occupied in the Petrograd movement.

Parade,[1] the first fruits of this influence, was, in spite of its novelty, a logical enough development of his pre-war activities. In choosing Picasso, Satie and Massine as collaborators Diaghileff showed the same type of choice as he had displayed in choosing Bakst, Ravel and Fokine for *Daphnis and Chloe*. The times had changed and Diaghileff had wisely changed with them, without actually altering his angle of approach. He did not, however, follow up the logically modernist path opened out by *Parade* for a number of reasons—not least among which may be mentioned the curious ill luck and disaster that usually accompanied any performance of this ballet. Diaghileff had not only the oriental love of luxury but the oriental love of power. *Parade* displayed only too clearly the guiding hand of Jean Cocteau, and a development along those lines would have meant a surrender of his power to the group that Jean Cocteau represented. As a space traveller, in fact, Cocteau was a little too quick for him. Diaghileff consequently evolved the most typical artistic device of the present age, that is to say, time travelling in more than one century or period at once. It is a device that is peculiarly well adapted to musical expression and in particular to ballet.

The various elements in painting being less easy to separate from each other than the various elements in music, it is obviously a little difficult to evoke deliberately more than one period at once, or to combine two periods of style, in any given painting. Picasso may change his style every five years, but during that five years each picture is strictly within its limited 'epoch'. Even in literature it is difficult to

---

[1] Although actually produced in 1917, *Parade* may legitimately be considered the first 'post-war' ballet, using the word in its social rather than purely temporal significance.

evoke more than one period in a given paragraph. James Joyce in the medical-student section of *Ulysses* gives us a brilliant pastiche of successive epochs in English literature, but it is a separate tour de force and does not represent the general texture of the book. As a pastiche it has a symbolic purpose and, moreover, the epochs succeed each other in logical and historical order. It can in no way be compared to the random and scrapbook methods of Diaghileff.

In music, though, the various elements, such as melody, rhythm, harmony, and counterpoint, all taking place in practically the same moment of time, can—though it is highly undesirable that they should—be so dissected and separated from each other, that a composer with no sense of style and no creative urge can take medieval words, set them in the style of Bellini, add twentieth-century harmony, develop both in the sequential and formal manner of the eighteenth century, and finally score the whole thing for jazz band. Similarly, in ballet it is possible to have décor, choreography and music in different periods and tastes, to throw abstract films on the back cloth while the orchestra turns out a laborious pastiche of Gluck and the dancers revive the glories of the nineteenth-century *Excelsior*.

It will be seen, then, that by his adoption or even invention of the particular type of present-day pastiche that can conveniently be described as time travelling Diaghileff immediately established a position of mastery again. It was not even necessary that his associates should be time travellers themselves—for by picking on collaborators sufficiently disparate in outlook he could achieve the required effect—but to start with, at least, he required a similar mentality on the part of his associates, and in Stravinsky, whose executive abilities so far outweighed his creative gifts, and who, like himself, was a somewhat déraciné figure, he found the ideal collaborator. *Pulcinella* was the first example of this movement, and though it may not seem on the face of it a very important piece of work it ranks as an historical date with *Pelléas*. It marks the beginning of the movement sometimes dignified with the name of neo-classicism.

Stravinsky was by far the best person for Diaghileff to send time travelling in the eighteenth century because, both temperamentally and racially, he was out of touch with the whole period. A Frenchman or an Italian might have felt some embarrassment about jazzing up the classics, but Stravinsky is like a child delighted with a book of eighteenth-century engravings, yet not so impressed that it has any twinges of conscience about reddening the noses, or adding moustaches and beards in thick black pencil.

Pulcinella combines the chic of today with the chic of the eighteenth century—always a safe period to consider 'good taste'. Yet there is something touchingly naïve about Stravinsky's attitude towards Pergolesi. His thematic material is all there for him, he does not even have to vamp up a pseudo-Russian folk song, and yet by giving the works a slight jolt, so to speak, he can make the whole thing sound up to date and so enjoy the best of both worlds. The jolt he gives the machine consists, on the whole, in a complete confusion between the expressive and formal content of the eighteenth-century style. In Stravinksy's adaptation the expressive element is treated in a mechanical way, and purely conventional formulae of construction are given pride of place. Like a savage standing in delighted awe before those two symbols of an alien civilization, the top hat and the *pot de chambre*, he is apt to confuse their functions.

Apart from the clash of periods shown in the music, *Pulcinella* was not a very complicated piece of pastiche. The choreography by Massine and the décor by Picasso were mild but pleasing. They were in keeping with the subject and did not imitate such strokes on Stravinsky's part as the use of jazz glissandos on the trombone by introducing 'black-bottoms' and skyscrapers. It was not until a later date that Diaghileff may be said to have deliberately introduced incongruity as an element to be admired.

Once the music of a ballet is allowed to be in two periods at once, there is no logical reason why the décor and choreography should share that particular type of pastiche or time travelling. Congruity between the various elements in a stage presentation is an essentially Wagnerian ideal, though as an ideal it lasted well into a period which, from the musical point of view, was anti-Wagnerian. Debussy, for example, revolted against the Wagnerian musical ideals in *Pelléas*, but it is safe to assume that he still desired the congruity of the Wagnerian music drama to be applied to the production of his own revolutionary work. Wagner's ideal of stage setting did not in fact reach full fruition until the early days of the Diaghileff ballet.

Diaghileff was always willing to wipe his boots on his earlier productions and to rise on stepping stones of his dead self to higher things, but he was astute enough, and in a way sincere enough, to demand a satisfactory reason for his own volte-face. By realizing that his earlier preoccupation with a sense of style and congruity was in essence Wagnerian he was able to invest with a revolutionary glamour the scrapbook mentality which in his later years he exploited with so marked a success. These scrapbook ballets were of course only a more grandiose and theatrical presentation of the scrapbook taste which is considered so modern and 'amusing' when applied to interior decoration.

It is a mistake to think that modern taste is really represented by Corbusier rooms, furnished with fitting mechanical austerity. Modern taste is to be found far more in the typical post-war room, in which an Adam mantelpiece is covered with negro masks while Victorian wool-pictures jostle the minor Cubists on the walls. In such a room a Picasso reproduction is not considered 'amusing' unless flanked by pampas grass or surrounded by a Gothic frame made out of walnut shells, any more than a Brancusi bird is considered 'amusing' unless set off by a cage of stuffed tits, and an effigy of Queen Victoria. To the post-war intellectual snob all periods are equally *vieux jeu*, including his own, and it is only by a feverish rushing from one period to another that he can disguise from others and from himself his essentially static intelligence.

The chic chaos of the type of room described above is reflected in the music of such a composer as Poulenc, the most 'amusing' of the many minor composers who were called on to vamp up the music for Diaghileff's fashionable dinners. Poulenc does not write in any particular style that he fancies to be fashionable at the moment, but in every style of the past and present that is not actually frowned on as pompous and outmoded. The easy charm of the folk song, the gay allure of the military band, the sparkle of the eighteenth century, the 'amusing' sentimentality of the nineteenth, the spicy harmonies of our own time, the saccharine smile of the prostitute, the extended tongue of the gamin, mazurkas, ragtimes, ritornellos, rigadoons, Stravinsky, Scarlatti, Chabrier, Gounod—all are paraded before us with bewildering rapidity, and the changes of style are executed with such abruptness that not the most lynx-eared of the fashionable cheka who are the self-appointed arbiters of vogue has the time to exclaim: 'A little dated—don't you think?'

Poulenc is the most accomplished and insouciant of time travellers, a Captain Spalding amongst musical explorers, and *Les Biches*, a witty social commentary reaching a high level of distinction from the point of view of choreography, was the most agreeable of the 'amusing' Diaghileff ballets in that it made no pretences. 'Amusing' rearrangements of sections cut through past periods keep a number of amateurs, who might otherwise set up business as artists, out of harm's way, and it is only when these poltergeists set themselves up as Demon Kings that it is time to call a halt. Unfortunately, the influence of Diaghileff and the Diaghileff type of mind has led to incongruous rearrangements being confused with genuine revolution and constructive progress. To take a homely sartorial example, the late Baroness Elsa von Frey-tag-Loringhoven—whose work will be remembered by readers of *The Little Review* and *Transition*—gained a reputation for revolution in dress by wearing a beaver hat trimmed with clocksprings, and using the frying pans out of doll's houses as buttons for her overcoat. This revolution in dress though superficial in nature was, however, of great interest as a forerunner of surrealism.

(c) Surrealism and Neo-Classicism

Putting on one side the political tenets of the surrealists, which, as occasion has convincingly shown, they themselves are perfectly willing to do when a chance of some bourgeois publicity turns up, surrealism may conveniently be defined as the free grouping together of incongruous and non-associated images. Whether these images are drawn from dreams and the unconscious mind, or whether they are the result of a particularly self-conscious and deliberate choice, is a question that only the artist can answer, and in no way affects the spectator. Cocteau has said that images in dreams are like flowers under the sea, in that they immediately lose their colour on being brought to the surface, and the spectator confronted with dream images set down on canvas may well feel the impotent boredom of a guest who is forced to share the dream experiences of a voluble host, experiences which, drawn from the mystery of sleep, have withered at the breakfast table. But not even the most exasperating of Dunne raconteurs expects to be paid, or claims aesthetic value for his account of how he was chased by a cow which eventually turned into the Eiffel Tower what time he himself was having his teeth removed by a lady dentist.

Big Business men must often have lain awake at night thinking how others, by sleeping, have become for a few hours commercially non-existent, wrapped in slumber, and devoting their precious time to useless dreams. It has been left to artists to achieve the final triumphant stroke of Big Business commercialization. They have valorized the dream. Beddoes' whimsical query: 'If there were dreams to sell what would you buy?' has now become a matter of hard fact. 'Some cost a passing bell, some a light sigh', and some cost many thousand francs in La Rue de la Boëtie. The fortunate poet need no longer say: 'I being poor have only my dreams', for dreams have now assumed a commercial value far exceeding the cloths of heaven.

One's reason for suspecting the validity—quite apart from the hypothetical interest—of these dream experiences is the extraordinary similarity and monotony of surrealist art. It is natural for one man trying to paint a guitar and a pair of boots to be influenced by another painter who is an admitted master of that genre, but it seems strange that a painter whose avowed object is the mere transcription of his dream should be influenced by the night fancies of some other painter. Perhaps dreaming is becoming an acquired accomplishment with its own standards of excellence. It may be that in the near future there will be schools of dreaming where you will be taught to do the thing properly. Dreamers will become classified into academic dreamers, who are chased by bulls, and modern dreamers, whose unconscious mind has more of a Viennese lilt. Dreaming, let us hope, will eventually assume a gossip-column value: 'Lady Trampleasure, best known perhaps as a breeder of Bedlingtons, has other interests besides. Her many friends who see her only at Goodwood would be surprised to learn that she is one of the most accomplished dreamers in the Dukeries.'

Turning from the future of dreams to their present-day first fruits in practical form, the surrealist school of painting may be described as being predominantly literary in content. Unlike previous schools of painting, such as the Impressionists or Cubists, which can only be classified by a consideration of their actual way of painting, the surrealists can be classified by what they paint. Their lack of formal content is the logical outcome of the overthrowal (in accordance with the famous manifesto of Breton) of the control exercised by the reason, and of any aesthetic choice, prejudice or preoccupation. Their academic realism of technique, though not actually demanded by their book of rules, is a natural corollary of their automatic-writing attitude towards painting. It is not necessary that an ouija board should be beautiful or significant in itself—it is only necessary that it should convey its message. Legibility rather than decorative effect is the quality to be prized in automatic writing.

Surrealist painting relying for its effect on the dreamlike association of incongruous images, it is necessary that these images should be as immediately recognizable as the easy-to-draw-but-hard-to-get cottage loaf of the pavement artist. There is no theoretical reason why a surrealist painting should not use the technique shown in such a work as 'The Doctor' by Sir Luke Fildes, and indeed if the doctor was given a cat's face for a head, the lamp beside him being a miniature railway signal, and the patient painted in the nude but with his various limbs scattered about the room, one detached hand giving the doctor a smart clip on the ear, the whole thing would be a remarkably successful example of surrealist painting.

The type of artistic experiment which tends to a slight, or even complete, obscuring of the immediately recognizable shape and function of the depicted object in the interests of formal unity, has no place in surrealism. The Cubists, for example, chose a guitar, a newspaper, a bottle of wine, and a pipe, as material for experiment, because they provided the right type of raw material for their purpose, and not because they were symbols of music, politics and self-indulgence. In spite of Jean Cocteau's lachrymose and Baldwinesque attempt to reduce Picasso to the stature of the *brave bourgeois* by pointing out that there was a pipe, a paper, and a bottle of wine in every true Frenchman's house, and also in every abstract of Picasso, it is reasonable to assume that this particular type of Home Sweet Home symbolism was the last thing that prompted Picasso's Cubist epoch. Between the Cubist epoch in painting and the surrealist movement lies as great a gulf as exists between the impressionism of Stravinsky's pre-war ballets and the neo-classicism of his post-war concertos.

Academic critics have, in the past, so covered themselves with ignominy by saying that anyone could paint like Van Gogh or that anyone could write like Debussy, that it requires no little courage to point out the short cuts and simplifications introduced by the surrealists into creative expression. It is possible to produce a poem that would satisfy surrealist canons by pasting together odd strips from a newspaper—this method is actually advocated by Breton—and it is possible to create a surrealist picture by pasting together, provided they are sufficiently contrasted in subject matter, odd scraps of old magazine illustrations—the more academic in style the better—a method followed by Max Ernst in his book *La Femme—Cent Têtes*.

81

Post-war Pasticheurs

That these methods can produce amusing and exhilarating results is shown by Max Ernst's book, but it is clear that all that is needed to produce this type of work is a quick wit and a modicum of sensibility. Instead of Max Ernst's nude statues and Fantomas illustrations, one can use old vintage years of the Royal Academy Illustrated and achieve equally striking results. One can even turn the tables and construct quite a good Max Ernst with incongruously superimposed fragments of pictures by Boecklin. A surrealist called upon to design a new costume need not display the invention of a Picasso or even the discrimination of a Poiret—he can simply trim a beaver hat with clocksprings, like the late lamented Baroness.

There might not, at first sight, seem to be any direct connecting link between the neo-romanticism of the surrealists with their sacrifice of form and texture to literary interest, and the neo-classicism of Stravinsky, with its apparent concentration on formalism and minute details of texture to the detriment of any emotional quality. But actually the mentality behind these two outwardly opposed manifestations is of much the same order, and the apparent disparity between the results achieved is due to the essential difference of the medium only. In the past the minor artist without any intense or personal vision usually relapsed into a mild form of academicism; today he is offered the exhilarating outlet provided by deliberate incongruity. In painting this is most simply achieved by a plain visual statement, and when an artist can satisfy both his conscience and his patrons by an unexpected arrangement of realistically painted objects it would be churlish to demand an equally unexpected development in their actual painting.

Music can offer no direct parallel to this type of surrealism for the very simple reason that realistic representation, except of the farmyard order, cannot be recognized without the aid of a programme. Strauss, the most accomplished master of photographic suggestion in music, can, it is true, suggest a flock of sheep by a bleating on muted trombones, a couple of monks by a modal passage on two bassoons, and a boat on the water by the usual aqueous devices; but it is highly improbable that by a combination of the three he could bring before our eyes a picture of two monks in a barge with a lot of sheep.

But although music provides no recognizable objects for rearrangement it provides certain recognizable styles and also certain formulas that are so familiar to us that they have almost the quality of a realistically painted object. The rapid time travelling from one period to another that we find in Poulenc's *Les Biches*, or in his concerto for two pianos, provides a parallel to the placing together of dissimilar objects in space that we find in the work of René Magritte or John Banting. The use of jazz glissandos in *Pulcinella* has much the same effect as a photograph of a Negro with a cocktail shaker pasted into the background of an Alma Tadema reproduction. The cadences in the chorales of *L'Histoire du Soldat* give one the same shock as the combination of classical statues with balloon ascents to be found in Max Ernst's *La Femme— Cent Têtes*.

If Poulenc's rapid changes of style may be compared to Ernst at his most facetious, Stravinsky's more subtle and more far-reaching pastiches may be compared to Chirico at his most characteristic. Both Stravinsky and Chirico stand a little outside the more unscrupulous and arriviste work of their disciples, and disdaining the beaver hat and clock-springs of the late Baroness they come before us like statues of early Victorian statesmen, clad in all the specious solemnity of the toga.

A background of classicism is by no means incompatible with the surrealist mind working in music. Like the realistic style of the surrealist painters it provides the essential norm without which the abnormalities would pass by unnoticed —it is significant that the sculptured head that appears with such monotonous persistence in modern paintings is always a Graeco-Roman head, never a primitive, or exotic, head. Stravinsky's researches into the past do not carry him as far back as the periods where you can never be quite certain what the composer is going to do next. He uses as his raw material either the formalized style of the eighteenth century as represented by inferior Bach, or else the sentimental clichés of Tchaikovsky which through their saccharine obviousness give a peculiar savour to the acidities of their incongruous accompaniment. A discordant harmonization of a familiar tune like 'God Save the Queen,' for example, would be much more of a shock to us than any given fourteen bars in an atonal work. Chirico can convey by his classically painted broken columns an effect which would fail were the columns to be painted in the manner of Rouault. The groups of geometrical planes which take the place of breasts in his gigantic philosophers are only remarkable through their contrast with the uninspired realism of the rest of the painting. Similarly, Stravinsky can achieve a surrealist incongruity by his wilful distortion of familiar classical formulas. A perfect cadence is broken across like a Chirico column, a suave and formal fugue leads, like the toga of Chirico's mobled sages, to a harsh and discordant collection of abstract patterns.

Although Diaghileff employed both Chirico and Stravinsky in his post-war ballets it will be remembered that with that genius for the chicly incongruous that made him the most successful of commercial surrealists he did not present two such kindred spirits at the same time. He also made use of the official surrealists—as represented by Ernst and Miró— though on one occasion only. To have given them his continued support would have destroyed his prestige as a time traveller and *marchand de nouveautés*. As a space traveller, before the war, he could occasionally afford to call a halt by the wayside, but as a time traveller he could not afford to be in the same epoch for any length of time. Besides, to have lent continued support to the surrealist school would have shown a congruity of thought and action hardly in conformity with surrealist theory.

It may seem that in concentrating so much attention on Diaghileff himself one is treating his collaborators in summary fashion. But Diaghileff was far more than a mere impresario. Though not, strictly speaking, a creative artist, he had very much more genius than many of the artists who worked for him, and it hardly seems worth while examining the work of such minor composers as Dukelsky, Sauguet, Nabokoff, and others, apart from their connection with Diaghileff. They were merely the gunmen executing the commands of their Capone, who, like all great gangsters, never touched firearms himself. Besides, Diaghileff's personality concentrated in a probably unparalleled way the spirit of a whole generation of artistic thought. His sensibility, if not always profound, was always rapid, and he had an astounding 'nose' for the growth of any particular movement of taste or snobbism. Being as near to a creative artist as any producer can be he was able to express things that were outside his own experience; but being a creative artist manqué, without a genuine urge or belief round which to orientate himself, he was always liable to become the tool of those whom he had brought into existence, and whose feelings he had formulated for them. He became a victim of the fashions he himself had set, and being an older man than his entourage he was correspondingly more afraid of fashionable reaction. When he was young he could afford to attach his name to certain movements, but in later years he did not dare to face the accusation of conservatism that such an attachment would imply.

Before the war he created a vogue for the Russian ballet, but after the war he merely created a vogue for vogue. All art became divided into 'choses fades' and 'choses vivantes' —'choses vivantes' meaning any novelty however futile, that he could use as a knout with which to lash the jaded public into enthusiasm. There was always the danger, though, that the knout might prove a fragile switch, easily broken and revealed only too plainly as a 'chose fade'. He thus became pledged to the sterile doctrine of reaction for reaction's sake, a doctrine which was well summed up by his henchman Stravinsky in the revealing phrase: 'Toute réaction est vraie'.

(d) 'Toute réaction est vraie'

Before the war Stravinsky's work was so intimately bound up with the mentality and organization of the Russian ballet that the idea of his breaking away from Diaghileff would have seemed as absurd as Alice trying to wake up the Red King. It is true that *Le Rossignol* showed a slight divergence from the narrow path of ballet mentality, but it had the excuse of being only a continuation of a work begun in pre-Diaghileff days, and its independent existence was shortlived, Stravinsky after a few years reducing it to a version which could take its place in the Diaghileff repertoire. As for the concert-hall works of this period, the *Chansons Japonaises* and the cantata *Le Roi des Étoiles*, although they contain excellent music they are the only works of his to achieve no notoriety. Until 1914, then, Stravinsky and Diaghileff may be treated as partners in the same firm. The war interrupted this collaboration but the Russian revolution provided a new link by throwing them into the same political and social situation. Willy nilly they became White Russians with all the trials such a role involves.

It is insufficiently realized how gravely political and social issues may affect what appear at first sight to be purely aesthetic problems, particularly when these problems concern—as in ballet—the public and the patron as much as the creative artists. The most striking successes of the pre-war Russian ballet depended very largely on Russian glamour, a Slavonic nostalgia either of the barbaric semi-Asiatic type, with its Tartar warriors, or of the more civilized semi-European type, with its wilting young women. The nostalgia was successful because it was false and because the oriental tradition and the imperial regime still existed. But the Russian revolution gave Russian glamour a severe setback; the nostalgia for old St. Petersburg became all too real a fact when the town was called Leningrad. The old Russian glamour was kept up in a sadly retrospective way by groups of émigrés with their unaccustomed balalaikas, but revolutionary pioneers like Stravinsky and Diaghileff could not afford to become professional exiles. The new glamour of revolt exploited in later years by the Soviet films had not yet reached artistic maturity and, even if it had, it is unlikely that an exploitation of this type of glamour would have best pleased the aristocratic patrons on whom Diaghileff was of necessity financially and socially dependent.

The national spirit that until then had sufficed Stravinsky and Diaghileff suddenly became an unreal shadow leaving them without a spiritual foundation for their work. Diaghileff, as we have seen, found his own solution to the problem; but whatever he did he had to stick to his own particular section of artistic expression, the ballet, and however much he reacted for reaction's sake he had always to be entertaining in the widest sense of the word. Stravinsky, although his greatest successes had always been in ballet form, was not so bound to the theatre, and his successive reactions led him to change not only the texture of his music, but also the angle of its appeal. It was necessary for him to be a pioneer, to create revolutionary sensation, but he had already exhausted the vocabulary of sensation, and there were no more buildings left to raze.

Like a spectacular sinner the only course left open to him was a spectacular conversion. If sensation could not be caused by a departure from the audience's norm it could at least be caused by a departure from his own norm, that of sensation—which, incidentally, the audience was gradually beginning to adopt as its own. His audience expected cocktails and jazz, but it was impossible to give them stronger cocktails, or louder jazz. They craved sensation—very well, they should have it. Cold water and a sermon for them. They expected to see their host in new and increasingly elaborate costumes. Very well, they should see the crowning *creation* of all—the Emperor's New Clothes. Stravinsky, in his last works, has achieved the final triumph of fashion, he has created a fashion for boredom.

In this country at least Stravinsky is best known by his early ballets and his later concertos, and it thus appears as if his chilly neo-classicism was an immediate volte-face from his barbaric impressionism. Such a conception is a dangerous telescoping of his musical progress. He has, it is true, proceeded by a series of reactions, but they have each been linked together by the presence of one or two qualities in common with the preceding epoch, and it is impossible to understand the true nature of the solemnities of *Oedipus Rex*, without examining the series of rather facetious miniatures he wrote during the war.

These works, *Renard*, *L'Histoire du Soldat*, *Pribaoutki*, the *Berceuses du Chat*, the *Pièces Faciles* for piano duet, and many

88

other works of similar calibre are chiefly marked off from the early ballets by a striking reduction in scale, both in texture and conception. The vast orchestra of *Le Sacre du Printemps* is supplanted by a handful of instruments, and the human panorama of *Petrushka* is replaced by a penny peep show. They are essentially marionette works. Petrushka is no longer even half human, he is merely stuffed with straw, and Stravinsky, the oriental magician, can play his little tunes of the flute with no ghost of emotion to disturb him.

Although written during the war they are an anticipation of the immediately post-war period of deliberate silliness in the arts. This silliness was sometimes almost inspired—as in the case of that admirable figure Erik Satie—but for the most part it had the flavour of an over-repeated practical joke. There is little doubt that it was a reaction against both the real and the false heroics of the preceding years. Heroics in music were apt to be all too reminiscent of the panache of 1914, and music-hall repartee was not unnaturally preferred to an oration. The logical spirit of 'I go to the theatre to make me laugh—after all there is enough sadness in life already without having to pay for it' became adopted towards all the arts. Unfortunately, music is not very well adapted to wit—as apart from the good humour of a composer like Haydn—and the only type of humour possible in music is buffoonery. A drearily forced wit and a species of intellectual and self-conscious buffoonery are the dominant literary characteristics of Stravinsky's wartime works.

Far be it from me to support the attitude of injured patriotism, almost, that so many critics take up when faced with the insignificant facetiousness of so much wartime music. Historical catastrophes can only become material for art when viewed in perspective. The only great treatments of historical and political events in music, Mussorgsky's operas, deal with periods remote from his own. Even the

Post-war Pasticheurs

Russian revolutionary films were made some time after the situations they celebrated were a fait accompli, and the finest of them, *Potemkin* and *La Nouvelle Babylone*, were constructed round the 1905 revolution and the Paris Commune respectively—revolutions easier to use as artistic material because they were not only separated from the present period but were also unsuccessful.

An artist must either take part in action or withdraw from it entirely. He cannot glorify it from outside. One can sympathize with the artist who enters with gusto into warfare and also with the artist who is a conscientious objector. But the artist who puts not himself but his art at the service of warfare, the composer who writes battle hymns, and the novelist who indulges in bellicose propaganda—those are the figures who should rightly incur the dangers of the trenches and the rigours of solitary confinement. When the death of some thousands seems to serve no other purpose than to inspire people like Lord Northcliffe and James Douglas to an ever purpler prose, and the sound of gunfire can be heard at the breakfast table, it is small wonder that the artist should turn aside to write lullabies for his cat or to record the adventures of the old colonel who never succeeded in shooting anything.

In Stravinsky's case the reaction against excess and brutality of any kind, particularly heroic excess and patriotic brutality, that every artist must feel during wartime, coincided with the period in his career when he himself had already reached the limits of excess and brutality achievable in his own medium. He had therefore a double reason for reaction. It is typical of the composer that his reaction should have been spectacular. The gargantuan forces of *Le Sacre* were reduced not to the sober dimensions of the classic orchestra, but to the mere handful of instruments called for by *Pribaoutki* and *L'Histoire du Soldat*.

'Toute réaction est vraie'

A work like *Renard*, though it may seem a reaction against the earlier ballets, is linked to them by its use of Russian material and by its concentration on purely rhythmic devices. But there is a significant difference between the niggling use of rhythm in Stravinsky's nursery-rhyme period and the orgiastic use of rhythm in his barbaric period. In *Le Sacre* rhythm is dissociated from its melodic and harmonic components for the purposes of emphatic expression, and the same may be said of the orchestration. It is used not abstractly but nervously and emotionally, and the lack of any intrusive melodic element is only a perverted and negative example of romanticism designed to give to the rhythm and orchestration a more romantically barbaric quality. In the nursery works of Stravinsky rhythm is dissected for dissection's sake— it is no longer used even in its lowest form, the purely physical. The glorious period of 'the objective investigation of aural phenomena' has begun. Music, from being an ordered succession of sounds, has become a matter of 'sonorities', and anyone who can produce a brightly coloured brick of unusual shape is henceforth hailed as an architect.

In *Renard* the obsession with rhythmic jigsaw puzzles is still tinged with the old national colour, though the Russian folk dance is by now no longer a live and kicking peasant but a dead kulak whose corpse is so much material for a lecture by the dissecting surgeon. The same type of fragmentary folk material is, however, put to far more significant use in *Les Noces* where the national spirit makes an impressive and galvanic death struggle. *Les Noces* is one of the masterpieces of this period and possibly the only really important work that Stravinsky has given us. It stands on one side of his main output, though, and will be more fully considered in the chapter on exotic influences.

Although *Les Noces* did not actually appear until 1923 it was conceived and practically finished in 1917, and by the time we reach *L'Histoire du Soldat*, written in 1918, the remnant of vitality provided by the Russian folk song is gone, and the material used is less picturesque and more international. The Russian folk dance gives way to the pasodoble of the street band, the polka of the musical box, and the valse of the mechanical piano. The constant rhythmic changes, which had some logic when applied to the asymmetrical line of the Russian folk song, acquire a new perversity when attached to the left-right-left and the one-two-three-hop of the wooden soldiers' march and the baby's polka.

The valse, ragtime and tango which the soldier plays on his violin are not parodies like the polkas of Walton and Berners, nor are they meant to have the René Clair-like evocative significance, the bal-musette sentimentality of the valses of Auric. They are like the familiar objects, the bottle of wine, the guitar, and the pack of cards used by the Cubist painters because their very familiarity would draw added attention to their geometrical distortion. To dance to these movements is really as absurd as it would be to read the news in the sections of *Le Journal* incorporated by Picasso or Juan Gris in one of their 'abstracts'. Stravinsky was quite right to protest against Massine using the *Ragtime*—a work of much the same type, and of roughly the same period—for dancing purposes. The *Ragtime*, like the piano *Rag Music*, is an abstract pattern created out of the raw material of certain syncopated devices. It has no connection whatsoever with either the technique or the emotional world of jazz.

L'Histoire du Soldat is chiefly of interest as the most elaborate and convincing work of Stravinsky's abstract period, that is to say, the period in which he uses popular and humorous material for the purposes of abstract rhythmical dissection. The abstraction of these nursery-rhyme works is more significant than their buffoonery, for there is singularly little geniality or gusto about their self-conscious clowning.

The paraphernalia of the harlequinade are not of necessity humorous in themselves. One man may laugh like a child when he sees the red-hot poker applied to the butcher's inviting rump, another man may use the occasion for a lecture on the origins of laughter, with some notes on the connection between sadistic impulses and the risible faculties in the mentality of the infant. In the hands of Stravinsky the red-hot poker becomes the ruler of the maths master. We should not allow the outré orchestration of this work—always, as with Stravinsky, the most accomplished side of it—to blind us to its essentially coldblooded abstraction.

Apart from the two short chorales, which point forward to his neo-classical period, *L'Histoire du Soldat* consists almost entirely of an objective juggling with rhythm, or rather metre, for there can be no true rhythm where there is no melodic life. Like Gertrude Stein, Stravinsky chooses the drabbest and least significant phrases for the material of his experiments, because if the melodic line had life dissection would be impossible. A statement like 'Everyday they were gay there, they were regularly gay there everyday', etc., from Gertrude Stein's *Helen Furr and Georgine Skeene*, has no particular value as content, least of all is it meant to be gay. It is merely material for a fantasia in rhythmic values whose effect would be equally appreciated by someone with no knowledge of English whatsoever. Similarly, the melodic fragments in *L'Histoire du Soldat* are completely meaningless in themselves. They are merely successions of notes that can conveniently be divided up into groups of three, five and seven and set against other mathematical groupings.

The melodic poverty, or even nullity, of such a movement as the *Petit Concert* reaches its logical development in the final section, a cadenza for drums alone that is actually the

93

most consistently satisfying feature of the whole work. It represents the goal towards which the earlier compositions of this period had been tending. Harmony, melody, all that could give the least emotional significance to his music, has been banished in the interests of abstraction, and musical purity has been achieved by a species of musical castration. The formula of sound for sound's sake is here reduced to its ludicrous essentials, and there is no further progress possible on these lines. The percussion solo which ends *L'Histoire du Soldat* has much the same satisfaction of finality as the map of that pioneer of abstraction The Bellman, which was, we are told, 'a perfect and absolute blank'.

Unlike Debussy, who was strong enough to conquer his early mannerisms and put his revolutionary technique to a flexibly expressive use, Stravinsky was caught in the mechanics of his technical mannerisms, and the deliberate exploitation of certain facets of musical thought for their own sake led him to a definite blind alley from which there was no escape except by a deliberate reaction. He is like a motorist who spends all his time with his head inside the bonnet. *Chi ha vissuto per amore, per amore si morì* ('Those who live for love are killed by love') sings the street musician in Puccini's *Il Tabarro*—and he might have added: 'Those who live for technique are killed by technique.'

(e) Synthetic Melody

The series of reactions by which Stravinsky has progressed have been imposed upon him not only by the exigencies of fashion, but by his complete lack of any melodic faculty. Even his greatest admirers, I think, would admit that from the pale Wagnerian reflections of the Scherzo Fantastique (*La Vie des Abeilles*) to the monotonous peasant fragments of

Les Noces there is nothing in his music that can be described as a typical Stravinsky tune. We can recognize him immediately by his scoring, by his rhythm and by the setting he gives to his themes, but the themes themselves are either traditional or characterless.

During the Impressionist period the excitement aroused by the new world of colour that had been opened up led to an almost complete neglect of the expressive possibilities of line, and melody through its traditional association with sentiment was tarred with the same brush as sentimentality. Melody came to be regarded merely as one of the elements in music, whereas it is not only the most important element but an all-embracing one. Harmony without melody is only an aural tickling, and rhythm without melody is not even rhythm—it is only metre, and can have at the most a vaguely mumbo-jumbo appeal, with no true musical significance. A melody, though, is a complete work of art in itself and the unaccompanied Gregorian chants still remain among the most perfect and satisfying achievements in music.

A composer may have a rudimentary harmonic sense or a rudimentary rhythmic sense, and yet remain a great composer on the strength of his line alone. To a composer gifted with melodic genius there may be problems of technique but there can be no problems of style, for a vital melody not only has intrinsic value but carries with it the implications of its harmonic, rhythmic and contrapuntal treatment. A complete and arbitrary change of style is unthinkable to a great melodist, for to him melody is a living thing, a part of himself—it is a tree which follows a natural growth and not a piece of wood which can be painted any colour, or used for any old piece of furniture. A composer like Tchaikovsky, for example, who, whatever his limitations as a symphonist, is undoubtedly one of the world's greatest melodists, shows no abrupt change of style at any moment in his career. His progress as a composer can be gauged by the increasing richness of his melodic powers. *La Belle au Bois Dormant* is a better work than *Le Lac des Cygnes* because melodically it is both more fertile and powerful, and the increasing richness of the harmony and orchestration is not an elaborate façade which conceals structural weaknesses, it is naturally conditioned by this melodic improvement.

Although a melodic gift does not force a composer to change his style it places no bounds on his developments, as does harmonic and rhythmic specialization. Delius obviously reached the extreme limit of what he could express by harmonic means by the time he had written *A Song of the High Hills*—or even earlier—and Stravinsky obviously reached the extreme limit of rhythmic expression in *Les Noces*. But a composer like Verdi, whose strength lay in his melodic line, arrived at no such cul-de-sac, either technical or emotional. He was not reduced to repeating his earlier manner like Delius, or to reacting against it like Stravinsky. He was able to pursue a logical process of development which resulted in those two masterpieces of expressive force and technical skill—*Otello* and *Falstaff*—both written in his seventies. It may be pleaded that the greater richness of the orchestral accompaniment is what chiefly distinguishes these operas from his earlier works, but, as in the case of Tchaikovsky, this richness is merely the logical counterpart of the greater power and flexibility of the melodic line.

One of the more deplorable results of the so-called speeding up of modern life is the credit for vitality given to an artist who satisfies the jaded appetite of his mondaine public by frequent changes of style. In any other age but the present it would be a truism to point out that frequent changes of styles argue a low vitality and undeveloped personality on the part of the artist—an inability to exploit more than the surface texture of his medium. When the mentality of the spoilt child who kicks his meccano to pieces out of boredom is valued above that of the man with the skill and patience involved in building a bridge, it is clear that some examination not only of the methods but also of the impulses of the modern artist is gravely needed. With the minor Parisian figures, the camp followers of Diaghileff, it is fairly safe to assume that lack of individuality and desire for chic were at the back of their changes of style, but with Stravinsky we may charitably assume that the reasons were more technical, for to do him justice there has always been an almost hieratic earnestness about his apparently facetious technical juggling. Les Six performed their little tricks with all the quips and cranks of the cheerily anecdotal nothing-up-my-sleeve type of conjurer, but Stravinsky approached his public with the pontifical solemnity of the oriental illusionist.

We have seen how the dissection of harmony and rhythm in the Impressionist period for expressive purposes was followed in Stravinsky's wartime period by the dissection of harmony and rhythm for abstract purposes. The one element that hitherto had not been dissected as such was melody. Melody, in fact, had been classed with the 'choses fades'. But given the type of mentality that can say with all sincerity: 'toute réaction est vraie', it is not surprising to find the once-despised melodic element suddenly enthroned as a 'chose vivante'. The time travelling of the *Pulcinella* ballet probably provided the impetus for Stravinsky's neo-classical period, which, apart from the adoption of eighteenth-century forms and titles, is chiefly noticeable for its attempt to create melody by synthetic means. Unfortunately melody cannot be learnt like counterpoint, nor is it capable of either dissection or synthetic manufacture. One cannot create a creature of flesh and blood out of fossil fragments.

It need hardly be pointed out that the sequences, cadences, and other stylistic features of the best classical tunes are not their most important element. They take their place in the scheme of things, they have formal and even emotional logic, but they are the façade, not the whole building. It is the easiest possible thing to take four bars out of one of the best-constructed and most moving of Mozart's arias and find that in themselves they have remarkably little value. This, in fact, is what Stravinsky often does without, however, realizing that he is confusing the periwig with the face beneath it. The turns of phrase that occur at the end of a melody with much the same conventional beauty and constructional logic as a Corinthian capital occurring at the top of a column are taken by Stravinsky, isolated from their surroundings and plastered over the façade with a complete disregard of their true function and a complete inability to add anything to them except a little incongruous colour. Lest I should be thought to be exaggerating the confusion between eighteenth-century thought and eighteenth-century mannerism exhibited by Stravinsky and his followers, I should like to recall the occasion when Diaghileff included as a symphonic interlude at the Russian ballet Mozart's *Musical Joke*, a brilliant parody of the stupid and mechanical application of eighteenth-century formulas to insignificant and ludicrous material. No one saw the joke except Diaghileff himself. His entourage took the piece with perfect gravity as an example of classicism to be admired and imitated.

To create even a synthetic melody—such as the one in the slow movement of Ravel's concerto—to any degree of satisfaction requires a power of sustained linear construction which it is only too clear Stravinsky does not possess. His melodic style has always been marked by extreme short-windedness and a curious inability to get away from the principal note of the tune. This was no matter in his earlier ballets where the abrupt fragmentary phrases and the repetition of one insistent note emphasized a barbaric quality which would have been destroyed by the introduction of a long and well-made melody. But the essence of a classical melody is continuity of line, contrast and balance of phrases, and the ability to depart from the nodal point in order that the ultimate return to it should have significance and finality.

That Stravinsky's shortwinded methods are incapable of producing even a satisfactory synthesis of this type of melody we can see by taking a concrete example, the theme which opens the slow movement of his Piano Concerto—a movement which may be said to set the type of Stravinsky's adagios for the next few years. It opens with a two-bar phrase in the eighteenth-century manner—commonplace enough, but still, capable of yielding results of a certain distinction in the hands of a composer such as Vivaldi. Stravinsky, however, is unable to continue this phrase or even find a contrasting two bars. He repeats it with a slight rhythmic variation—the only type of treatment that comes easily to him—twists its tail for a moment and then lets it fall gradually back on itself, the process of extinction being artificially held up by the mechanical application of sequential figures, which derive not from eighteenth-century lyricism, but from eighteenth-century passage work.

The repetition of the theme, by the orchestra, adds even less to the very insignificant content of the opening phrase which, like Stravinsky's earlier themes, is restricted to a small interval centred round the one note. The second subject strikes a more convincing atmosphere at the outset because, consisting of a little minor phrase repeated three times over a double ostinato, it takes us back to the peasant mentality of the old Stravinsky. But here again the phrase is illogically extended by eighteenth-century passage work, whose origin is not thematic, but harmonic. That is to say, in a quick eighteenth-century movement for a keyboard instrument

99

the harmonies are often split up into toccata-like figures for the sake of the texture alone, the figures thus produced having no significant content as pure melody. Their *raison d'être* is the harmony that lies beneath them, and to use them as Stravinsky does as melodic material over a totally different harmonic base is a complete misunderstanding of their value and function, and a convincing proof, if any such is needed, of the artificial and synthetic quality of his alleged classicism.

A phrase like 'Ladies and gentlemen, unaccustomed as I am to public speaking' is flat enough in all conscience, but if it occurs at the beginning of a speech as a prelude to a remark of some weight we can accept it readily enough as an unavoidable and inoffensive formula; but we can hardly be expected to keep patience with a speaker whose whole oration consists of a portentously solemn Mene Mene Tekel Upharsin delivery of a Stein-like fantasia such as 'Ladies and gentle ladies and gentlemenu-manumissionaries unaccustomed as I am to a Siamese customary una-menu-mina-mo ('alf a mo' ladies) to a ladies' public bar and gentlemen's speakeasy I mean to easy public speak I-N-G spells ING.'

Stravinsky's later slow movements, it is true, show a greater flexibility—due mainly to the greater vocabulary of formulas that are drawn upon—but the artificial method of construction remains the same. In his quick movements a certain effect of logic and continuity is obtained by adopting the shape and type of an eighteenth-century toccata, but the form thus achieved is purely extrinsic, and has none of the intrinsic form and inevitability of shape which is independent of formalism. Like the material itself the form is synthetic.

Once we have realized the synthetic nature of Stravinsky's neo-classicism we can follow, step by step, the various applications of this method to material drawn from different and later sources. To the melodic formulas drawn from Bach which are used in the Piano Concerto are added, in later works, fragments from Beethoven, Bellini, Chopin, Tchaikovsky and even Johann Strauss—who enters with ludicrous effect into Jocasta's air at the beginning of the second act of *Oedipus Rex*—while to synthetic calm succeeds synthetic drama, and to synthetic austerity synthetic charm.

Stravinsky is essentially a decorator, not an architect, and he must always find new shapes to decorate. *Oedipus Rex, Apollo Musagetes, Le Baiser de la Fée,* may differ in outward shape, but the mentality behind their fabrication remains the same. They are not so much music as renowned impersonations of music. *Oedipus* has all the paraphernalia of a tragedy, and the only thing wrong with it is the complete lack of any genuine pity or genuine terror. It attempts to move us by reviving the dramatic restraint and formalism of Gluck without realizing that this austerity is apparent to Gluck himself, who, on the contrary, sought the most passionate form of expression his technique and period allowed him. It is surprising to find Jean Cocteau, who so truly remarked: 'One may derive art from life, but not from art', associated with a work which is so triumphant a proof of his dictum. *Oedipus* is a synthetically emotional work, created by the use of type-material associated in our mind with the genuine emotion of classical opera.

There is no essential difference between the mock tragedy of *Oedipus* and the mock gaiety of the piano *Capriccio*. They are both examples of frustrated ectogenesis. The finale of the *Capriccio* imitates the sound and the methods of gay music without once achieving the quality of gaiety. Jazzed-up Johann Strauss, with neither the sentimental appeal of Strauss nor the exhilaration of jazz, it has the depressing effect of a gramophone record of someone laughing.

The same methods of fabrication, more openly avowed, can be seen in the ballet *Le Baiser de la Fée* where a series of Tchaikovsky's lesser piano pieces are treated in the Procrustean manner once applied to Pergolesi's innocent charms. Here the neglected element of melodic charm is exploited with all the mechanical solemnity of *Oedipus*, though the necessary element of chic and time travelling is provided by the sour and deliberate harmonic distortions of such a saccharine melody as 'None but the Weary Heart'. The effect is like a collaboration between Marcus Stone and Picabia, and *Le Baiser de la Fée* is perhaps the most sur-realist of his works, combining the nationalist charm of *L'Oiseau de Feu* with the neo-classical solemnities of his later period. This analysis of charm is not so much a killing of the goose that lays the golden eggs, as a dissection of the egg that might have produced another Golden Bird. At the same time the very fact that the thematic material is drawn from the always fecund Tchaikovsky gives to *Le Baiser de la Fée* a certain character, which is lacking in the later works, such as the Violin Concerto. Stravinsky's brilliant sense of orchestral colour, which for some years he had rigorously suppressed, is here allowed full and charming play, and has much the piquant effect of Sickert's coloured transcriptions of Victorian engravings.

The extreme lack of thematic distinction shown in the first movement of the Violin Concerto—which in this respect recalls the earlier Concertino for string quartet—and the negative nature of the finale of that superb example of Musica Celestia the *Symphonie des Psaumes*—which bears much the relation to true melody that the finale of *L'Histoire du Soldat* does to true rhythm—suggest that Stravinsky has reached a turning point in his career similar to that which he reached after the war. But while it is interesting to specu-late about the future of most contemporary composers of note, the mentality revealed by Stravinsky, both in his compositions and in his spoken pronouncements, gives us little hope that his future reactions will be based on anything more urgent and compelling than the exigencies of vogue.

As an example of Stravinsky's attitude towards reaction for its own sake I may quote an instance of his urging young composers to give their tunes to the violins and not to the trumpet on the grounds that too many people had been writing tunes for the trumpet in the last few years. So might Patou and Poiret forecast the colours for the coming season. It does not seem to have occurred to him that orchestration has any relation to the technical nature or expressive quality of a given theme, that one writes for the cor anglais because that is the tone colour one wants, and not because it happens to be a Tuesday. Similarly Stravinsky's followers will say with all the withering self-satisfaction of those who have caught the last seat in a crowded bus: 'It's no use writing that sort of harmony *now*', and will themselves admittedly falsify their originally conceived harmonies purely with a view to giving them a more strictly contemporary quality.

It really is of no great significance which period of music Stravinsky chooses to exploit next. His time travelling is like the space travelling of a character like Douglas Fairbanks who finds a golf club and an American bar wherever he goes, whether it be Malaya or Madagascar. At one time we were told that the truth lay in Bach, at another that it lay in Tchaikovsky, and if tomorrow Stravinsky took to producing synthetic Grieg—and there are remoter possibilites —no doubt we should be told that it was towards the melodic freshness and harmonic charm of the Norwegian composer that Stravinsky had been aiming all his life. The 'chose vivante' of today becomes the 'chose fade' of tomorrow, and when every reaction is equally true then every reaction becomes equally insignificant.

The somewhat melancholy catalogue of Stravinsky's later works has been worth examining not so much for their individual merit as for their significance as types. Like Diag-hileff, Stravinsky stands for more than he himself has achieved, and it is as a group soul or *Zeitgeist* that he is a figure of weight. The enormous influence exerted by his technical dexterity, and previously won prestige, has un-doubtedly helped on a movement which, although it might have existed without him, would not have received such sharp definition.

It is not necessary to study in detail the reactions of his various Parisian and would-be Parisian followers, who, with touching unanimity, mimic his different movements and changes of style much as the minor painters who group them-selves round Picasso automatically switch over from 'abstracts' to Ingres, and back again, in accordance with the whims of their leaders. They are like the confidante in *The Critic* who imitated her mistress even to the point of coming in mad, dressed in white satin. To examine seriously their synthetic imitations of an already synthetic product would be to lose all sense of proportion.

At the same time we should distinguish between Stra-vinsky's use of pastiche—which may more accurately, though laboriously, be described as the synthetic creation of music by a rearrangement of previously existing formulas —and the more obvious use of pastiche in the accepted sense of the word such as we find in the parodies of Walton and Berners, or the genre pieces of Ravel. Nor should we confuse it with the natural classicism of Prokofieff whose music has from the outset shown affinities with the academic generation of Russian music represented by Glazunoff and Medtner. The contrast between *Daphnis and Chloe* and *Bolero*, between *Ala and Lolly* and *L'Enfant Prodigue* is significant as showing a general trend in modern music, but it is Stravinsky who is the key-figure of our times. As Mr. Cecil Gray has rightly remarked, if he had not existed it would have been necessary to have invented him. The only thing that prevents him from becoming a lay figure on which to drape the latest intellectual fashions is a pleasantly atavistic trait which peeps through the austerities of his later period much as the homely African features of Francis Williams, the eighteenth-century Negro Scholar of Jamaica, belie the periwig on his head and the geometrical instruments in his hand. Like so many Russians Stravinsky has adopted and been adopted by a Parisian intellectual world that is not his by racial right. You cannot, or so I have been informed, scratch a Russian without finding a Tartar, and the formula applies even to those Russians who are more at home on the boulevard than on the steppe.

It stands to reason—as Norman Douglas would say—that the composer of *Le Sacre* and *Les Noces* cannot entirely suppress his natural leanings and genuine impulses even when these impulses have been intellectually classed as 'choses fades'. The healthily barbaric tradition of Russian music will insist on breaking through the chilly austerity of his neo-classical works, and the most impressive moments in these compositions are undeniably those when he returns to the ostinatos, the short repeated phrases, the primitive incantations and the rhythmical emphasis of his early ballets; such moments as the kaleidoscopic cadenza in the first movement of the piano concerto—which recalls *Les Noces*—the fine Gloria in *Oedipus*, the sombre pulsing on two notes that accompanies the opening and final chorus in the same work, and the closing bars of *Apollo* with their repetition at varied rhythmic intervals of the same little figure. This last device is Stravinsky's favourite method of bringing a movement to an end, and can be traced back to the first tableau of *Petrushka* and the first tableau of *Le Sacre*. The final page of *Apollo* has an entirely different tempo and quality of sound, but in spite of its suavity it displays essentially the same primitive use of rhythmic emphasis to achieve finality. This effect may be compared to the use of the word Shantih in the final section of Eliot's *Waste Land* and the most successful example of it in Stravinsky's work is to be found in the final pages of *Les Noces* where a short phrase for bass voice is presented in curtailed form by the pianos and finally reduced to three strokes on the bell recalling the Shantih, Shantih, Shantih, that brings the *Waste Land* of Eliot to an equally impressive end.

It is typical of Stravinsky's art that to achieve an air of finality he should curtail a phrase and not extend it. It is an essentially primitive attitude and in spite of his dazzling and outward sophistication Stravinsky is essentially primitive and naïve. His real talent is *au fond* nationalist and illustrative, and it is only the forces of mechanical reaction and vogue, that we have been examining in this chapter, that have slowly driven him to being the apostle of abstraction and internationalism in music.

Although it is a truism to say that art has no boundaries and that music is the purest of all of the arts because it is non-representational, it is worth while pausing for a moment and asking whether any but a small proportion of the world's greatest music can be called international and whether any of it can be called abstract.

(f) Abstraction in Music

Nothing is more typical of the superficial nature of most modern or rather modernist critisicm than its slip-shod use of the word abstract, particularly as applied to music.

The word abstract has, of course, a certain definite significance when applied to painting, and it is a tenable hypothesis that the best modern paintings and sculptures have been abstract. Even so it would be reasonable to point out that, by denying himself realism, the painter, though he thus avoids the pitfalls of anecdotage, at the same time cuts himself off from the variety and significance of forms that intelligently used realism can provoke. The modified realism of Cézanne can be of far greater interest from the purely formal point of view than the abstractions of Léger; but even though we may grant that the highest form of plastic art consists in a significant organization of shapes devoid of all purely representational sentiment and literary association, it by no means follows that this hasty and sweeping thesis holds good for music. It is all very well to hammer out a theory, however mistaken, that applies to an art functioning in space; it is quite another matter to apply this to an art that functions in time. Most of the modern fallacies about abstraction, literary sentiment, representationalism, romantic contamination, etc., in music are due to ignoring this elementary distinction.

A picture with a narrative element in it is vaguely unpleasing not because it is literary, but because it is trying to represent time by cutting a section through it in space. *The Last Day in the Old Home,* for example, relies for its appeal not only on its own representational qualities and arrangement of forms, but on the associative and imaginative powers of the spectator, who is irresistibly led to reconstruct the events that have led up to this moment of time, and to speculate sympathetically on the future. The interest of the spectator is forced away from the scene as it occurs in space to the event as it occurred in time. The picture is, therefore, in the nature of an uncompleted sentence. The artist has only suggested a line of thought and depends for his final effect on an element of time that he cannot define in his own medium, that of space. The same incident, however, could obviously occur in a novel and be perfectly satisfactory, for then it would be one of a series of events in time and could balance the other events from the formal point of view, acquiring architectural value, as well as sentimental appeal.

Conversely, a pair of boots painted by a master like Van Gogh is a perfectly finished artistic statement in space, whereas the most detailed literary description of a pair of boots would hardly have much artistic value except, perhaps, as a prelude to the treatment of boots in time, as it were, by attaching to them a series of events like those that befell Andersen's goloshes.

Neither of the two paintings mentioned above is exactly an ideal subject for musical inspiration. Not even Strauss, that master of realism in music, could produce the musical equivalent of Van Gogh's boots. At the same time, while the prospect of a Strauss symphonic poem based on Martineau's *chef-d'œuvre* may seem too grisly to be envisaged, it is undeniable that he might achieve something by trying to express the underlying emotion of the scene, and by attempting to follow the sequence of implied events in terms of musical form. The impure picture, in fact, is nearer to music because of its emotional appeal, and its time element.

It is highly undesirable, of course, that the time element in musical design should be put to the purposes of sentimental narrative, but the mere fact that it can be so used distinguishes it from plastic design. The repetitions of a certain underlying curve in an abstract or representational picture have no dramatic content because they occur in the same moment of time—one's eye can choose which it looks at first, or take in the various statements of the same form simultaneously. But the return of the first subject after the development in a symphonic movement has an inevitable touch of the dramatic, merely through the passage of time that has elapsed since its first statement. Time, in fact, is rather vulgarly dramatic; it is the sentimentalist of the dimensions, and small wonder that *visuels*, like Wyndham Lewis, feel that it is occupying too much space in our lives.

Quite apart from this expressive time element, which grows in effect in direct proportion to the length of the work —the reminiscences of earlier themes in *Götterdämmerung* having a more powerfully associative and expressive quality than similar reminiscences in *Valkyrie*, for example—there is a naturally expressive element in all types of music, whether primitive or sophisticated, that it would be un-necessary to insist on, or even mention, in any other age but our own. The type of modern composer and critic who would have us believe that the greatest music consists of an abstract succession of tastefully arranged notes is fond of contrasting the pure classicism of the eighteenth century with the deca-dent romanticism of the nineteenth century, enthroning the pure Mozart as hero and casting the impure Wagner in the role of villain. Music—or so we are led to understand—was written in an objective spirit until the nineteenth century, when contamination from romantic sources set in, and com-posers, led by Beethoven, began to exploit emotional expres-sion, pictorialism, their own personalities and other extra-musical qualities.

Mr. Alan Pryce-Jones has actually gone so far as to say that 'the present-day function of a tune is to prompt emo-tion, and its power to do so is almost entirely a legacy of Beethoven.' He has evidently, like so many critics, mistaken the cool restraint of the eighteenth-century masters for a deliberate frigidity and not troubled to look further back than this much-vaunted golden period of music. To borrow a phrase from Edmund Dulac, he is like a man who would write a history of the horse by giving us a list of famous Derby winners.

Even if one were to grant for a moment that the greatest

music of the eighteenth century is abstract and unemotional, to assume that this holds good for the earlier classics argues a complete lack of historical perspective. Actually, the subjective spirit in which Wagner sat down to write an opera is a far more common attitude in the history of music than the objective spirit in which Bach sat down to write a concerto. Emotional and romantic expression in music is not a late and decadent excrescence, but a natural tradition, that only became temporarily eclipsed in a few minor eighteenth-century works.

Music, far from being an abstract art, is as naturally emotional as painting is naturally representational. If we speak of Mozart as a pure composer it is only in the sense that we speak of Renoir as a pure painter. *Figaro* is pure compared to *Elektra*, just as *La Première Sortie* is pure compared to *When Did You Last See Your Father?* but that does not mean for a moment that Mozart or Renoir believed in abstraction in art. Mozart's best music, as is well known, was found unpleasing by many of his contemporaries because of its intensely melancholy and romantic nature. Those present-day critics who see in Mozart nothing but a glorified craftsman making a concord of sweet sounds in a spirit of angelic detachment offer convincing proof of their complete insensitiveness to all save the purely stylistic aspects of music.

The romantic and emotional nature of music is latent in its origins. The earliest forms of music were, as far as can be ascertained from history and from the examination of still primitive races, unaccompanied folk songs and ritual drumming. A folk song, it stands to reason, is expressive and even programmatic. The best examples represent in embryo, as it were, the balance between emotional and formal content that has been struck by the greatest symphonists. As for primitive instrumental music, need one point out that the

Negro beating a tomtom is aiming not so much at an abstract dissection of rhythm in the manner of Stravinsky, as at the creation of an altogether unobjective state of physical excitement?

Without in any way wishing to link the primitive origins of secular music with the primitive origins of religious music, one may recognize that in spite of its deliberately restricted manner Gregorian chant still remains one of the most moving expressions of the musical spirit. As befits religious music, the emotion is to some extent impersonal, that is to say it embraces the individual in a communal feeling. But there is a world of difference between this impersonal expression of a devotional spirit and a cold objectivity. If it be pleaded that an unaccompanied vocal line, whether sacred or profane, hardly provides a parallel to the later complications of instrumental and choral music, one has only to look at the great period of choral writing to realize the folly of those who would hold up pure music as the classic norm. The religious music of the sixteenth century displays a great concentration on technical device, but this concentration is not objective, it is adapted to deeply expressive ends. The emotion may vary from the serenity of Palestrina to the passion of Vittoria—which recalls El Greco in its violence—but it is an integral part of the music. To suggest that these masters were merely fabricating musical material in the spirit of Hindemith and later Stravinsky, would be pure impertinence.

The same lack of objective spirit is to be found in the secular and instrumental music of the period which shows, particularly in England, a vein of romanticism and pictorialism which anticipates the least austere of nineteenth-century composers. A title like the *Pathetic Symphony* is looked on as an example of decadent romanticism by purists who have forgotten Dowland's *Lachrymae or Seven Teares figured in Seven Passionate Pavans*. Ravel's *La Vallée des Cloches* is considered too pictorial and onomatopœic, yet as a piece of impressionism it is outweighed by Byrd's *The Bells*. Mussorgsky's word painting is considered a sacrifice of pure melody to extra-musical interests, yet he cannot be held to have exceeded Purcell in this respect. It is true that with the development of musical instruments grows the development of display with its inevitable thinning out of musical content. The Fitzwilliam Virginal Book, for example, contains a number of pieces in variation form whose aimless and facile figuration foreshadows the pattern making of the minor eighteenth-century harpsichordists; but these are, by common consent, the least interesting and characteristic pieces in the collection. They do not typify the spirit of their time.

Objective pattern making is, roughly speaking, a product of the eighteenth century and it marks not an artistic progress, but a social and spirtual decline. Those who listened to a motet such as Vittoria's *O Vos Omnes* took part in it spiritually if not actually; those who listened to a madrigal such as Weelkes' *O Care thou wilt despatch me* as likely as not were all actually performing it—they each took a part and the part was worth taking. The same is true of the seventeenth-century consorts of viols whose decline is so lamented by those two splendid critics, Roger North and Thomas Mace. With the advent of the professional violinist, and the decline of the amateur viol player, part writing gave way to fireworks and pattern making.[1] Music ceased to be a vital and spiritual experience and degenerated into a mere aural decoration—as which it is defined by that typical child of his time, Dr. Burney.

[1] For an excellent short account of the decline of music during this period see Peter Warlock's introduction to Purcell's 3, 4, and 5 Part Fantasias for Strings (Curwen).

Abstraction in Music

If you play music in your home, then you choose music of emotional content and technical interest; but if you are going to treat music as a background or ornament to social life in general, such qualities would be a positive disadvantage and all you require is something that is brilliant, easy and consonant. The eighteenth century produced a mass of such occasional music with nothing to recommend it except a certain elegance of style. It is only this elegance combined with an absence of actual vulgarity that entitles it to any more serious consideration than the average present-day foxtrot. (In absolving the eighteenth-century minor composers from vulgarity we must remember that musical vulgarity, though a pungent enough smell to the composer's contemporaries, is a quickly fading scent. It may only be that our noses are not keen enough to catch the faint odour of corruption. The dung of today becomes the potpourri of tomorrow. The vulgarities of Auber have already taken on a period charm, like Victorian woolwork, and it is only a matter of time before the vulgarities of Wagner and Liszt achieve in turn an old lavender quality.)

Although the greatest achievements of the eighteenth century have probably never been surpassed, the general level of every-day music has probably never been lower. There is a certain distinction about the minor composers of earlier periods, but the minor eighteenth-century composers are merely garrulous and perfunctory. The same is true of the minor works of even such great masters as Mozart and Haydn. The trouble with modern enthusiasts for the purity of eighteenth-century music is their apparent inability to distinguish between romantic and subjective masterpieces, like Mozart's G Minor Quintet and G Minor Symphony, and the many divertimenti that he cynically turned out in order to pay for the rent and a little champagne.

The pièces d'occasion of this period are sufficiently lacking in intellectual and emotional content to justify the admiring epithets of abstract and objective applied by the present-day exponents of purity in music. But they also achieve the well-known combination of purity and dullness. In fact, it may safely be said that the only classical music that is abstract is bad classical music. The Romantic movement which is still held by a certain school of critics to have dethroned purely musical interests in favour of dramatic expression and literary associations actually was a perfectly reasonable reaction back to the true tradition of music, a tradition of far greater force and far greater duration than the elegant divagation provided by all but the finest eighteenth-century masters. The reaction inevitably took an extreme turn with the result that perfunctory sentiment was apt to take the place of perfunctory pattern making. Classical technique became confounded with classical coldness, and the desire to achieve romantic atmosphere and warmth at all costs led to an unnecessary overthrowal of formal devices and to the creation of a false distinction between classicism and romanticism that has lasted to this day.

We are still apt to regard formalism and emotional expression as opposed interests instead of as an indissoluble whole. That is why at the present time even sympathetic critics are sometimes puzzled by the combination of mathematical methods and melodramatic atmosphere to be found in so much atonal music. If we were to forget the arbitrary distinction between classic and romantic we should realize that a composer like Alban Berg, who uses a carefully wrought and alembicated technique for highly expressive ends, stands nearer to the true tradition of music as represented by the sixteenth- and seventeenth-century masters than any of the self-conscious classicists of the eighteenth, or the self-conscious romanticists of the nineteenth centuries. Berg's music itself would have sounded strange to seventeenth-century ears, but his aims were much the same as theirs. At that period there was no divorce between intellectuality and emotionalism. Mace, lamenting the decline of the seventeenth-century string fantasias, refers to these 'solemn and sweet delightful ayres' not only as 'so many pathetical stories', but as 'subtle and acute argumentations'. Could one not also describe *Pierrot Lunaire* as a series of pathetical stories and acute argumentations? The atonal school, whatever its faults and in spite of its superficial air of mathematical frigidity, can in no way be described as abstract.

(g) Erik Satie and his Musique d'ameublement

The only modern composer whose music, in its complete lack of any romanticism, pictorialism, or dramatic atmosphere, can be described as abstract is that much-maligned and misrepresented figure, Erik Satie. It was once said of Delius that he divided English critics into two camps, those who did not know his works disputing the opinions of those who did. Of Satie the same cannot be said. English critics have been unanimous in their disapproval, and one has yet to see that their contempt is based on any knowledge of his work as a whole.

Satie is looked upon in this country as a farceur and an incompetent dilettante. Before examining his work, then, it is perhaps necessary to point out that in spite of his verbal wit, and his many blagues and cocasseries, no composer, not even Debussy, took a more essentially serious view of his art. As for his being incompetent, we have it on the eminent authority of Albert Roussel from whom he took lessons: 'Il n'avait rien à apprendre. . . . Il était prodigieusement musicien', while far from working in a careless and dilettante manner few composers have devoted such unceasing labour to the revision and remoulding of phrases and the perfection of detail—for instance, the limpid opening bars of *Socrate* are preceded in his notebooks by six alternative and rejected versions of the phrase.

One cannot, it is true, add to one's musical stature by taking thought, but if Satie's technical skill and probity of outlook do not in themselves make him an important composer, they at least distinguish him from the opportunists and Dadaists with whom he is still thoughtlessly classed.

Satie's reputation as a humorist and eccentric has unfortunately outweighed his reputation as a composer. Few people know his works, but most people have heard of his remark: 'Monsieur Ravel has refused the Legion of Honour but all his music accepts it', or of the occasion when he went up to Debussy after a rehearsal of the first movement of *La Mer* (*De l'aube à midi sur la mer*) and said he liked it all, but particularly the little bit at a quarter to eleven. His verbal humour used to overflow into his compositions to which he would add ludicrously inappropriate titles and elaborate programmes, and some of his most charming music is to be found in the *Aperçus Désagréables* and the *Airs à Faire Fuir*. These, and other more fantastic titles which were aimed at the precious pictorialism of the Impressionists, have undoubtedly had their designed effect of repelling those too insensitive to see beyond their superficial buffoonery. However, both those who find this type of humour agreeable, and those who find it exasperating, should try to forget this side of Satie's mentality when examining his music, for too great an obsession with Satie's humour— whether in the archaic or present-day sense of the word—is apt to distract one from realizing his position as a composer.

What chiefly distinguishes Satie from the other representatives of post-war Parisian mentality is the fact that while they were catching up with the times he had the no doubt gratifying sensation of seeing the times catch up with him. Stravinsky's post-war works represent a reaction from his pre-war activities, but Satie's are a logical continuation of what he had been aiming at since 1900 and earlier. When Satie starts off *Parade* with a chorale[1] and fugue he is not wittily reacting against the pictorialism of the previous decade—as represented by *Petrushka*—he is quite simply following his own established manner.

The reaction against Impressionism with its appeal to the nerves; the insistence on line, not colour; the development of popular melodies and forms; the revival of fugal devices —all these typical traits of the post-war movement are already to be found in Satie's early suites for piano duet *En Habit de Cheval* and *Trois Morceaux en forme de Poire*. For that reason Satie's post-war music has a sincerity and above all an easiness which is lacking in many of his contemporaries.

He was an old practitioner amongst over-zealous students and, like an Italian priest, could allow himself an occasional bottle of wine or a risqué story which the English convert would regard as a lapse from devoutness. In *Socrate* and other works he was able to achieve a classical calm that was in no way due to pastiche, because there had always been a a classical element in his work, even in the early *Gymnopédies* and *Sarabandes*.

These pieces with their anticipation of Debussy's harmonic style have been considered by some as a precursor of Impressionism, while others have indignantly denied Satie's influence on Debussy, maintaining that Satie himself had been imitating Debussy's unpublished compositions. The point is immaterial, for Satie's method of using so-called Impressionist harmony is entirely different from that of

---

[1] This chorale, together with a long penultimate movement, is, unfortunately, not included in the piano duet arrangement.

Debussy. Debussy uses his chords for their own sake, Satie as an accompaniment to a beautifully formed melodic line. The *Gymnopédies* in spite of their harmonic basis foreshadow not Impressionism but neo-classicism. Although the Rosicrucian flavour of these early pieces gives way in his later ballets to a more robust and popular tang, the *Gymnopédies* establish the constructive methods that he was to follow all his life.

Technically speaking, his music is rather difficult to analyse in words and without the use of music type, but one can draw attention to certain traits that appear in works as widely separated in date and superficial style as the early *Gnossiennes* and the late *Relâche*. Melodically speaking, we find the juxtaposition of short lyrical phrases of great tenderness with ostinatos of extreme and deliberate bareness. Harmonically speaking, Satie's methods differ as much from Debussy's static use of chords for their own sake as they do from Liszt's rhetorical use of chords as so many points in a musical argument. His harmonic sense—of which a particularly happy example is to be found in the posthumously published *Jack in the Box*—is rich and pleasing but, like his lyrical sense, displays a curiously objective and unatmospheric quality. The strangeness of his harmonic colouring is due not to the chords themselves, but to the unexpected relationships he discovers between chords which in themselves are familiar enough. There is, however, no instance in his works of the spicing up of a simple harmonic basis by the addition of what are popularly—and rightly—known as 'wrong notes', such as we find in Auric. Nor is there any suggestion of the illogical distortion of recognized classical methods such as we find in Stravinsky. His progressions have a strange logic of their own, but they have none of the usual sense of concord and discord, no trace of the *point d'appui* that we usually associate with the word progression. They may be said to lack harmonic perspective in much the way that a cubist painting lacks spatial perspective.

The lack of any feeling of progression that we find in his personal use of harmony is emphasized by his equally personal use of form. By his abstention from the usual forms of development and by his unusual employment of what might be called interrupted and overlapping recapitulations, which cause the piece to fold in on itself, as it were, he completely abolishes the element of rhetorical argument and even succeeds in abolishing as far as is possible our time sense. We do not feel that the emotional significance of a phrase is dependent on its being placed at the beginning or end of any particular section. On Satie's chessboard a pawn is always a pawn; it does not become a queen through having travelled to the other side of the board.

Satie's habit of writing his pieces in groups of three was not just a mannerism. It took the place in his art of dramatic development, and was part of his peculiarly sculpturesque views of music. When we pass from the first to the second *Gymnopédie* or from the second to the third *Gnossienne* we do not feel that we are passing from one object to another. It is as though we were to move slowly round a piece of sculpture and examine it from a point of view which, while presenting a different and possible less interesting silhouette to our eyes, is of equal importance to our appreciation of the work as a plastic whole. It does not matter which way you walk round a statue and it does not matter in which order you play the three *Gymnopédies*.

The same may almost be said of the two acts of the ballet *Relâche*. They are so formally linked together by thematic repetition and transformation that the second act is like a reflection of the first in a mirror. Yet it is arguable that the work would retain its formal logic were the order of the acts to be reversed, or the work to be played backwards as regards the order of the movements. This type of formal logic which is independent of all dramatic or narrative element is, of course, in the most complete contrast to the formal logic of the Romantic school. We have only to imagine the effect of playing the march in Liszt's *Mazeppa* before the opening section to realize how far Satie had travelled from all that the music of the preceding century stood for.

There is no romance about Satie's music, not even of the modern type that takes the form of anti-Romanticism. Auric in his preface to *Parade* has wrongly suggested that the work has a vein of mechanical romanticism by saying that Satie's score 'se soumet très humblement à la réalité qui étouffe le chant du rossignol sous le roulement des tramways'. This is far from being even approximately true, for the most striking feature of *Parade* is its combination of monotonously repeated and mechanical figures with passages of great lyrical charm. Satie was too objective in his standpoint to side with either the nightingales or the tramcars. If while riding on a tramcar a nightingale had flown on to the same seat he would not have seen in it a symbolization of two opposed worlds and indulged in either philosophy or regrets. He would have accepted it quite naturally as a simple occurrence, just as we accept the fantastic items of general information—such as 'Owl steals pince-nez of Wolverhampton builder'—detailed in the papers as News from Far and Near.

If Satie's music is difficult to appreciate it is not due to any obscurity in his technical style, which is always clear cut and limpid, but to his habit of abruptly changing his mood within the course of a single bar. He does not, like his followers, present us with stylistic incongruity, but he does present us with a far more disturbing emotional incongruity. The *Prélude en Tapisserie*, for example, consists of about half a dozen thematic fragments which though carefully wrought into a formal balance are totally opposed in mood. This emotional incongruity may be taken by some to be almost realistic in the effect, an echo of the lack of congruity to be found in the sights and sounds that impinge on our consciousness during a haphazard walk through the streets. But I feel that it is more likely to be a deliberate refusal on Satie's part to create an effect of logic and continuity by any save strictly technical means.

Occasionally this incongruity is used pictorially, as in the movement representing Chaos in *Les Aventures de Mercure*. Here, instead of the harmonic and orchestral outburst and the avoidance of line that an impressionist composer would have brought to bear on the subject, Satie presents us with a clear pattern in two parts, a skilful blending of two previously heard movements, one the suave and sustained *Nouvelle Danse*, the other the robust and snappy *Polka des Lettres*. These two tunes are so disparate in mood that the effect, mentally speaking, is one of complete chaos, yet it is achieved by strictly musical and even academic means, which consolidate the formal cohesion of the ballet as a whole. Even such very modified pictorialism, however, is an exceptional case in Satie's work, and in *Socrate*, the most extended of his later works, the music refuses to reflect in any direct way the meaning and emotion of the words.

It has been suggested by René Chalupt, in his preface to *Socrate*, that Satie's music is like a series of illustrations by Ingres to the dialogues of Plato. But the simile is hardly accurate. Satie steadfastly refuses to illustrate, and his music may be more aptly compared to the printer's art. The lettering is graceful, the margins well proportioned, and the occasional decorative capitals have a grave charm, but there is no alteration in style and make-up because one page happens to be more tragic in content than another.

The surprising restraint of *Socrate* is again no stunt on Satie's part, but the logical application of theories that he had always held. Many years before he had objected to the instrumental melodrama of Wagner's operas, remarking: 'A property tree does not grimace because the hero walks on to the stage.' He felt that music should supply a suitably coloured background to the words, but should never usurp the dramatic and narrative element supplied by the text.

Socrate is the logical continuation and reductio ad absurdum of the musical restraint shown in certain sections of *Pelléas and Mélisande*. The music, always limpid and serene, pursues a modified rondo form which has no connection with the argument of the text, or the change of character; it is an unobtrusive background against which the characters of the dialogue appear in undramatic contrast. The greatest concession made to the dramatic element is in the death scene where the music far from gaining actually loses intensity, fading out to the monotonous repetition of a bare fifth as if it feared to draw one's attention away from the tragedy of the text. *Socrate*, though perfectly successful as the logical application of a theory, has something of the rigor mortis always associated with overtheorized music. Satie's refusal to reflect the incidental emotion of the words becomes, in the end, as irritating as the insistence on detailed word painting that we find in Dargomizhky's *Stone Guest*, or Mussorgsky's *Match Maker*. There are two kinds of chastity in music, as in life, and it is easy for the composer to confuse restraint with impotence. The restraint of *Socrate* degenerates at times from the calm of a philosopher to the passivity of a dead object.

Though written in Satie's most serious vein *Socrate* has a certain affinity with his most flippant pieces, the *Musique d'ameublement*, which, though of no intrinsic importance, throw an interesting sidelight on his outlook on music. He felt that the entr'acte between two parts of a concert provided too great a break in the general atmosphere, and that music should be played in the foyer, to which music, however, people would pay no more concentrated attention than they would to the furniture or the carpet. He accordingly wrote a ludicrous set of pieces for piano duet, bass trombone, and small clarinet in which themes from *Mignon* and *Danse Macabre* were mingled with his own. The players were put in different parts of the room and the short pieces were played over and over again, it being hoped that the audience would not listen but would talk, move about and order drinks. Unfortunately, the moment the placard *Musique d'ameublement* was put up, the audience stopped talking and listened as solemnly as if at the opera until, at the thirtieth repetition of one of the furniture pieces, Satie, exasperated beyond reason by this uncalled-for respect, dashed furiously round the foyer shouting: 'Parlez! Parlez! Parlez!' This may seem merely a typical example of Satie's blague, but it also indicates his detached and objective view of music and explains why even in his serious works, like *Socrate*, the music sometimes takes on a deadly and static quality.

There is a moment, almost impossible to analyse, when a piece of sculpture, through excessive simplification on the part of the artist, ceases to be a living form however simplified and becomes an abstract object. However much we may admire Brancusi's fish, for example, we may ask ourselves at times whether the process of simplification has not been carried to a point when not only the inessentials, but the essentials of sculpture have been thrust on one side. Like Brancusi, Satie states a certain problem in its most acute form, but his work is even more open to question because he is dealing with a dynamic medium functioning in time, and far less suited to the static objectivity which both these artists undoubtedly achieve.

Post-war Pasticheurs

We may well ask ourselves if, to obtain the static abstraction of Satie's best work, it is worth while throwing over the dynamic movement and expressiveness which has hitherto always been considered an essential part of music. At the same time, one must admit that in such movements as the *Bain des Graces* in *Mercure*, Satie achieved a more complete objectivity than any other composer has done. Stravinsky's essential dynamic qualities keep breaking through even in so outwardly abstract a work as the *Concertino* for string quartet, and his abstract music must therefore be considered less complete as an artistic statement than that of Satie—though some may find it more vital for this very reason. A statement, however, is not necessarily valuable because it is complete, and although Satie is of great interest both as an individual figure and as a curious anticipation of the post-war *Zeitgeist* he can hardly be said to be a major composer. In spite of his intensely musical faculties it is impossible not to feel that the mentality that directed these instincts would have found truer expression in one of the plastic arts.

This warping of the medium to use it for a form of expression best suited to another art is by no means confined to composers, amongst modern artists. While Satie and Stravinsky may be said in their objective compositions to be taking up the work of the painter, the surrealist painters are working on lines which would obviously find more convincing and fluid expression in writing, while transitional writers like Gertrude Stein are aiming at rhythmic patterns and formal arrangements of sound that would have far more weight if expressed in musical form. By working out of focus with one's medium one can undoubtedly achieve results of the utmost experimental interest; but it is rarely that these experiments have led to anything but a technical and spiritual cul-de-sac.

Although Satie's formal and harmonic methods are full

of suggestions for future development, he has up to the present had hardly any real followers, and must be looked upon as a figure rather on the margin of music. His experiments, though fascinating, have in no way altered the path of music because the abstraction at which he aimed, if not an essentially unmusical ideal in itself, led to the denial of so much that is essentially musical, just as a concentration on abstract form in painting leads to the denial of so much that is essentially paintable from the formal point of view. Even in Satie's own music the partial pictorialism and expressiveness of *Mercure* yields more interesting results from the abstract point of view than the deliberate abstraction of *Socrate*.

Satie is not a sufficiently powerful figure or dominating influence to lend support to those who uphold abstraction in music. Least of all does he lend support to those who preach internationalism. For his music, in spite of its objectivity, has at times a very strong French flavour and it is probably this quality that is mainly responsible for the hasty dismissal of his work by English critics, who only seem favourably disposed to those French composers such as Berlioz and Debussy, who, from the French point of view, are in the nature of an exotic culture.

Much as one may deplore the narrow critical outlook which is one of the concomitants of nationalism in music, it may be doubted whether it is possible or even desirable at the present moment that music should regain the internationalism which it displayed in the eighteenth century. It may even be doubted whether the style of the eighteenth century was as international as it appears to us today. The British Empire does not become international because it is far flung, nor does a musical style become international because it is shared by a number of different countries. The style of the eighteenth century was mainly Italian, that of the nineteenth century—until broken up by foreign influences—mainly German, and twentieth-century dance music, which provides the most genuinely international style of today, is international only at the cost of submission to America.

There is no denying, however, that compared with the composer of the present day the eighteenth-century composer possessed an international language comparable to the Latin in which medieval savants carried on their arguments. But the nationalism of the intervening century has made any attempt to revive this type of musical language as fruitless as the efforts of the neo-classical composer to achieve intrinsic form by copying the extrinsic formality of classical masters.

One cannot erase the results of nationalism any more than one can erase the results of Romanticism. What the eighteenth century achieved with ease and by traditional means we much achieve with difficulty and in our own individual way. When we look at Sibelius's *Finlandia*, and then at his Seventh Symphony, we may well agree with George Moore that art must be parochial in the beginning to become cosmopolitan in the end.

Internationalism, like simplicity, is a desirable end but, like simplicity, it is found only in the highest and the lowest forms of art. The paintings of Giotto speak an international language and so do lavatory drawings. We must beware lest in aiming at one we produce the other. It is fatally easy for the modern composer, reacting against the passionate nationalism of recent musical movements, to rid himself of parochialism not by intensifying his thought but by denuding it, and to reach universality through nullity.

We cannot, however, understand the present-day problem of nationalism versus internationalism without going back a little in history and examining the influence on musical style and form of nineteenth-century nationalism—a musical influence as potent as that of religious thought or romantic feeling.

PART THREE

NATIONALISM AND THE EXOTIC

(a) Nationalism and Democracy

The theory that music is an international language may be compared to the statement that blood is thicker than water. They are both so obviously untrue that no one worries about them any longer or is likely to protest at their frequent occurrences in public speeches. I doubt if anyone would notice were a speaker to use one for the other, forgetting for the moment whether he was addressing the Empire League or the Worshipful Company of Musicians. At the same time the present neo-classical revival in music has led not only to a revival of eighteenth-century formulas but to a revival of what we imagine eighteenth-century ideals to have been, and one of these is internationalism.

Internationalism in the eighteenth century was not so much a political ideal as a social fact. From Major-General Fuller's *War and Western Civilization* we learn that even the art of war was an aristocratic profession, conducted with as little national feeling as possible. When, as late as 1813, Sir Humphry Davy and Faraday were entertained by French scientists in Paris, during the Napoleonic Wars, their visit was not looked on as an international gesture or anti-patriotic move—it was taken as a matter of course. We have only to compare this attitude with that of the scientists and artists on opposed sides during the late war to get the exact measure of the growth of national feeling in the arts; for the freedom and impartiality shown by the scientists was of course shared by the artists of that time and earlier. In the eighteenth century there was an artistic league of aristocrats instead of a political League of Nations, and aggressive nationalism in music would have been considered as parochial an offence against good manners as aggressive nationalism in behaviour. It would have been regarded not so much as an artistic freak as a social degradation.

The most natural and powerful form of national and racial expression in music is to be found in the folk song, and the average eighteenth-century composer faced with an unpolished folk song felt like Millamant faced with Sir Wilful Witwoud—'Ah rustic, ruder than Gothick'. When Millamant said: 'I nauseate walking, 'tis a country diversion,' she was making a remark not only in the character of her part but in the character of her time. In the eighteenth century untutored nature gave way to the urban grove, and the countryside, which is the basis of nationalism in music, took a secondary place in art.

Occasionally a periwig is ruffled and a shapely leg cuts unexpected capers—the Croatian peasant and the English sailor peep out for a moment in the symphonies of Haydn and Boyce—but for the most part eighteenth-century composers chose to address their audiences in a cultivated Esperanto with its roots in Italian. A light accent was the nearest approach to dialect allowed. A person with a 'nose' for national inflections will of course be acutely sensible to these provincial variants, will realize from certain harmonic traits that Scarlatti was at one time in Spain, will be able to tell which parts of Handel's *Time and Truth* were written in England, which in Italy, and so forth; but at no time will he find national feeling expressed with such directness that it stands between him and the musical thoughts of the composer. He may prefer Arne to Locatelli, Paisiello to Méhul, but it is unlikely that in his preferences he will be directly influenced by national prejudices as he might be in preferring Vaughan Williams to Bartók, or Milhaud to Sibelius.

We must not think, however, that the modified internationalism of the eighteenth century is any more a permanent and integral part of musical tradition than the objective pattern-making of the period. When we go back to earlier musical epochs we find, in spite of the obscuring patina of time, a far more decided national tang. Dowland and Byrd and their French contemporaries are as distinctly national as Borodin or Mussorgsky. The difference being that they wear their nationalism easily and unconsciously—it gives a positive and piquant flavour to the music without ever becoming a negative and excluding influence. Dowland could absorb as much Italian influence as he wished without any fear of losing his own unconsciously English personality.

Similarly, in a later period, when music was already beginning to show the formal and cosmopolitan imprint of aristocratic tastes, Purcell was able to graft the Italian manner on to his early post-Elizabethan manner with no loss of national individuality. The happy and homogeneous duality of his style is indeed symbolized by *Dido and Aeneas* where the exquisite classicism of the Italianate court scenes is set against the rowdy nationalism of the sailors' stews. Such a scene as the drunken sailors' chorus in *Dido* would have been considered in the eighteenth century not only barbarously national but intolerably vulgar. We get similar scenes in *The Beggar's Opera*, it is true, but only as a burlesque which forms the most powerful comment possible on the artificial taste of the time, for such a burlesque would have been impossible in Purcell's day when mythological goddesses, woodnymphs, dairymaids and ladies of the street met on equal terms.

Romanticism and nationalism are, in fact, to be found just as much in earlier music as in the nineteenth century, but they are never exclusive and dominating elements, and are invested with none of the pseudo-political significance of a 'movement'. The later extreme specialization of these elements is due not only to the democratic movements of the nineteenth century whose connection with nationalism is pointed out in Major-General Fuller's book, but also to the constricting influence of the classical and aristocratic tastes which eighteenth-century society imposed upon the music of the time.

The reaction against this constriction gave a special impetus to the romantic and national elements which had previously been either latent or taken for granted. Decorum gave way to fine frenzy and cosmopolitanism to jingoism. The romantic and national elements which were latent qualities in the older music became enthroned as conscious and guiding impulses, much as the macabre element in *Macbeth* and the patriotic element in *Richard II* became specialized into such forms as the Tale of Terror and the Imperial Ode.

M. Georg Brandes has devoted many considerable volumes to the influence of romanticism on literary form, and it would require at least an equal number fully to analyse its influence on musical form. Mr. Cecil Gray has admirably summed up the literary side of the romantic movement in music in the prelude to his *Survey of Contemporary Music*, and in a study like the present, which is mainly devoted to post-war problems, it is hardly necessary to do more than docket fullblooded and self-conscious romanticism as an artistic movement which has little direct influence except of a negative or distorted order on the present-day composer.

Nationalism and Democracy

The romantic and nationalist movements in music, though to some extent interlinked (as in the case of Weber for example), are more easy to separate from each other than the similar movements in literature, and their separation becomes more marked as the nineteenth century wears to an end. Romanticism as a conscious movement is of little weight in modern music because its original impulse is by now faded; the effects of the nationalist movement, however, are still at work in music, and in many countries nationalism is as much a battlecry today as romanticism was a hundred years ago. The explanation, as is so often the case, is as much political as artistic. The nationalist movement in music was not only a temperamental and stylistic reaction against the frigidity of the preceding epoch—it was intimately bound up with the growth of racial and political consciousness. The romantic movement may be held to be only an extreme statement of something that had always been latent in music—even in the classical music against which the romanticists were reacting—whereas the nationalist movement brings in a new and extra-musical element.

In spite of the fact that music is held to be an international language we can trace the growth first of racial then of proletarian consciousness as easily through Russian music, for example, as through Russian literature—more easily in some cases, as music is not so ruled by the censor. The most obvious example of the connection between nationalism and music is, of course, the somewhat bastard one of the patriotic or revolutionary song, where the presence of actual words is apt to confuse any estimate of the evocative power of the music qua music. We must try carefully to distinguish between those tunes that are moving in themselves and those that are only moving through political and verbal associations. It would be childish, for instance, to pretend that the growth of the Communist party in England has been in any way influenced (save perhaps negatively) by the music of *The Red Flag;* but in the case of a song like the *Marseillaise,* the most far reaching of popular songs, the effect is clearly dependent for its major appeal on the music itself and it is significant that the tune if not actually popular in technical origin is popular in general allure and non-classical in construction.

It is doubtful if the Marseillais of 1792 indulged in the splitting of technical hairs, but it is more than likely that the tune had for them an added, if unrealized, significance through its denial of the principles of taste and construction which mark the music of the aristocratic régime. We have only to compare it with a classically constructed tune written by a professional composer, like *Rule, Britannia,* to see the difference between a work which though national in feeling places musical construction first, and a work in which national or political feeling is paramount, sweeping technical considerations on one side through its intensity of mood.

Although *Rule, Britannia* is the best written of national songs, and the *Marseillaise* shares with the Toreador's Song from *Carmen* the distinction of being the most clumsily constructed tune that has ever become universally popular, it is not surprising to find that the latter has had more far-reaching effects. We can imagine *Rule, Britannia* being played by a ship's band or being hummed on the quarter-deck by some dilettante admiral, but we can hardly hear it being sung by sailors as they go into battle. The classical construction and the operatic nature of some of the vocalization—particularly in its original form—immediately give to it an aristocratic quality which prevents if from becoming truly popular in the fullest meaning of the word.

These two tunes conveniently symbolize not so much the difference between two countries as the difference between two ages—the difference between the political and artistic ideals of the eighteenth century and those of the nineteenth. *Rule, Britannia,* a song written in honour not only of patriotism but of aristocracy, is embedded in the style of its day, whereas the *Marseillaise* points forward to the style of the succeeding epoch, to Auber and Berlioz, to the age when operas and even symphonies began to assume an extra-musical and even politically national quality. It was not only due to the political situations that Auber's *Masaniello* once caused a revolution, and that in later years Verdi's *O Signore dal tetto natio,* Smetana's cycle of symphonic poems *Ma Vlast,* and Sibelius's *Finlandia* were almost to assume the quality of revolutionary anthems. These emotional reactions are latent in the style of the music as apart from its associations. No amount of association with revolutionary sentiment could turn an opera by Grétry into a call to action or make a Haydn symphony a symbol of the Croatian Separatist movement.

From the purely musical point of view the direct association of political feeling with a piece of music is the lowest and least desirable form of nationalism; but it is necessary to insist on its existence and not to regard it as a regrettable side show. No political pamphlet or poster can get a hundredth of the recruits that are enrolled by a cornet and a bass drum; and it is doubtful whether the war would have lasted six months without the aid of that purest of the arts, music, whose latest gift to civilization is the notorious Horst Wessel Song.

We must realize the social and political bases of nationalism in music in order to realize the artificiality of those present-day composers who, on purely musical grounds, would revert to the international musical style of the eighteenth century with none of the physical and mental background which makes such internationalism sincere, natural and convincing.

Nationalism and the Exotic

The present reaction in some quarters against excessive nationalism in music is in some ways an aesthetic reaction against the abuse of folk-song material, but we shall not rid ourselves of nationalism by refraining from use of the folk song. The nationalist movement of the nineteenth century is of course inseparably connected with the folk song, the simplest and most agreeable form of national expression. It would be a mistake, though, to think that the nineteenth-century composers sound national because for purely musical reasons they chose to base their style on folk songs and folk-song material. They chose to use this type of material in order to express as fully as possible a national and racial feeling that was already there from the social point of view, and which was sufficiently strong to influence even such purely aesthetic problems as symphonic development, for example.

The composer who is more concerned with political destruction than with musical construction may seem hardly worthy of the name; but we must remember that the same attitude, intensely sublimated, is to be found in the work of such undoubtedly important figures as Bartók and Vaughan Williams. In a work like Vaughan Williams's *Pastoral Symphony* it is no exaggeration to say that the creation of a particular type of grey, reflective, English-landscape mood has outweighed the exigencies of symphonic form. To those who find this mood sympathetic, their intense and personal emotional reaction will more than compensate for the monotony of texture and lack of form, of which a less well-disposed listener might perhaps be unduly conscious.

This symphony is one of the landmarks in modern English music, and to many English critics it is one of the masterpieces of recent years. Yet it is a well-known fact that few English works have met with less understanding and appreciation abroad. In this case music, far from proving an international language, has produced a work more baffling to the foreign mentality than a translation of a dialect novel of English country life. You can say to a Czechoslovakian who does not appreciate the symphonies of Elgar: 'However unsympathetic you may find this mentality you must admit the mastery of technique, the virtuosity of orchestration', but to a Czechoslovakian who dislikes the *Pastoral Symphony* you can only say: 'Oh, well, I suppose you don't like it.'

Elgar's music is as national in its way as the music of Vaughan Williams but, by using material that in type can be related back to the nineteenth-century German composers, Elgar avoids any suspicion of provincial dialect, even though his national flavour is sufficiently strong to repel certain countries—France in particular. Similarly, Walton (who, reacting against the music of the immediately preceding generation, has far more in common with Elgar than with Vaughan Williams), by using material that can be related to Handel on the one hand and to Prokofieff on the other, addresses an international audience in easy terms without losing his national and personal qualities.

Vaughan Williams, however, whose style is based on material without classical or international precedent and which, without necessarily being folk-songy in the picturesque way, is intimately connected with the inflections and mood of English folk music, cannot be said to share the freedom from provinciality shown by Elgar and Walton. His appeal is undoubtedly more intense but it is also more limited. This limitation of appeal proceeds not only from the intensely national quality of the material itself but from the formal treatment, which is logically evolved from this material. This logicality is the strongest feature of the work and yet is the most potent force in restricting its appeal.

Unlike so many composers, notably Brahms, with whom the creation of musical material and its subsequent treatment appear to be two separate mental processes, Vaughan Williams nearly always evolves his form from the implications of the melody and rarely submits his themes to a Procrustean development. In this he recalls Debussy who, however, wisely refrained from attempting the balanced four movements of a symphony. The form of the *Pastoral Symphony* follows logically enough from the material, but hardly achieves either the contrast or sense of progression that is usually associated with symphonic form, and is the essential feature of classical symphonic writing. By refraining from the conventional type of symphonic development Vaughan Williams avoids the complete contrast between mood and method shown by such a fabricated symphony as Dvořák's *From the New World*, but this negative virtue does not in itself mean that the *Pastoral Symphony* satisfies us as much from the architectural point of view as it does from the point of view of mood and colouring. Just as the form, though logical, is restricted through its dependence on the thematic material, so the thematic material, though beautiful, is restricted through its insistence on a specifically local mood.

We can appreciate Debussy's *Rondes de Printemps* without knowing or liking French landscape, but it is clearly difficult to appreciate either the mood or the form of the *Pastoral Symphony* without being temperamentally attuned to the cool greys and greens, the quietly luxuriant detail, the unemphatic undulation of the English scene. Beautiful as this work is, one feels that it is too direct a transcription of a local mood and that the material has not undergone that process of mental digestion, as it were, which can make the particular into a symbol of the whole and can, as in Sibelius's symphonies, give to local and individual characteristics the quality of universality.

The *Pastoral Symphony* not only raises the problem of how

Nationalism and Democracy

far it is wise for an artist to detach himself from cosmopolitan tradition in order to reach individual and national expression: it also represents in acute fashion the clash between local colour and classical construction which is the main drawback to nationalism in music. The clash is particularly noticeable in that this work comes so late in the nationalist movement. Like a germ which gathers force as it sweeps through the population, striking with added virulence the final victim of an epidemic, so the nationalist movement in music has acted most strongly on those countries which have received its influence late in the day.

The débâcle of the nineteenth century has put English music a little out of focus with time, and the English nationalist movement thus constitutes a special case, an isolation ward of more value to the specialist than to the student.

The effects of the nationalist movement on German music, though marked, are a little difficult to disentangle because in Germany the romantic movement and the nationalist movement are not only closely interwoven but carry on almost imperceptibly from the previous century. One realizes, listening to Schumann's *Rhenish Symphony*, that here is music as exclusively and deliberately German as *Prince Igor* is Russian, but it is difficult to say exactly where, between *The Magic Flute* and the *Rhenish Symphony*, this element has crept in.

The pros and cons of nationalism can be examined most clearly in the Russian schools partly because it has a stronger and more convincing racial background than in England, partly because its origins and results are more clear cut than in Germany, and partly because it is sufficiently distant, both from the point of view of date and culture, to be examined without local or contemporary prejudice.

(b) The Russian Nationalists

Glinka is one of those convenient historic figures, like Sir Walter Raleigh, to whom almost all discoveries can be ascribed—and in his case with justice. The task of reviewing the influence of nationalism on musical style and structure is enormously simplified in the case of Russian music by the fact that Glinka had the field entirely to himself for about thirty years, and also by the fact that whereas every Russian composer since Glinka has been enormously indebted to his influence, he himself appears to have sprung fully armed from the racial womb.

It is impossible to say when music written in Germany became specifically Teutonic; but we can say with no exaggeration that Russian music became specifically Russian in the year 1836, the year of the first performance of *A Life for the Czar*. *Russlan and Ludmilla*, which appeared six years later, is of more importance from the purely musical point of view, but *A Life for the Czar* inaugurated a period whose tail end is still with us, and in spite of its many dubious qualities it must be considered one of the turning points in music.

There is no Russian composition of importance—unless Scriabin's orchestral poems be considered important—that is not directly indebted to one or both of these operas. Even Mussorgsky who, on the whole, was influenced more by Dargomizhky—Glinka's 'spiritual nephew', if one may steal a phrase from Edward Lear—pays open homage to him in several pages of *Boris* and more particularly *Khovantchina*. We are apt to forget this, merely because such music of Glinka's as is known in this country has for the most part appeared some time after that of his later followers. Those who, knowing their *Coq d'Or* and *L'Oiseau de Feu*, expect much the same degree of sophistication from Glinka, forget that *Russlan and Ludmilla*, although the direct forerunner of these two works, is actually nearer in date to *The Magic Flute* to which, indeed, it provides a Russian counterpart.

It is necessary to emphasize the fact that not only Rimsky-Korsakoff, Borodin and the avowed followers of Glinka owe much of their inspiration and their methods to him, but that his direct influence is to be observed as late as *Le Sacre du Printemps* and Debussy's *Iberia*—for example, the middle section of the first movement of *Iberia* is constructed on the principle laid down by Glinka in *Russlan* and crystallized in *Kamarinskaya;* while as for the reflections of Glinka in Stravinsky's music they are too clear to require further definition. What may be called Franco-Russian scoring—as opposed to the Strauss-Elgar treatment of the orchestra—is the direct legacy of Glinka, and it is not too much to say that the whole of the movement in taste known as 'Russian Ballet' is implicit in certain pages of *Russlan*.

Among nineteenth-century composers Glinka is second only to Liszt in historical importance; but he was more than a gifted amateur who happened to pop up at the right time. In spite of the sedulously fostered impression to the contrary, he was in every sense—save the financial—a professional composer, and the occasional weaknesses in even his best work are due not to any technical deficiency on his part but to the method of his approach and the angle of his appeal. In considering the pros and cons of nationalism we need not really go further than Glinka for our case. It is essentially as unnecessary to drag in such excellent but minor figures as Rimsky-Korsakoff and Liadoff as it would be to drag Strauss into a discussion on the symphonic poem when we have Liszt's thirteen examples before us.

Glinka's importance as a composer is very largely due to

a fortunate coincidence of temperament and period. In the eighteenth century a figure like Glinka would, in all probability, have cheerfully gone on composing in the fashionable Italian manner. As a matter of fact he had a great sympathy for the Italian style and was at times as worthy an exponent of the Bellini bel-canto as Verdi himself; but he lived in the period when Russian national consciousness was beginning to awake and find concrete expression in the works of Pushkin. His spiritual background was not so much the fashionable emulation of Western manners as the nostalgic appreciation of Russian peasant life that we find so superbly presented in Oblomov's dream.

Admirably loyal and law-abiding as the plot of *A Life for the Czar* may be, the fact remains that it is an opera not about Czars but about peasants. From the patriotic sentiments of Glinka to the revolutionary sentiments of Mussorgsky is a comparatively small step. The real break comes between the mythological operas of the eighteenth century and Glinka's national epic. At a time when cultural Russians spoke in French and sang in Italian Glinka thought in Russian and wished, in his own words, to write music 'that would make his countrymen feel at home'. It is not surprising that to do so he turned to the shortwinded but intensely felt songs that he heard sung by his nurse at home and by coachmen in the streets. One should notice that Glinka speaks not of himself but of his countrymen. The choice of words is significant. It indicates not only his personal reactions but also the growing racial consciousness and pride in purely local as opposed to sophisticated Western tradition that is to be found in the Russian literature of the time. He succeeded in making some of his countrymen feel too much at home, and some of the more popular choruses in *A Life for the Czar*, notably the one whose accompaniment imitates the balalaika, were contemptuously dismissed as 'coachmen's music'. The condemnation was of course an unintentional tribute to the genuinely vital and racial qualities of the opera. No one would refer to Vaughan Williams's works as 'farmhands' music'.

A Life for the Czar is admittedly a most unequal work and much of it is written in an amiable but rather debased Italianate style. What is surprising though, considering its date, is not how little genuinely Russian music the opera contains, but how much. It is noticeable that the most characteristically and movingly national passages are invariably given to the chorus. This is typical of the whole of Russian music from Glinka to Stravinsky and can be seen in such widely different operas as *The Snow Maiden, Prince Igor* and *Boris Godunoff*. While the music given to the soloists is sometimes conventional, superficial and Italianate in style, the music given to the chorus is national and deeply felt.

We have only to compare the cantilena solos in *The Snow Maiden* with the choruses in the carnival scene, to compare the duets and cavatinas in *Prince Igor* with such a chorus as the incomparable 'Gsak the Conqueror' in the fifth act, to realize that Russian music at its best is not only national but proletarian. It is a truism to point out that in *Boris Godunoff*, the greatest of all Russian operas, the hero is not Boris but the people; and this would be seen still more clearly if the opera, instead of being presented in a distorted and mutilated version as a peg on which to hang a piece of admittedly brilliant ranting, were given to us in its original form with the personal tragedy of Boris set as an incident against the real background provided by the Russian people. Even in the case of Stravinsky his most important work is *Les Noces*, a choreographic oratorio in which solo singers and solo dancers are banished in the interests of the chorus and corps de ballet.

This proletarian quality, though only hinted at in *A Life for the Czar*, is nevertheless clearly apparent in many of the choruses, of which the most striking from an historical point of view are the previously mentioned balalaika chorus and the wedding song in five-four time. The first struck right through the classical-toga snobbery of the period and was a direct forerunner of the use of popular and jazz-band timbres which is so great a feature of contemporary music. The second, by its introduction of what were then considered exotic and barbaric rhythms, opened up the way to the rhythmic experiments of Borodin and Stravinsky and freed music from the restricting and lumbering rhythms of the German Volkslied. Though it would obviously be too much to trace the broken rhythms of Stravinsky's *Danse Sacrale* back to the regular five-four wedding chorus in *A Life for the Czar*, we can without exaggeration trace a direct line of descent through this chorus to the slightly more elaborate hymn to Lel in *Russlan and Ludmilla*—with its five-four broken by two-two—the eleven-four chorus to Yarilo in *The Snow Maiden*, the chorus to Ladou in Act IV, Scene 3 of *Khovantchina*, and the finale of *L'Oiseau de Feu*.

In spite of the significance of a few individual passages in *A Life for the Czar*, Glinka would have remained a figure of historical rather than intrinsic importance had he written nothing after this opera. It is *Russlan and Ludmilla*, written six years later, which clinches Glinka's position as a composer. There are still weak and conventional numbers, it is true, but they are in a great minority. Written with far more skill than was displayed in the earlier opera *Russlan* not only establishes the heroic national style on a firm basis but, for the first time, introduces with success and significance the oriental or exotic element which has since played such enjoyable havoc with tradition. It would take a whole book to enumerate the technical devices—harmonic, orchestral and rhythmic—which, found for the first time in *Russlan*, have altered the whole face of European music. Even so extreme a development of modern technique as the *Adoration de la Terre* section in *Le Sacre du Printemps*, held at one time to have no connection with any tradition save that of primitive instinct, can in its essence be traced back to the astounding passage at the end of the Caucasian Lezginka, which was considered so daring even in the present century that it was always cut at the Imperial Opera. As *Russlan* is known chiefly by its pleasing but quite uncharacteristic overture my estimate of this opera's importance may seem a little far fetched. The present study not being a history of Russian music or a treatise on modern orchestration I must deny myself technical proof and ask my readers to take these statements on trust.

Glinka changed and enriched every branch of music but one—construction—and this formal weakness is evidently part not only of Glinka's make-up but of the whole make-up of Russian music, or deliberately national music anywhere. It was not, as is so often thought, a question of technical deficiency or amateurishness on Glinka's part. We have only to glance at the comparatively conventional but extremely skilful overture to *Prince Kholmsky* or the brilliant finale to the first act of *Russlan* to dispel that legend. The weakness is due to the inherent struggle between national expression and symphonic form.

Spiritually speaking, this struggle is symbolized by the contrast between the sonata and the fugue on the one hand, types of aristocratic, international and intellectual expression, and the folk song and folk dance on the other, types of popular, national and instinctive expression. More technically speaking, it is due to the fact that folk songs—round which national expression in music centres—being already finished works of art with a line of their own, obstinately refuse to become links or component parts in the longer and more sweeping line demanded by the larger instrumental forms. One cannot use a small watchchain as a link in an anchor cable.

(c) The Conflict between Nationalism and Form

Glinka, though not specifically admitting this technical and spiritual conflict, implies it in a letter referring to the difficulty he had in developing his themes symphonically when engaged on the symphonic poem *Tarass Bulba*. It was not that Glinka was unable to master the mechanics of conservatoire construction—it was that in trying to reflect the particular atmosphere of Gogol's heroic tale he was bound to invent material of a type that would not submit to traditional methods of treatment. The question of too literary an attitude does not enter into this particular instance. Nothing could be more literary than the programmatic framework of Berlioz's *Symphonie Fantastique*, yet formally speaking it is among the finest of nineteenth-century symphonies.

Although excessively romantic and literary programmes are hardly compatible with the true symphonic tradition they do not capsize symphonic form to the same extent as the use of folk-song material. The romantic movement as exemplified by such typical though widely separated examples as Byron's *Manfred* and Villiers de l'Isle Adam's *Axel* is marked by its insistence on the individual as opposed to the crowd; and the musical reflection of this insistence finds its most satisfactory expression in the monothematic symphonic poem, such as Liszt's *Tasso*, rather than in the symphony. But symphonies like Berlioz's *Fantastique* and Liszt's *Faust* show that this hero-worship or self-concentration—call it what you will—by no means disintegrates the formal instinct. The classical symphony has as its spiritual background the aristocratic and international qualities of eighteenth-century society. The romantic movement gives an individualist twist and an added picturesqueness to the eighteenth-century symphony which alters its technical form without seriously striking at its spiritual foundations. Nationalism, however, destroys both the aristocratic quality of the eighteenth-century abstract symphony and the individualist quality of the nineteenth-century programme symphony.

The conflict is not only technical and emotional, it is almost a class conflict, and it is hardly too far fetched a play upon words to suggest that the phrase 'first subject' is in itself undemocratic. In Mussorgsky this conflict is openly avowed. Symphonic development was repellent to him because it symbolized not only foreign domination but aristocratic domination. In *Boris* and *Khovantchina* we find the strongest expression in any art form, up to the present day, of the conflict between aristocratic internationalism and proletarian nationalism.

It may be pleaded that Wagner was a self-conscious nationalist and that yet his operas are remarkable for their formal continuity and almost symphonic shape. We should remember, though, that Wagner's nationalism lay more in his theoretical pamphlets than in his actual music. *Die Meistersinger* which, with its comparatively popular atmosphere, its crowd scenes and occasional folk dances, stands closer to the Russian school than does the rest of his output, is the only opera of his which does not display his usual symphonic qualities.

The two most common forms of nationalism in music are the evocation of a landscape background of a specifically local type and the evocation of a popular gathering—for example, Balakireff's *Russia*, Sibelius's *Finlandia*, Rimsky-Korsakoff's *Grande Pâque Russe*, Albeniz's *Fête-Dieu à Seville*, Vaughan Williams's *Norfolk Rhapsody*, etc. These two forms of expression are obviously incompatible with the avoidance of the realistic and picturesque, which is one of the essentials of the symphony, and also incompatible with the idée fixe, the internal monologue that lies at the back of the Lisztian symphonic poem.[1] It is important to emphasize once more the spiritual conflict that lies at the back of the obvious technical conflict between the folk song and classical form.

To put it vulgarly, the whole trouble with a folk song is that once you have played it through there is nothing much you can do except play it over again and play it rather louder. Most Russian music, indeed, consists in ringing changes on this device, skilfully disguised though the fact may be. If we look at *Russlan and Ludmilla*, for example, we see that, except in those sections which are conventional in colour, the composer never gets further than a repetition of an unvarying folk song or folk-type tune with a varied harmonic and orchestral background. Within these limits he produces an extraordinary range of colour, as can be seen by comparing the chorus of the Giant's Head at the end of Act II with the Persian chorus at the beginning of Act III, but by the time we reach the end of the opera this short-winded method of construction begins to interfere with our enjoyment of the continuous flow of melodic and harmonic invention. The same is true of his purely instrumental works. *Kamarinskaya*, the most typical of these, is a little masterpiece, no doubt, but Tchaikovsky was wrong in describing it as the acorn from which the oak tree of Russian music grew. It is an acorn that has miraculously produced

---

[1] What may be called the externalized symphonic poems of Liszt, such as *Festklänge*, are patently inferior to those that centre round some individual figure, like *Hamlet*.

a series of larger and more decorative acorns. The marches and ballets in *Prince Igor* are more technically advanced, more powerful and opulent than those in *Russlan*, but they show no advance in conception. And if this is true of Borodin it is doubly true of Rimsky-Korsakoff who spent his life producing a charming but essentially unimportant series of operas in which various facets of Glinka's genius are gently developed.

Borodin's two symphonies[1] are thoroughly enjoyable continuations not so much of the Beethoven tradition as of the Haydn tradition, but they do not constitute a symphonic school. It is noticeable too, that the second and more powerful symphony, with its heroic and national colouring reminiscent of *Prince Igor*, is, from the formal point of view, far less satisfactory than the first symphony which achieves an admirable symphonic texture at the cost of a partial denial of purely Russian and popular atmosphere. Balakireff, more of an individualist and less of a nationalist than Borodin, did not provide a solution to the problem of reconciling national colour and formal tradition. The folksong finale of his first symphony, hopelessly at variance with the mood of the first movement, is a typical instance of a piece of music delightful in itself that has no place in a symphony. In *Thamar* and *Islamey* he produced two masterpieces of their genre, but they can hardly be considered as specifically national in feeling. Combining the stylized exotic atmosphere of *Russlan* with a Lisztian technique they are both more Eastern and more Western than the works of Mussorgsky, the Russian par excellence.

The outstanding masterpiece of the Russian school is by

---

[1] The third symphony being pieced together by Glazunoff after Borodin's death cannot be taken as an example of Borodin's formal methods. In any case it is a work more noticeable for melodic charm than for constructional merit.

general consent Mussorgsky's *Boris Godunoff*, a work whose content it would be impossible to overpraise but whose form leaves us much where we were before. *Boris* depends for its effect on the direct transcription of the emotional implications of the scene before the spectator, relying on no formal or extrinsic device to aid its inherent worth. The method, in fact, is the simple one of hit or miss—if a scene is bad or dull we cannot say, as we do of Wagner, that it is essential to the formal unity of the work. Fortunately Mussorgsky's inspiration in this particular opera was at such white heat that there is not a single dull bar and we are never conscious of the possibility of his missing. But, like Debussy after him, Mussorgsky established no method and no tradition.

Human nature being what it is, no art can depend entirely on inspiration. It was possible for a second-rate but able musician of Mozart's time to produce quite admirable results by following Mozart's methods—how many people indeed, without being primed, can tell when listening to the *Requiem* where Mozart ends and Süssmayr begins? It is impossible, though, to produce neo-Mussorgsky or neo-Debussy. There is indeed no more convincing proof of the dangers of the hit-or-miss method than Debussy's minor piano pieces.

This, however, is a slight digression. The point about *Boris* is that, while admittedly the highest peak achieved by Russian nationalism, it represents the greatest divagation possible from the classical, aristocratic, formalized opera of the Mozart type or the romantic, individualist, and symphonic opera of the Wagner type. Mr. Calvocoressi, it is true, has made an interesting attempt to prove that the whole of *Boris* is based on the opening phrase; but this, I am convinced, is no more than an able scholastic theory displaying a crossword-puzzle ingenuity of which Mussorgsky was palpably incapable.

That *Boris* lacks formalism or symphonic continuity is, in

148

itself, no fault; nor is it a fault that certain scenes can be taken away from the opera without absolutely injuring the effect of the whole. The same is true of most of Shakespeare. We do not condemn his chronicle plays because they lack the deliberate formal unity of Euripides on the one hand, Ibsen on the other; nor do we say that *Hamlet* is second rate because we can follow the plot after it has been severely cut. I am not trying, however, to determine the intrinsic merit of *Boris*. I am only trying to point out that this national and proletarian opera represents the complete break-up of the formal tradition of the eighteenth century. A sympathetic critic of the day might well have thought that one opera of this sort was worth half a dozen more carefully constructed operas of the German school, and personally speaking I find that to go from *Boris* to any of Wagner's operas is like going from a Shakespeare play to one of the nineteenth-century poetic dramas like *Becket*. This, however, is a purely individual reaction which in no way affects my argument that it is to nationalism even more than romanticism that we owe the destruction of the classical tradition that so many contemporary composers are trying to revive by a species of artificial respiration.

Boris and *Prince Igor* possess such extraordinary vitality and colour that to a contemporary observer it might have seemed that one could well spare a school of symphonic writers when faced by such virility and genius. Unfortunately, *Boris* and *Prince Igor* are not only the climax of the Russian nationalist school but to all intents and purposes its finale. After the death of Borodin we find little of any genuine interest. Rimsky-Korsakoff continued his series of operas, in which the fresh primary colours of Glinka became gradually effaced by the weary pastel shades of Wagner. Liadoff, a real petit-maître, produced at rare intervals a few miniatures of extraordinary felicity but of little weight.

Glazunoff, whose earliest and best works, such as *Stenka Razin*, are in the Borodin tradition, relapsed into premature middle age, producing a series of well-wrought symphonies whose occasional touches of national colour only throw into greater prominence the conservatoire qualities of the rest of the work. The Diaghileff ballet, by providing the plastic equivalent of the musical atmosphere of the national school, gave a sort of strychnine injection to the practically defunct body of the Glinka tradition and produced in Stravinsky's pre-war ballets its final impressive and galvanic death struggles. But Russian nationalism had by then already lost its psychological background, and Stravinsky's ballets had in them that element of pastiche which was to be openly avowed in his post-war works.

The Russian national tradition, therefore, may now be considered as dead as mutton and, as it is the only national movement in music whose beginnings and whose end we can so clearly trace, it is worth while pausing a moment to see what it has given us that is good—and also what harm it has done. On the credit side are one opera of outstanding genius, another half-dozen of remarkable merit, one great symphonic poem—also with its train of satellites—a couple of symphonies of unequal merit, and a host of short orchestral and piano pieces of undeniable albeit monotonous charm. Permeating all this a wealth of vitality, colour, and primitive nostalgia which breaks through the stuffy conservatoire tradition of the central European composers as refreshingly as the painting of Gauguin and Van Gogh breaks through the traditions of the French Salon. But, as I have said elsewhere, Russian music produced no Cézanne. In its lack of any genuinely architectural element it carried with it the seeds of its own ultimate collapse.

The constructive shortwindedness to be found in Glinka —which as we have seen was the inevitable counterpart of

Glinka as a Russian composer, not of Glinka as an individual composer—is echoed faithfully in every work which continues his tradition. There is an extraordinary lack of formal as opposed to merely colouristic progress in Russian progress, and during the seventy years that separate *Russlan* from *Le Sacre du Printemps* there is less real advance, save of a purely decorative and two-dimensional order, than there is in the thirty years that separate Beethoven's first symphony from his ninth. On the debit side, then, is this one grave accusation. Russian music had the vitality to break up the eighteenth-century tradition, but not the vitality to build up another. Like nomad Tartars, the Russians razed the Western buildings to the ground but put up in their place only gaily painted tents.

(d) Nationalism and the Modern Scene

There is no other country, however, which has produced a purely national school for which we can say so much. The Spaniards can show no *Boris*, no *Prince Igor*, no *Coq d'Or*—nothing but a series of glorified and tasteful picture postcards of the come-to-sunny-Spain order. The grandeur of Spain's historical and artistic past, the austerities of its inhuman and inspiring landscape, are conquered by the monotonous *espièglerie* of the cabaret dancer. In Russian music the voice of a street singer is sometimes the voice of the people, but in Spanish music it remains the voice of the street singer—charming, alluring, nostalgic no doubt, but essentially limited both in its appeal and in its potentialities.

The whole of Spanish music so far is summed up in a few of Albeniz's piano pieces: notably *Evocación*, *Malaga*, *El Polo* and *Triana*. These, within their narrow range, have a unique charm and an unexpectly profound emotional appeal; but they are exceptional examples of an unvarying formula which soon becomes wearisome in the extreme. Manuel de Falla, after continuing the Albeniz tradition in a somewhat desiccated manner, has only found an escape from this obvious cul-de-sac by grafting on to his national style a chilly neo-classicism. Most other modern Spanish composers seem unable to realize that they are in a cul-de-sac at all, and figures like Turina still rely on the picturesque glamour of the folk dance and the religious procession to disguise the essential thinness of their musical thought. With the inevitable and not-far-distant conquest of the jazz band, and the already established conquest of an anti-religious government, this glamour will suffer a severe set-back even if it does not disappear altogether.

It would hardly be an exaggeration to say that the Spanish national style was invented by a Russian, Glinka, and destroyed by an Englishman, Lord Berners; for after the latter's amazingly brilliant parody of Spanish mannerisms it is impossible to hear most Spanish music without a certain satiric feeling breaking through. The self-conscious concentration on purely local characteristics which is the hallmark of all Spanish composers without exception, the eternal stamping of heels and clacking of castanets, is at times as irritating and embarrassing as the self-conscious racial exhibitionism of those who unconvincingly remark: 'Wouldn't I be telling you that it's Irish I am', or those who suddenly break into a 'black-bottom' to cries of 'Vo-dodeo-vo' and 'Whoopee-e-e' in a vain effort to persuade others and themselves that they are instinct with the overbrimming vitality of the New World.

This irritating sense of artificiality is doubled by the time we get to the modern English school of nationalist composers. To the technical disadvantages inherent in the use of folk song as musical material, that we have already examined, is added the depressing fact that English folk songs have for the average twentieth-century Englishman none of the evocative significance that the folk songs of Russian had for the average nineteenth-century Russian. The Petrograd coachmen would have been found singing tunes of the type that occur quite naturally in *Boris*, but the London bus conductor is not to be found singing the type of tune that occurs in *Hugh the Drover;* if he sings at all he is probably singing a snatch of *Love is the Sweetest Thing*, in an unconvincing though sickening imitation of the American accent.

Folk songs in England are not a vigorous living tradition, as they were in Russia, nor have they the power to graft a foreign influence on to themselves while retaining their own individuality, like the Catalan sardanas which have added to their primitive basis sophisticated and foreign elements without losing their essentially Catalonian qualities. The English folk song, except to a few crusted old farmhands in those rare districts which have escaped mechanization, is nothing more than a very pretty period piece with the same innocent charm as the paintings of George Morland. The particular type of self-conscious Englishry practised by the folk-song composers is in itself curiously un-English. England has never produced an artist so 'echt-English' as Mussorgsky is 'echt-Russian', or Renoir 'echt-French'. The strength of the English tradition in art is that it has always been open to fruitful foreign influences, which have been grafted on to the native plant without causing it to wither away. The Elizabethans, and Purcell after them, drew what they could from their Italian contemporaries without in any way submerging their own personalities. Even in our day Elgar and Delius have, in their widely different ways, written music that is essentially English in feeling without having to dress itself up in rustic clothes or adopt pseudo-archaic modes of speech.

Nationalism and the Exotic

Although at the time it started the English folk-song movement probably provided an excellent pied-à-terre for those who not unnaturally wished to rid English music of the intolerable accretion of German clichés that had been strangling its growth for a hundred years or so, it is by now —if it was not always so—a definitely exotic and 'arty' movement completely detached from any genuine life. That English folk songs are indeed an exotic growth to even those composers who exploit them is suggested by the way in which they mingle homely English with barbaric Irish songs. In Borodin the Russian and Tartar tunes are always kept severely apart, the latter being recognized as a definitely exotic element opposed to the natural expression of the former. The English composers have invented a species of synthetic Anglo-Irish melodic line which conjures up the weakest passages in Housman and Yeats at one and the same time.

There is about this music something both unbearably precious and unbearably hearty. Its preciosity recalls the admirably meant endeavours of William Morris and his followers to combat the products of those dark satanic mills with green and unpleasant handwoven materials, while its heartiness conjures up the hideous faux bonhomie of the hiker, noisily wading his way through the petrol pumps of Metroland, singing obsolete sea chanties with the aid of the Week-End Book, imbibing chemically flavoured synthetic beer under the impression that he is tossing off a tankard of 'jolly good ale and old' in the best Chester-Belloc manner, and astounding the local garage proprietor by slapping him on the back and offering him a pint of 'four 'alf'.

It may seem unreasonable to condemn a school of composers for what some people might consider extraneous social reasons; but it is essential that we should see music against its social background. The recent invention by certain critics of a hitherto unknown art described as 'pure music' has resulted in the criticism of music becoming more and more detached from any form of life, composers being treated as though they produced patterns of notes in a spiritual vacuum, uninfluenced by the landscape, social life, and political situations surrounding them. For every technical argument for or against a method of composing, there is at least one social argument, and the social argument is often the more far reaching and convincing.

At the present time the arguments against deliberate nationalism in music are twofold. The first point is a minor technical one, but it is yet worth establishing. Modern harmony has progressed to such a point that the application of it to a modal folk song is as absurd as an atonal setting of *Land of Hope and Glory*. The harmonic style of Glinka and Borodin, like the harmony of the sixteenth century but unlike the harmony of the eighteenth century, provides a natural counterpart to the modal line of the folk song, the reason being that it is based roughly on the harmonic implications of the melody itself. Though the harmony may give an unexpected twist to the melody, the two exist in a state of amity up to the end of the century. But with *Le Sacre du Printemps* we begin to get folk tunes treated in an harmonic style that has not the remotest emotional or technical relation to the harmonies suggested by the melody itself. The relation between the melodic line and its harmonic setting is no longer friendly. It resembles more that between the unfortunate yokel in the dock and the cynical barrister prosecuting him.

The lack of rapport between the tune and harmony is particularly noticeable in some of the later works of Bartók. Although in his earlier works, such as the first two string quartets and the opera *Bluebeard's Castle*, Bartók achieves a melodic line which, like that of Vaughan Williams at his best, is intensely individual while yet drawing its inflections from national song—a line which is at one with its stark harmonic background—in his later works, such as the piano sonata, a dangerous split is apparent between melody and harmony, the melody becoming definitely simpler, squarer and more 'folky' while the harmonic treatment becomes more cerebral and outré. The gap between the two becomes such that in some passages, notably the finale of the piano sonata, the composer gives up all attempt to bridge it, merely punctuating each pause in an innocent folk song with a resounding, brutal and discordant crash, an effect which, did it not remind one of a sadistic schoolmaster chastising some wretched country bumpkin, would verge on the ludicrous. This is an extreme example, perhaps, but it is obvious that the less consonant harmony becomes, the more artificial is the effect provided by the introduction of folk-type material.

There is a far more profound argument, however, against the deliberate fostering of a national style at the present day, and that is the lack of any genuine spiritual or social background to lend force to such a movment.

We have only to think of the average large street in twelve different European capitals, streets distinguished from each other only by the names painted over the shops or the way the windows open, filled with men in precisely the same drab clothes following precisely the same drab occupations, supporting wives or mistresses wearing the same cheap French models and using the same cheap French perfume, going to the same Garbo film, listening to the same American light music, watching the same kind of sports and driving the same kind of motor-car, to realize the absurdity of conjuring up one street by a can-can, another by a hopak, a third by a tango, a fourth by a morris dance and so forth through the stock list of national dances. Specific and

stylized national forms, such as the folk dance with its characteristic rhythm, are now become symbols as artificial as the
various types of hat—the flat top hat of the sturdy Rowland-
son John Bull, the tall top hat of the dyspeptic goatee'd
Uncle Sam, the astrakhan hat of the bearded Bolshevik,
the Phrygian cap of the matronly tricoteuse—by which
political cartoonists try to disguise the fact that we are all
represented by much the same type of tired and harassed
business man wearing a characterless and standardized
bowler.

It is true, of course, that you don't destroy a nation by
destroying certain national customs, that the fact that the
delegates at Geneva look alike does not prevent their dis-
liking each other, that England is England still, the spirit
of Drake, etc.—any journalist can be asked to fill in the rest
of this paragraph. . . .

Music however, being the most instinctive of the arts is
more than any other art susceptible to the purely mechanical
differences of civilization in so far as they affect our emotional
life. The argument that England is England still is an
intellectual one to which the musical nerves refuse to listen.
If the composer imagines that he can treat present-day
Surrey with its charabancs, filling stations, hikers, road
houses, dainty tea rooms, and loud speakers discouraging
cosmopolitan jazz, in the way the Elizabethan composers
treated the 'woodes so wilde' he is living in a narrow world
of escape, incapable of producing anything more than a
pretty period piece.

A composer cannot, without performing a spiritual
amputation, entirely detach himself from his times. One does
not require that his work should be a strictly contemporary
record, but one does require that it should not be a series
of studio pictures.

Boris Godunoff, though dealing with an earlier period than

157

Mussorgsky's own, was in no way a period piece, for the Russian people and its relations to the Czar and his government were still much the same in Mussorgsky's day as they had been for centuries past. The spiritual foundation of *Boris Godunoff* was the spiritual foundation of Mussorgsky's Russia, and that is why every scene has such extraordinary realistic force quite apart from its purely musical value. But the spiritual background of a modern people's-opera, like Vaughan Williams's *Hugh the Drover*, is something that no longer exists and which nothing will bring back and the work in consequence fails to move us except in a detached nostalgic way.

Tristan, again, though laid in legendary Cornwall is no more a period piece than *Boris*, for the setting is not an integral part of the opera but a frame to the expression of Wagner's feelings about himself and about love in general. There is no possibility of a modern *Tristan* either, because this particular type of romantic feeling has crumbled away just as much as the national feeling of Mussorgsky's time. There was nothing forced about Wagner's and Liszt's romanticism. It was the most natural thing in the world for Liszt to take his young countesses on Lake Como and read them Tasso and Victor Hugo. If anyone still thinks this spirit exists let him visualize himself taking his young woman on the Serpentine and reading her T. S. Eliot. I don't want him to dismiss the argument as facetious or trivial, I just want him to spend a minute or two visualizing the scene. The various inhibitions, social and personal, which would prevent this scene taking place, or being in any way moving did it improbably take place, exactly explain why the modern composer cannot hope to write a movement like the Gretchen section in the *Faust* symphony.

If we go further back in history for a great opera that owes much of its greatness to its firm spiritual and social background, we find that Mozart's operas are not a symbolic but an exact reproduction of the spirit and society of his day. He himself could have walked into one of his own operas, which combined the most delicate spiritual beauty with the social topicality of a play by Somerset Maugham. The essential falsity of modern attempts to revive the delicious formality of the Mozartian period of opera lies in the fact that the whole framework of society, whose relation to the individual symbolizes the cadences and codas that gently restrain the flow of Mozart's passionate line, is crumbling away if not already completely desiccated.

If we take *Figaro*, *Tristan*, and *Boris*, as representing three of the highest peaks in the history of music, we see that they symbolize three phases of human thought without which background they would have taken on a very different shape and quality. (The same is true of the instrumental works of these three periods, but the relation is more clearly grasped in a stage work.) Mozart represents the aristocratic internationalism of the eighteenth century, Wagner the passionate individualism of the romantic movement, Mussorgsky the equally passionate democratic nationalism of the nineteenth century—which has its basis in emotion not in economics. The people who, in effect, say to the modern composer: 'Why don't you stop making those beastly noises and write lovely tunes and pleasant harmonies like those in *Figaro*, *Tristan* and *Boris*, etc.?' may not realize that even were a modern composer sufficiently endowed with invention and technique he is totally lacking in the artistic faith, conscious or unconscious, that these phases of thought provided.

It is hardly worth while pointing out that the aristocratic internationalism of Mozart's time is gone, once and for all. As for the romanticism that inspired Liszt and Wagner, it may still beat in a few isolated breasts, but the latter-day individualist must feel painfully déraciné—unless he happens to be a temporary dictator, in which case his twenty-four-hour day hardly leaves him time for composition. The decline of individualism has been so devastatingly exposed in Lewis's *The Art of Being Ruled* that there is no need for me to expatiate on it at length.

Manfred and Don Juan would not be allowed to walk about Europe alone today. They would have to buy a guitar, join a band of Wandervogel and put up at special hostels. Axel and Sara would neither renounce the world nor enjoy it—they would carefully invest their money, and spend it on the improvement of the Axel estate or the construction of an emancipated school on Bertrand Russell lines for the benefit of the villagers. Tristan would not have entered into his regrettable emotional entanglement, either because he had been carefully brought up to realize the folly of such anti-social behaviour, or because his experimental marriages with both Isolde and Brangäne had already been proved a failure—in any case he would be a teetotaller and would say: 'No, I am afraid I never touch potions in any form.'

The decline, not so much of romanticism but of the individualism and obstinacy without which it cannot exist, is aptly symbolized in the gradual transformation of the Rowlandson-like John Bull into the Little Man of Strube, the black-coated citizen at the beck and call of the Press barons, docile, smiling and obedient, capable only of mass indignation, herd pleasures and community singing.

Although most people would admit that the aristocratic internationalism of Mozart's time and the romantic individualism of Wager's were both, if not extinct, completely enfeebled in our own day, it might be thought that the nationalism that inspired *Boris* is more rampant now than ever. At first sight this may seem to be so but, just as there is more food than ever in the world and also more starvation, just as there is more music than ever in the world and also less genuine musical experience, so at the present there is more petty nationalism than ever combined with a less genuine basis for national feeling. As this is not a political pamphlet and was indeed intended—as a glance at the title page will show—to be a book on music, I cannot enlarge on this aspect of present-day life even if I were competent to do so. No one, however, whatever his political opinions, can fail to distinguish between the liberal spirit of nationalism that inspired political figures like Mazzini and musical figures like Mussorgsky, and the retrograde spirit of nationalism that inspires the petty dictators and juntas of gangsters, with their pathological worship of violence and hatred of all true intelligence, even from their own nationals, that are becoming our leaders today. Does anyone imagine that the dictators of today and the tariff wars they engage in will inspire works like *Boris Godunoff* and *Prince Igor?* The gangster film or the comic strip would seem more suitable mediums in which to treat the self-appointed puppet leaders and would-be leaders of the people.

However much inspiration the composer may draw from the contemporary scene it is unlikely that he will draw any from the Press-fomented patriotism of the present political situation. More particularly as the recent increase in political separatism coincides with a period when, through the advance of mechanical communications, mechanical reproduction of music and wireless, the physical and psychological separatism is decreasing.

The physical texture, the uniform drabness of modern urban life is far more vividly presented by Hindemith and his followers than by any of the self-conscious nationalists. For not only does Hindemith produce busy and colourless music without any distinguishing spiritual or national quality, but his followers and pupils, whether they write in

F   161

Nationalism and the Exotic

Serbia or in Golders Green, produce precisely the same type of busy and colourless music. Their works differ as much from each other as a Cook's office in one town differs from a Cook's office in another. They represent the final decline of the aristocrat, the romantic and the peasant, of the three types of whose psychology the composer must in some degree partake. Here at last is the musical equivalent of the robot and the adding machine. Whatever its merits as psychological realism this is obviously, from the audience's point of view, the least desirable form for the reaction against excessive nationalism to take—it is like exchanging Burns's poems for Mr. Ogden's basic English. Moreover, its avoidance of essential psychological differences in national musical thought is as false as the insistence on superficial differences in national musical style.

Whatever we think of nationalism in music we cannot sweep aside the whole of music since Glinka. The only solution is an absorption of national feeling in an intellectually self-supporting form such as we find in the symphonies of Sibelius. While the peculiar atmosphere of Sibelius's music is no doubt as influenced by intense national feeling as anything in Bartók or Vaughan Williams, we are never conscious of his allowing local atmosphere to interfere with formal and expressive preoccupations. He is a citizen both of Finland and the world. His symphonies, in which incidentally nothing approaching a folk song appears, are not Finnish symphonies but symphonies by a Finn. He alone among modern composers has combined the national intensity of Mussorgsky's operas with the formal intensity of Beethoven's quartets; and listening to his works we realize that our whole quarrel is not so much with nationalism as with that particular form of provinciality that has degraded nationalism to the level of the exotic.

162

(e) The Cult of the Exotic

In literature the exotic and the nationalist keep rather severely apart. As far as I can remember Swinburne is the only poet to deal both with legendary oriental queens and Northumbrian fisher-lasses, and he took great care that they should not occur in the same poem. In music, however, the cult of the exotic and the cult of the peasant are curiously intermingled in the works of the same composer and, very often, the same composition. This may be due to the fact that the cult of the exotic was 'established', so to speak, by the same phenomenal genius who established nationalism— namely, Glinka. The fact that Glinka was a Russian strengthens the link, for in Russian folk tales, more than any others, do we get the familiar treatment of fabulous oriental czars side by side with homely Russian peasant heroes. At a later date the link between the two may signify, as I have suggested in the previous section, that nationalism itself has become something of an exotic culture.

The exotic elements in Glinka's music are of two kinds. First of all we get the exploitation of the exotic atmosphere suggested by the music of those countries nearest to his own, such as Persia and Caucasia. These have a certain authenticity of conception and feeling that marks them off completely from the usual oriental fantasies of western composers, so brilliantly pilloried by Kaikhosru Sorabji in his *Around Music*. It is natural that exoticism of a convincing kind should have its foundation in Russia, for Russia on the one hand, and Spain on the other, form the boundaries of Western music.

It is an interesting experiment to put on gramophone

records of native music, starting from Catalonia, going on to Andalusia and over the sea to Morocco, eastwards through Persia and India as far as China and Japan, then back through Siberia to Central Asia and Caucasia. It will be seen, in spite of the striking differences between these various forms of so-called native music, that the real break comes between the squarecut and breezy melodies of Catalonia and the oriental arabesques of southern Spanish flamenco music, between the modal tunes of European Russia and the chromatic tunes of eastern Russia. Oriental influences have occasionally been grafted on to European music directly, as when Debussy became influenced by the Cambodian music heard at the Paris Exhibition, but on the whole they have percolated naturally through these racial frontiers, and undoubtedly the Mongolian element in Russian music and the African element in Spanish music give a firm basis to the exoticism to be found in the music of these two countries.

Exoticism of a certain sort existed, of course, before Glinka, but only in the form of a deliberate type of chinoiserie. Mozart's Turkish rondo is like a Negro page in an eighteenth-century salon—there is no feeling that Mozart's spiritual home was Stamboul rather than Vienna or Prague. Glinka was the first to establish in music that particular type of nostalgic world of escape which has now become so familiar and, unfortunately, vulgarized that it hardly requires further definition.

The Persian chorus and oriental dances in *Russlan and Ludmilla* are the fountain head of a tradition that is still with us and whose course it is unnecessary to trace. Glinka's particular genius lay not so much in his introduction of oriental tunes into Western music as in the harmonic justness and taste with which he treated them. We have only to compare the particular tune which occurs in act three of *Russlan* in one of Ratmir's recitatives (page 160 of the piano score, Fürstner edition) with the setting of the same tune in Félicien David's *Le Désert* to realize the difference between objective and subjective exoticism. Besides his happy gift for investing an oriental tune with an appropriate harmonic atmosphere, Glinka may be said to have invented the particular type of stylized tune we get so often in Rimsky-Korsakoff which, convincing the Western listener as being oriental in atmosphere, bears much the same relation to oriental music as Bilibin's charming illustrations do to Persian painting. A parallel to this stylized treatment of the exotic music closest to one's own national tunes may be found in the Irish tone poems of the English composers, such as Bax's *Garden of Fand*, and the Spanish rhapsodies of the French school, such as Chabrier's *España*.

Besides this comparatively authentic exoticism Glinka may be said to have established, in his *Jota Aragonesa* and *Summer Night in Madrid*, the even more familiar form of exoticism which consists in exploiting the atmosphere of an alien music—a type of musical cabotage, in fact. These two innocent fantasias have had an even more numerous and fantastic progeny than the oriental passages in *Russlan*, and there are few modern composers who do not owe something to Glinka's typically northern nostalgia for the south.

At first sight it might seem that exoticism in music, by opening up to the Western composer a new world of melody, timbre, and above all rhythm, would have the same healthy effect as exoticism in sculpture; and it is true that the exotic influences in the Russian and Spanish schools have superficially broken up and fertilized the academic nineteenth-century Teutonic tradition in much the way that the appreciation of Egyptian, Chinese, Mexican and African sculpture has broken up and fertilized the Graeco-Roman tradition; but the comparison is not a true one, for whereas the Western and Eastern sculptors were working in the same medium with approximately the same tools and facing the same formal problems, the Western musician and the Eastern musician cannot really establish a technical point of contact.

We can say without falsity that we prefer the design of a Utamaro print to that of a Puvis de Chavannes panel, or that we admire Maya carvings more than those of Mr. Moore; but we cannot say that we think that classical Indian music shows a more highly developed sense of form than classical Italian music, because the whole basis of thought and principle of construction is so entirely different. Nor can we compare the orchestration of Chinese theatre music with the orchestration of European theatre music, for there is hardly an instrument common to the two. Any attempt of a Western composer to approximate to oriental instrumentation by the use of exotic drums, bass flutes, etc., is monstrously crude when compared to the genuine article, partly because it is impossible to rival the virtuosity of the oriental performer, and partly because the melodic instruments cannot execute the minute and subtle divisions of the scale found in non-European music.

More important, however, than these technical considerations is the fact that while we can appreciate oriental plastic art without altering our angle of approach, or adopting a different criterion, we cannot appreciate oriental music without a violent dislocation of our usual critical processes, if indeed we can appreciate at all an art that lives in so different an emotional world and depends to so great a degree on improvisation. Exoticism in music is therefore more artificial than exoticism in literature or the plastic arts, and for this reason it might be expected to produce even fewer works of ultimate importance and architectural value than self-conscious nationalism. But actually its artificiality is in its favour, for it induces in the composer a certain degree of stylization that is often to be preferred to the verism of the nationalist composer. Moreover, the imitation of the arabesques of oriental melody—though appalling at its worst—can, in the works of a composer of sensibility like Balakireff or Debussy, produce themes of a far greater plasticity than the rigid folk songs which the nationalists plump down in the middle of a symphony.

Sorabji, himself an authority on oriental music, has spoken of the Asiatic affinities shown in the suppleness of rhythm, the richness and delicacy of colouring, and the flexibility of melodic line in Debussy's best works. A tune of an exotic type, unless it is to be accompanied merely by a Maskelyne and Devant tom-toming, compels an equally unconventional and supple formal treatment, and thus exoticism, though even more disruptive of the eighteenth-century spiritual tradition than is nationalism, has produced a greater variety of valuable architectural experiment. Balakireff's *Thamar* is a more closely knit and convincing piece of construction than any of Brahms's symphonies—the programme in this case actually aids the form, for Lermontoff's poem has a convenient element of recapitulation—while Debussy's *Iberia* has a far greater formal compactness and invention than the symphonies of Elgar—or, should this comparison seem too far fetched, let us say those of Glazunoff or D'Indy.

Even amongst Stravinsky's work we find that *Les Noces* is by far his most interesting ballet from the architectural point of view. At first sight *Les Noces*, with its simple peasant background, might seem his most nationalist work, but its orchestration and its peculiarly African use of rhythm and form remove it from the peasant expression of Mussorgsky's operas. It is equally far removed from the oriental lushness of Rimsky-Korsakoff's operas. The exoticism of *Les Noces* is of the 'darker' D. H. Lawrence order and we feel at any moment that middle-aged Englishwomen are going to slip out of the stalls and join in the singing, like the heroine of *The Plumed Serpent*.

In *Les Noces* all influences of Debussy's impressionism have disappeared and we are no longer worried by the disparity between the vocal line and its harmonic background. It is impossible indeed not to admire the consistency of this work, even though we may feel that the consistency is of a negative order, achieved by rejecting most elements in musical composition rather than by blending them into one harmonious whole. Whereas the orgiastically rhythmic sections of *Le Sacre* were contrasted with other sections that relied more on melodic, harmonic, or colouristic appeal, in *Les Noces* rhythm is paramount. The harmonies on the pianos are merely there to fix a rhythmic shape in space, as it were; they have no value as sound if examined vertically. The occasional appearance of counterpoint in the choral part, again, is due not to any actual contrapuntal feeling but to an antiphonal use of melodic phrases reminiscent of primitive African singing. The resultant harmonies are really quite arbitrary. This particular attitude towards rhythm links up *Les Noces* not only with African music but with certain types of Asiatic music—notably the Laotian orchestras, whose use of conflicting rhythmic passages on two or more marimbas provides an exact parallel to Stravinsky's use of four pianos.

Seen on the stage, where the dynamic rhythms are given an additional force by Nijinska's monumentally constructed and austere choreography, *Les Noces* has an undoubted nervous and emotional appeal; but heard in the concert hall, the ear soon wearies of a design on one plane only. The pleasure we get from the cross rhythms in Elizabethan music comes largely from the way they are fitted into the melodic and harmonic scheme, just as the pleasure we get from the design of a Cézanne picture is largely due to the skill with which he has been able to base it on three-dimensional realism without seeking the easy path of two-dimensional abstraction. The trouble with exotic music is that so much of it is emotionally and technically two-dimensional. The austere exoticism of Stravinsky's rhythms soon becomes as wearisome as the lush exoticism of Delius's harmonies.

I do not wish, when faced with exoticism, to adopt an attitude which can best be described by the admirable expression 'po-faced'. We cannot live perpetually in the rarefied atmosphere of the austerer classics, whether ancient or modern, and it is absurd not to enjoy a work merely because it is essentially sterile in influence. Personally speaking, if it is a question of choosing between an exotic work and a so-called abstract work, give me exoticism every time. But as we are examining in this chapter the decline of the classic tradition it is necessary to lay more emphasis on the fatality of that *femme fatale* exoticism, than on her feminine charms.

(f) Exoticism and 'Low Life'

If we compare the average titles of present-day orchestral pieces with those of twenty or thirty years ago, we might think that exoticism had died out of music save in the brilliant parodies of Lord Berners or the works of a few isolated figures like Villa Lobos. *Pur-sang* exoticism of the fruity Oscar Wilde order is indeed extinct, but it would be a great mistake to imagine that the type of mentality it represents has died out, either among artists or audiences. The world of escape which lies behind exotic expression has shifted its *venue*—that is all.

Nationalism and the Exotic

Even the most austere amongst us occasionally feel a desire to escape from our drab physical surroundings and our drab spiritual surroundings into a more highly coloured and less moral world, and with certain types—not, I admit, major artists but often minor artists of distinction—this momentary desire may become an obsession. In the nineteenth century, and more particularly during the 'nineties, this desire usually expressed itself in a series of oriental and pagan daydreams laid in regal surroundings, ranging from Lermontoff's *Thamar*—'Péri mystérieuse, cruelle, astucieuse et divine à la fois'—to Swinburne's innumerable processions of legendary queens.

Apart from the natural reaction against any overdone literary fashion, oriental daydreaming has suffered a slight setback since American travelogues, emancipated potentates and shoals of scrutable Indian students have brought the East unromantically near, but America, in destroying the romance of other countries, has created a romance of her own and the 'gangster's moll' has overthrown the 'veiled houri' of the 'nineties. Unable to find exoticism in the strange and distant, we force ourselves to dive down into the familiar, and what is conveniently called Low Life provides the exotic motive for the post-war artist. The grubby gamins and snotty little brats that haunt the pages of Gide and Cocteau have taken the place of Pierre Louÿs's pitiless courtesans; and Swinburne, were he alive today, would write about a very different sort of queen. The worship of violence for its own sake which we find disguised as a piece of antique fancying in *Aphrodite* is openly avowed in present-day French literature; and the connection between violence and romanticism has been so perfectly summed up by Proust when discussing the medieval proclivities of M. de Charlus (see page 200 of the first volume of *Le Temps Retrouvé*) that it need hardly be emphasized again.

Exoticism and 'Low Life'

Without wishing to bring a Freudian element into the argument, I think we can, without exaggeration, see a certain connection between this neurasthenic and sophisticated nostalgia for the world of the apache and the modern composer's obsession with café tunes, dock life, and Negro bands. As might be expected, this neurasthenia is far more marked among central European composers than among those of Paris, whose satiric feeling has usually prevented them from sentimentalizing modern life, to the same extent as Krenek and Kurt Weill for example. Kurt Weill for all his deliberately sordid topicality is as essentially romantic as Marschner, only the romanticism is more localized and the poor white, the racketeer and the bum provide the element of rakishness once sought in Lord Ruthven and his attendant Gadshill. In the nineteenth century they cried for the moon and today we cry: 'Oh, show us the way to the next whisky bar.' The sense of frustration is the same, however.

This neurasthenic exploitation of popular themes is almost exclusively a post-war development, and there is certainly no hint of it in the 'aise aimable qui rayonne' of Emanuel Chabrier, who technically speaking may be considered— far more than Erik Satie—the father of the post-war movement associated with the names of Les Six and the École d' Arceuil. It is impossible to praise too highly the wit, charm and skill of this composer, whose works are still airily dismissed with the label 'light music'. His *España* and *Fête Polonaise*—typically French in spite of their titles—his *Bourrée Fantasque* and *Joyeuse Marche* have all the verve and reckless gaiety of Offenbach at his best, combined with the harmonic and orchestral subtlety of Ravel. As an harmonic innovator, his influence, though acting within a smaller range, is no less far reaching than that of Glinka himself, though this fact will not be fully realized until *Le Roi Malgré Lui* is better known. He is, too, the only composer to have equally influenced both generations of modern French music—the pre-war aesthetic period and the post-war 'tough' period.

Above all, Chabrier holds one's affection as the most genuinely French of all composers, the only writer to give us in music the genial rich humanity, the inspired common-place, the sunlit solidity of the French genius that finds its greatest expression in the paintings of Manet and Renoir. There was, too, a touch of Toulouse-Lautrec about him if we can imagine Toulouse-Lautrec without any of his sinister qualities.

Although he unfortunately spent half his time trying to become a French Wagner, his best work is a musical summing up of the anti-Wagnerian aesthetic which was not to find concrete verbal expression until much later—in Cocteau's *Coq et Arlequin*. He was the first important composer since Mozart to show that seriousness is not the same as solemnity, that profundity is not dependent upon length, that wit is not always the same as buffoonery, and that frivolity and beauty are not necessarily enemies,

It is little wonder that the post-war French composers, reacting equally against German romantic heaviness and French impressionist tenuity, should have seen in this genial figure an ideal to be followed. There is unfortunately the gravest of differences between the composers who uncon-sciously establish an aesthetic and those who consciously follow it. The mere fact that Chabrier wrote *Gwendoline* shows that his *Joyeuse Marche* and similar works were not the result of a deliberate artistic formula, similar to that proposed by Cocteau. After listening to the abundant gaiety of Chabrier's music, which flows forth with all the natural ease of his period, Cocteau's post-war exhortations to the younger French school to rid themselves of pomposity, to be typically Gallic and gay, and to draw inspiration from the bal-musette and street band, read painfully like one of Doctor Crane's once famous 'Tonic Talks'.

The typical French gaiety of the bal-musette school of composers is really as artificial as the typical English jollity of the country-pub school of composers. They both draw their inspiration from a side of life which is either dying out altogether or taking on an American accent. The curious lack of any rhythmic sense shown by the average French dance-band player has prevented French dance music becoming so rapidly Americanized as the dance music of other nations: but it has suffered all the same. René Clair would not dare to synchronize one of his scenes with the sound of a real bal-musette band taken on the spot, for most of the while they would be playing some atrocious version of 'Broadway Melody'.

The low-life exoticism of Les Six and the École d'Arceuil started off, then, with a definitely sentimental handicap, a period lag which became more noticeable every year. Chabrier's gaiety had a solid period backing, so to speak, and his tunes, though evocative of the café-concert, are in no way pastiches of café-concert tunes, being indeed of a far superior order. But the post-war composers, lacking Chabrier's spontaneous gaiety, could only be evocative of the café-concert by deliberately aping its methods, producing a synthetic gaiety through means of association: thus, most of the tunes in the ballets of Poulenc, Auric, and Milhaud are not gay in themselves—they recall the type of tune played in places popularly supposed to be gay.

In the heyday of the music-hall aesthetic it was often urged that since painters like Manet could produce their best work in such paintings as the Bon Bock or the Bar at the Folies Bergère, etc., there was no reason why composers should not achieve work of a similar greatness, taking their inspiration from similar scenes—I am speaking of course of some years ago, before the invention of 'pure music'. This theory is an obvious fallacy. The painter in treating the bar of the Folies Bergère or the basement of the Boeuf sur le Toit does not have his formal methods and his texture dictated by the subject. Provided the picture is ultimately recognizable, the associative effect is much the same whether it is painted in the style of Degas or Severini. To the musician, however, the essence of the scene lies in its associations and emotional reactions, which can only be expressed by a certain type of tune involving certain formal and harmonic limitations, as may be seen even in Chabrier, the least shackled of popular composers.

There is a definite limit to the length of time a composer can go on writing in one dance rhythm (this limit is obviously reached by Ravel towards the end of *La Valse* and towards the beginning of *Bolero*). The sudden changes of rhythm open to him in a symphonic work are not open to him in a dance work, because they involve not only a change of time but also a change of atmosphere. It is not a question of going from three-four to four-four, but of going from valse time to foxtrot time. There is also a limit to the amount of harmonic gingering up and melodic distortion that a composer can impose on a dance tune while yet retaining its associative qualities. A dance tune cannot really be submitted to the same variety of treatment that can be imposed on an object by a painter. Picasso's cubist bottles of wine still remain bottles, but Schönberg's atonal valses emphatically do not remain valses. As the melodic shape is clearly the most important factor in pre-jazz popular music, composers have usually contented themselves with harmonic rather than formal and melodic developments of popular tunes, and hence has arisen what is vulgarly known as the 'wrong note' school of modern music or, in order not to hurt people's feelings, shall we say the school which applies to melodies of a naïve and popular character harmonies of a piquant and sophisticated nature?

The obvious disadvantage of this style of writing—which can, on a small scale, be quite amusing—is its inflexibility, which combines the technical disadvantages of the nationalist school with an even more limited emotional background. If a tune depends for its vitality on the unsuitability of its harmonic background, it is impossible to develop it, use it contrapuntally, or add anything to it after its first statement. Although the harmony may seem wildly at variance with the tune from the vertical point of view, it is yet indissolubly linked with it from a horizontal point of view. This type of writing is seen at its worst in the ballets of Auric, which consist for the most part of a string of boyscout tunes with an acid harmonic accompaniment, hopelessly lacking in either development or continuity.

Even Milhaud, who shows considerably more technical skill, cannot disguise the weakness of his methods in those of his works which are based on exclusively popular material. In *Le Boeuf sur le Toit*, the most amusing of the highbrow music-hall ballets, he achieves a certain continuity and shape by the adoption of an ingenious key scheme and a variant of the rondo form—both essentially academic devices. But this extrinsic form does not disguise the essential inflexibility of his methods which consist not in developing the melodic line, but in embedding it in a series of ineluctable ostinatos, or presenting it in three keys at once. The mechanical imposed polytonality of Milhaud's earlier works, which jump sharply from the most academic euphony to the most startling cacophony, remind one of a host who having forgotten to put gin in the first round of cocktails puts methylated spirits in the second round to make up for it. In his later works, it is true, Milhaud's polytonality is softened down into a flexible use, not so much of different keys as of different modes at once, and in *La Création du Monde* the treatment of the melodic material is far more plastic than in *Le Boeuf sur le Toit*. This work, however, one of the best examples of popular material put to genuinely constructive use, belongs more properly to the later movement of Negro influence and will be more fully treated in the section on jazz.

On the whole, it may be said that since Chabrier's day the only successful examples of sophisticated music with a popular allure have been works on a small scale. William Walton's brilliant accompaniments to Edith Sitwell's *Façade*, for instance, avoid the monotony and lack of continuity of Auric and Milhaud by their concentrated brevity. They are not examples of the sentimental and exotic attitude towards lowbrow tunes but satirical genre pieces—over in a flash, but unerringly pinning down some particular aspect of popular music, whether foxtrot, tango or tarantella. They represent only one facet of the composer's personality, however, a facet that is not shown to us in his symphonic works and, although to my mind the most enjoyable of the modern pieces based on tunes of a popular kind, they are not from the psychological or historical point of view as important as those works where the popular element is paramount and treated with a certain emotional seriousness.

Although the belated attempt to revive the glories of Chabrier in the shape of the bal-musette sentimentalities of Auric, the military-band exoticism of Poulenc and the wide-cracking South Americanisms of Milhaud, has produced little work of even temporary value—and certainly no work of anything like permanent value—this self-consciously popular movement has been worth examining if only for the fact that it provides the link between pre-war national exoticism and post-war international exoticism. It is strange indeed that the slangy squarecut vulgarity of Auric and Milhaud, as exemplified by *Les Matelots* and *Le Boeuf sur le Toit*, should be the bridge between the sturdy provincialism of the folk dance and the emasculated cosmopolitanism of the foxtrot.

(g) The Spirit of Jazz

By jazz, of course, I mean the whole movement roughly designated as such, and not merely that section of it known as Afro-American, or more familiarly as 'Harlem'. The Negro once enjoyed a monopoly of jazz, just as England once enjoyed a monopoly of the industrial revolution, but for the Negroes to imagine that all jazz is their native province is as if an Englishman were to imagine that all locomotives were built by his compatriots. Even the Harlem section of jazz is by no means so African as might be supposed.

There is a double yet opposed conspiracy to persuade one that modern dance music represents a purely negroid tradition. On the one hand, we have the crusty old colonels, the choleric judges and beer-sodden columnists who imagine they represent the European tradition, murmuring 'swamp stuff', 'jungle rhythms', 'Negro decadence' whenever they hear the innocent and anodyne strains of the average English jazz band, hugely enjoying their position of Cassandra prophesying the downfall of the white woman. On the other hand, we have the well-meaning but rather sentimental propagandists of the Negro race, only too eager to point out that the Negroes are the only begetters of a movement that has admittedly swept all over the world and that provides an exotic influence far exceeding the localized exoticism of Cocteau and his followers. The only flaw in both these arguments is that most jazz is written and performed by cosmopolitan Jews. Were this fact sufficiently realized, it would hardly abate the fury of the colonels and the columnists, for from their point of view the Jew is just as much an enemy of the

British and Holy Roman Empires as the Negro; but it might slightly curb the hysterical enthusiasm of the poor-white Negro propagandists whose sentimental effusions must be so embarrassing to the intelligent Negro himself. The particular type of white inferiority complex responsible for this propaganda has been so ruthlessly dealt with by Wyndham Lewis in his *Paleface* that one can add little to his conclusions except to point out that in music also the same game of intellectual 'pat-a-cake' is taking place.

The European's enthusiasm for so-called Negro music is in equal ratio to the Negro's appropriation of European devices, and the more the European tries to imagine himself 'down on the Delta' the more the Negro tries to imagine himself in an aristocratic salon. In this connection, it is amusing to recall the situation that arose recently when a well-known Negro dance arranger was called in to produce a ballet for a highbrow company trained in the classical tradition. While all the Europeans flung aside their carefully won training to indulge in an orgy of pseudo-Charlestons the Negro himself was moved to tears, not by his own work but by the classic elegance of *Lac des Cygnes*.

If anyone doubts the essential element of European sophistication in jazz, it is a simple matter for him to compare a typical piece of jazz music, such as Duke Ellington's *Swampy River*, first with a lyric piece by Grieg and then with a record of native African music. It must be clear to the most prejudiced listener that apart from a few rhythmical peculiarities the Ellington piece has far more in common with the music of Grieg. I am not denying for a moment the racial characteristics implicit in these rhythmical peculiarities —I am only pointing out that Ellington, like all Negro composers, has to use the European harmonic framework. Ellington's works are no more examples of African folk song than James Weldon Johnson's poems are examples of the Dahomy dialect;[1] they both represent the application of the Negro temperament to an alien tradition and an acquired language.

The emotional appeal of jazz depends not only on its rhythms which, though childishly simple compared with those of African folk music, may legitimately be accounted African in origin, but also on its harmonic colour, which cannot conceivably be traced back to Africa for the simple reason that harmony as we understand it does not exist in primitive African music. Hornbostel in his admirable handbook on African music records only one example of pure harmonic writing in the whole history of his discoveries, and that consisted of two chords at the end of a satirical song about the local missionary, the intention of which was obviously to parody the lugubrious effect of his harmonium.

The harmonic element in Afro-American music is an acquired element mainly due to the religious music of the Anglo-Saxon, an influence that naturally had a more powerful effect on the déraciné Negroes of America, bereft of their language and their cultural traditions, than on the self-satisfied if not contented Negroes of Africa. We find it hard now to realize not only the emotional effect but the full sensual effect of the hymns of John Bacchus Dykes and his followers. They were, however, the first real popularization of what is known as 'juicy' harmony, and the force of their influence can be judged by the fact that the modern English composer brought up in their tradition often hits on exactly the same type of variant of their harmonic style as does the Negro composer—possibly Delius, who has been subjected to the influence of Anglo-Saxon church music and its Negro variants, provides the link. The reaction of the

---

[1] Paul Morand tells us that African natives, far from reacting favourably to jazz records, find records of Russian folk songs more exciting and sympathetic.

sentimental and oppressed Negroes to the rich and unctuous melancholy of nineteenth-century religious music was of course enormously enhanced by the religious nostalgia of the words—the oft-repeated desire to escape from this vale of woe into a better and happier land.

Another factor in the growth of harmonic sense on the part of the Negro was the popularization not of the banjo but of the guitar, an instrument which, in the hands of the improviser, easily gives rise to remarkable harmonic combinations. The phrase 'barber-shop chord'—which denotes a chord of unusual succulence—dates back to the days when a guitar hung in every Negro barber's shop, and a client who was waiting would vamp about on the instrument until at a lucky *trouvaille* everyone would shout: 'Hold that chord'. It need hardly be pointed out that this type of harmonic experiment is as sophisticated in its method as that of the contemporary composers who—deny it hotly though they may—compose 'at the piano'.

The lack of any innate harmonic sense in the Negro can be realized by listening to the bands in the poorer bals nègres in Paris, where the orchestra consists of unsophisticated Negroes who have been brought up in the French colonies and not subjected to the influence of the succulently harmonized Anglo-Saxon religious music. Here we can find no hint of the typical 'blue' harmony of the Negro New York composers. The same rhythmic and improvisatory sense is there, but applied to the rudimentary harmonies of the French musical song.

The superiority of American jazz lies in the fact that the Negroes there are in touch not so much with specifically barbaric elements as with sophisticated elements. Negro talent being on the whole more executive than creative, and modern Negro music being essentially an applied art, jazz is naturally largely dependent for its progress on the progress of the sophisticated material used as a basis for its rhythmic virtuosity. The sudden post-war efflorescence of jazz was due largely to the adoption as raw material of the harmonic richness and orchestral subtlety of the Debussy-Delius period of highbrow music. Orchestral colour, of course, is not a thing that can really be appreciated in itself; it is largely dependent for its colour on the underlying harmonies. The harmonic background drawn from the impressionist school opened up a new world of sound to the jazz composer, and although the more grotesque orchestral timbres, the brute complaints of the saxophone, the vicious spurts from the muted brass, may seem to belie the rich sentimentality of their background, they are only thorns protecting a fleshy cactus—a sauce piquante poured over a nice juicy steak.

Jazz, or to be pedantically accurate, 'ragtime', from having a purely functional value—a mere accompaniment to the tapping of toe and heel, the quick linking of bodies and the slow unburdening of minds—has suddenly achieved the status of a 'school', a potent influence that can meet the highbrow composer on his own terms. Though popularly regarded as being a barbaric art, it is to its sophistication that jazz owes its real force. It is the first dance music to bridge the gap between highbrow and lowbrow successfully. The valse has received august patronage from Beethoven onwards, it is true, but the valses of the nineteenth-century composers are either definite examples of unbending or definite examples of sophistication—somethimes both. Chabrier's *Fête Polonaise* has an harmonic and orchestral elaboration far beyond anything imagined by the popular valse writers of his time, but the modern highbrow composer who writes a foxtrot can hardly hope to go one better than Duke Ellington, if indeed he can be considered as being in the same class at all. In the nineteenth century the split between the classical and popular came between a follower of Liszt, let us say, and a follower of Gungl. Today the split occurs between a composer like Kurt Weill and a composer like Jarnach—both of them pupils of Busoni.

The same rapprochement between highbrow and lowbrow—both meeting in an emotional *terrain vague*—can be seen in literature. Though Byron wrote a poem about the valse there is little in common between his poems and the popular songs of the period; Rossetti kept his limericks and his sonnets severely apart; and though Dowson frequented the breezy music halls of his day there is no touch of Dolly Gray about Cynara. In the poetry of T. S. Eliot, however—particularly in *Sweeney Agonistes*—we find the romantic pessimism of the nineteenth century expressed in the music-hall technique of the twentieth-century lyric writer, not ironically but quite genuinely. 'This is the way the world ends, this is the way the world ends, this is the way the world ends, not with a bang but a whimper' echoes not only the jingle of the jazz song but its sentiment. Whimpering has indeed become recognized as one of the higher pleasures.

The words of jazz songs mark the first popularization of that well-known modern vice—the Inferiority Complex. Until recently a certain exuberant self-confidence has usually formed the spiritual background of a popular tune. 'What fine fellows we all are' is the predominant sentiment of *Liberty Bell, On to Victory* and the other magnificently extrovert marches of John Philip Sousa. A general air of physical attractiveness, sexual bounce and financial independence is naturally assumed by the writers of pre-war song hits. The singer's hat is at a jaunty angle, his gloves are in his hand, he suffers from no inhibitions or self-consciousness as he walks down the pier, receiving the glad eye from presumably attractive girls with whom he ultimately and triumphantly 'clicks'. Even if he 'can't afford a carriage' he can at least stump up enough for a tandem bicycle, which is considerably more than the hero of 'I can't give you anything but Love, baby' can claim to be able to do.

In modern songs it is taken for granted that one is poor, unsuccessful and either sex-starved or unable to hold the affections of such partner as one may have had the luck to pick up. Even when the singer says that he has a woman crazy about him he hastens to point out that her attitude is clearly eccentric and in no way to be expected. For the most part, though, the heroes and heroines of modern songs meet with the rebuffs they deserve and take refuge in the unmute reproach of 'Ain't misbehavin' ', and 'Mean to Me', or the facile melancholy of 'Dancing with Tears in my Eyes', 'You've got me Cryin' again, you've got me Sighin' again', and 'When you Want Somebody who Don't want You, perhaps you'll Think of Me'.

The other side of the medal, the series of crazy words, crazy tune numbers, with their assumed galvanic energy has an equally neurasthenic basic. The so-called 'hot' songs are as depressing as the so-called 'sweet'; they spring from no genuine gaiety such as inspires the marches of Sousa, the sardanas of Bou and the valses of Waldteufel—they are a desperate attempt to hide an underlying boredom and malaise. The difference between the gallops of Offenbach and the 'black-bottoms' of today is the difference between a champagne party at eleven in the morning and a gin-jag in the small hours.

The most irritating quality about the Vo-dodeo-vo, poo-poop-a-doop school of jazz song is its hysterical emphasis on the fact that the singer is a jazz baby going crazy about jazz rhythm. If jazz were really so gay one feels that there would not be so much need to mention the fact in every bar of the piece. Folk songs do not inform us that it's great to be singing in six-eight time, or that you won't get your dairy-maid until you have mastered the Dorian mode. In the nineteenth century there are occasional references to 'Valses endiablées', but for the most part the music is left to tell its own tale. It is almost impossible to find a quick fox-trot, however, that does not inform us that it is in a particular variant of common time, and that it is very gay in consequence. Martin Tupper, who claimed to be the first since King David to set words to a dance tune, has a heavy onus to bear if he is the father of the numerous technical songs such as 'I'm going to Charleston, back to Charleston', 'Crazy Feet, I've got those Crazy Feet', and 'I tell you Rhythm is the Thing, Rhythm is the Thing, Rhythm is the Thing of today'. What should we think of a concert aria which kept harping on the fact that the singer's mouth was open and that her vocal chords were in prime condition?

The third type of song—that which describes a dream world in some remote American state which the singer apparently is permanently prevented from visiting—is now happily on the wane, but in its hey-day it provided an amusing reversal of the more mawkish 'There is a Happy Land' type of hymn tune. The prosperous Anglo-Saxon having held out unctuous consolation to the poor Negro, it is now, apparently, the turn of the prosperous Negro to hold out unctuous consolation to the poor White. That is, if we assume that the tunes are actually written by Negroes. In point of fact, jazz has long ago lost the simple gaiety and sadness of the charming savages to whom it owes its birth, and is now for the most part a reflection of the jagged nerves, sex repressions, inferiority complexes and general dreariness of the modern scene. The nostalgia of the Negro who wants to go home has given place to the infinitely more weary nostalgia of the cosmopolitan Jew who has no home to go to. The Negro associations of jazz, the weary traveller, the comforting old mammy, the red-hot baby, have become a formula of expression only, as empty and convenient as the harlequin and columbine of the nineteenth century. The pierrot with the burnt-cork face symbolizes not the England of yesterday but the Jewry of today.

The importance of the Jewish element in jazz cannot be too strongly emphasized, and the fact that at least ninety per cent of jazz tunes are written by Jews undoubtedly goes far to account for the curiously sagging quality—so typical of Jewish art—the almost masochistic melancholy of the average foxtrot. This masochistic element is becoming more and more a part of general consciousness, but it has its stronghold in the Jewish temperament. As Blaise Cendrars has said: 'Y a-t-il eu un peuple au monde plus profondément masochiste qu'Israël? . . . Israël se contortionne, Israël verse des larmes de sang. Mais Israël jouit de sa bassesse et se délecte de son avilissement. Quel volupté et quel orgueil! Être le peuple maudit . . . avoir le droit de se plaindre, de se plaindre à haute voix . . . avoir la mission de souffrir. . . . Les Juifs seuls ont atteint cet extrême déclassement social, auquel tendent aujourd'hui toutes les sociétés civilisées, et qui n'est que le développement logique des principes maso-chistes de leur vie morale. Tout le mouvement révolution-naire moderne est entre les mains des Juifs, c'est un mouve-ment masochiste juif, un mouvement désespéré, sans autre issue que la destruction et la mort: car telle est la loi du Dieu de Vengeance, du Dieu de Courroux, de Jéhovah le Masochiste.'

There is an obvious link between the exiled and persecuted Jews and the exiled and persecuted Negroes, which the Jews, with their admirable capacity for drinking the beer of those who have knocked down the skittles, have not been slow to turn to their advantage. But although the Jews have stolen the Negroes' thunder, although Al Jolson's nauseating blub-bering masquerades as savage lamenting, although Tin Pan

Alley has become a commercialized Wailing Wall, the only jazz music of technical importance is that small section of it that is genuine negroid. The 'hot' Negro records still have a genuine and not merely galvanic energy, while the blues have a certain austerity that places them far above the sweet nothings of George Gershwin.

The difficulty of estimating the contribution of the Negro to jazz is largely due to the fact that a jazz record, unlike a valse by Johann Strauss, is rarely the work of one man; more often than not it is the work of three composers and three arrangers plus a number of frills that are put on by the players at the spur of the moment. Of this synod only one member may be coloured and usually the Negro element is confined to the actual arabesques of the execution. These arabesques may be of the most fascinating order; but the fact remains that they are improvisations over an accepted basis and not true composition at all. (It is the greatest mistake to class Louis Armstrong and Duke Ellington together as similar exponents of Negro music—the one is a trumpet player, the other a genuine composer.)

Improvisation is all very well in its way, so long as its expressive and formal limitations are realized. At first sight it might seem that improvisation would lead to a greater freedom in music, but in actual practice it proves a considerable restriction—at least in music based on the European harmonic system. It is possible that a purely melodic improvisation based on a more varied range of modes than our own, such as we get in Indian music, might provide a melodic line of greater expressive and formal interest than our squarecut classical tunes; but when it comes to a number of players improvising dance music together they can only avoid complete chaos by sticking to a simple and mutually recognized ground as a basis for their cadenzas. It is the monotony and paucity of musical interest in this perpetually recurring harmonic ground that eventually makes us lose interest in the cadenzas themselves.

An artist like Louis Armstrong, who is one of the most remarkable virtuosi of the present day, enthralls us at a first hearing, but after a few records one realizes that all his improvisations are based on the same restricted circle of ideas, and in the end there is no music which more quickly provokes a state of exasperation and ennui. The best records of Duke Ellington, on the other hand, can be listened to again and again because they are not just decorations of a familiar shape but a new arrangement of shapes. Ellington, in fact, is a real composer, the first jazz composer of distinction, and the first Negro composer of distinction. His works—apart from a few minor details—are not left to the caprice or ear of the instrumentalist; they are scored and written out, and though, in the course of time, variants may creep in—Ellington's works in this respect are as difficult to codify as those of Liszt—the first American records of his music may be taken definitively, like a full score, and are the only jazz records worth studying for their form as well as their texture. Ellington himself being an executant of the second rank has probably not been tempted to interrupt the continuity of his texture with bravura passages for the piano, and although his instrumentalists are of the finest quality their solos are rarely demonstrations of virtuosity for its own sake.

The real interest of Ellington's records lies not so much in their colour, brilliant though it may be, as in the amazingly skilful proportions in which the colour is used. I do not only mean skilful as compared with other jazz composers, but as compared with so-called highbrow composers. I know of nothing in Ravel so dexterous in treatment as the varied solos in the middle of the ebullient *Hot and Bothered* and nothing in Stravinsky more dynamic than the final section.

Nationalism and the Exotic

The combination of themes at this moment is one of the most ingenious pieces of writing in modern music. It is not a question, either, of setting two rhythmic patterns working against each other in the mathematical Aaron Copland manner—it is genuine melodic and rhythmic counterpoint which, to use an old-fashioned phrase, 'fits' perfectly.

The exquisitely tired and four-in-the-morning *Mood Indigo* is an equally remarkable piece of writing of a lyrical and harmonic order, yet it is palpably from the same hand. How well we know those composers whose slow movements seem to be written by someone else—who change in the course of the same section from slow Vaughan Williams to quick Stravinsky and from quick Hindemith to slow César Franck. The ability to maintain the same style in totally different moods is one of the hallmarks of the genuine composer, whether major or minor.

Ellington's best works are written in what may be called ten-inch record form, and he is perhaps the only composer to raise this insignificant disc to the dignity of a definite genre. Into this three and a half minutes he compresses the utmost, but beyond its limits he is inclined to fumble. The double-sided ten-inch *Creole Rhapsody* is an exception, but the twelve-inch expansion of the same piece is nothing more than a potpourri without any of the nervous tension of the original version. Ellington has shown no sign of expanding his formal conceptions, and perhaps it is as well, for his works might then lose their peculiar concentrated savour. He is definitely a petit maître, but that, after all, is considerably more than many people thought either jazz or the coloured race would ever produce. He has crystallized the popular music of our time and set up a standard by which we may judge not only other jazz composers but also those highbrow composers, whether American or European, who indulge in what is roughly known as 'symphonic jazz'.

(h) Symphonic Jazz

There is, on the face of it, no reason why the jazz idiom should not prove a more stimulating and fruitful *materia musica* than the cult of the neo-classic, the exotic, or what the French describe as 'très folk-lore'. The barbaric and vital Negro element, though small, provides the same stimulus for the present day as oriental exoticism did for the 'nineties, while the sophisticated and masochistic Jewish element provides a far more convincing and natural background to contemporary thought than any school of folk song. Much as we may deplore the latter fact, there is no getting away from it. The sheer anger aroused in 'hearties' of the Beachcomber order by such different manifestations of contemporary depression as jazz songs and the poetry of Eliot is an unconscious tribute to the strength of this negative spirit. The intoxicating low spirits of jazz do not, like the music-hall songs of the 'nineties, express a certain mood of a certain class in a certain country; they express, whether we like it or not, the constant tenor of our lives. They are not a cordial which changes in every country, like schnapps; they are a universal anodyne, like aspirin.

The curiously delocalized and declassed atmosphere of jazz was aptly symbolized in the film version of Noel Coward's *Cavalcade*. Whereas in the earlier part of the film the barrel-organ tunes were used to hit off the atmosphere of London lower-class life at a particular date, towards the end of the film the jazz song, 'Twentieth Century Blues,' was used to hit off the atmosphere of post-war life in any venue. Mr. Coward's symbols are, in their way, so trite and vulgar that the mind rather boggles at accepting them. We hardly like to face the fact that they are not only good theatre but

189

sober truth. Yet, in spite of its facile melancholy, is not Mr. Coward's 'City'—with its 'unbelievably tiring, Life passes by me, noise and speed are conspiring to crucify me'—as perfect a symbol of the nineteen-twenties as Pierce Egan's 'Oh, London, London Town for me'—with its 'masquerades, grand parades, famed gaslights, knowing fights, such prime joking, lots of smoking', etc.—is of the eighteen-twenties?

Jazz considered as a musical idiom has other qualities besides the somewhat melancholy one of psychological truth. The American style in popular music of today fulfils much the same function as the Italian style in classical music of the eighteenth century. It is internationally comprehensible, and yet provides a medium for national inflection more convincing than the very modified and occasional provincialities of Boyce and Grétry. Although linked together by a common derivation, nothing could show more subtle racial variations than the highbrow jazz of such composers as Milhaud, Kurt Weill, Copland, Schulhoff and 'Spike' Hughes. These subtle variations are a far more accurate symbol of the differences between the urban life of different countries than the highly coloured, exotic differentiation provided by folk song, yet they avoid the drabness of the purely internationalized Hindemith manner, with its evocation of underground railways and hygienic tiling.

From the technical point of view, of the jazz idiom is a more plastic basis than the folk song or the pre-jazz popular song. Jazz, like so much exotic music, depends more on rhythmic and melodic inflections than on a squarecut rhythmic and melodic scheme. An Irish folk song or a Sousa march depends on balance of phrase and melodic form for its atmosphere; it does not exist in sections, and as a whole it is too clearly cut and rounded off to be of any use as material. But the cadences of a jazz tune do not so restrict the composer, nor are they incompatible with construction of a classical and even academic kind.

To take a striking instance, Darius Milhaud in *La Création du Monde* represents the primeval incantations of the gods Nzamé, Mébère and Nkwa by a three-part jazz fugato over a percussion accompaniment. The rhythm and inflections of the fugue subject are clearly derived from jazz arabesques, yet, at the same time, the subject is an admirable one from any save the most crusty academic view. Crudely and naïvely analysed, the percussion background provides the necessary barbaric atmosphere, the jazz inflections of the tune suggest a stylized Negro speech, the counterpoint provides the element of mingled and growing effort, while from the objective point of view the passage, theatrical atmosphere apart, is an excellent and logical 'arrangement of notes'. Had Milhaud used a Negro folk song for this scene, he might have obtained the requisite dark atmosphere, but he would have been unable to add to this the constructional plasticity allowed by the jazz idiom he has chosen. This whole work and in particular the final section, with its brilliant blending of themes, is a most remarkable example of the compromise possible between popular idiom and sophisticated construction. Though perhaps not great music in itself, it opens up an avenue of progress which this too versatile composer has unfortunately passed by with a careless gesture.

It is often suggested that jazz rhythm, though exhilarating at first, ends by becoming monotonous through its being merely a series of irregular groupings and cross-accents over a steady and unyielding pulse. This is true in a way, and certainly nothing is more wearisome than the mechanical division of the eight quavers of the foxtrot bar into groups of three, three and two; yet in the best Negro jazz bands the irregular cross-accents are given so much more weight than the underlying pulse, that the rhythmic arabesques almost completely obscure the metrical framework, and paradoxically enough this 'bar line' music often achieves a rhythmic freedom that recalls the music of Elizabethan times and earlier, when the bar line was a mere technical convenience like a figure or letter in a score. On paper the rhythmical groupings of a tune like 'Step on the Blues' (from *The Girl Friend*) bear a striking resemblance to the irregular groupings to be found in the music of Edmund Turges (*circa* 1500) who, it need hardly be added, was roundly condemned for his metrical eccentricities by the august Dr. Burney.

We make a mistake in considering these rhythmic arabesques abnormal or artificial. It is the lack of rhythmic experiment shown in the nineteenth century that is really abnormal—at least as regards English music and the setting of English words. Without wishing in any way to denigrate the magnificent achievement of the German romantic school from Weber to Mahler, we can without exaggeration say that it is remarkably deficient in purely rhythmic interest. Wagner himself was conscious of this failing and admitted it with a deprecatory 'Well, you can't expect everything' air.

Yet we in this country have a musical upbringing based on the German classics plus a strong leavening of hymns— 'ancient and modern'. We still go on setting English poetry in the totally unsuitable rhythms drawn from the German Volkslied. Actually, had not the course of English music been interrupted first by Handel and then, more gravely, by Mendelssohn, we should probably have found the rhythmic tradition of English music very much more eccentric and more full of 'conceits' than the tradition of jazz. As it is, certain jazz songs show a more apt feeling for the cadence of English speech than any music since the seventeenth century.

Symphonic Jazz

There is, of course, no reason why the composer who draws inspiration from contemporary dances should limit himself to the metrical frame imposed by the ball-room. The rhythmic pattern of Walton's *Portsmouth Point* is clearly derived from jazz, yet after the sturdy opening in four-four time, the composer, having established his norm, proceeds to juggle with the bar line in a manner which is unfortunately denied to the commercial composer. We need not expect the symphonic jazz of the future to bear any more superficial resemblance to the foxtrot of the night club than the scherzi of Beethoven's symphonies did to the minuets of the eighteenth-century salon. We should remember that most of Richard Strauss's *Elektra* owes as great a debt to the rhythms of Johann Strauss as even Ravel's *La Valse* itself.

Whether the composer can afford to treat the harmonic basis of jazz so freely is a little doubtful. Much of the emotional stimulus of jazz is due to the piquant contrast between the terse and slangy rhythm and the somewhat glucose harmony. Although *Portsmouth Point* is a successful example of jazz rhythm used apart from jazz harmony to produce an atmosphere that is in another world from Harlem, there is always a danger that jazz rhythm so used may become a purely synthetic means of giving to a work some surface vitality. An atonal foxtrot is as disturbing a thought as an atonal waltz. Nothing indeed is more irritating than the way in which atonal and neo-atonal composers sometimes use dance rhythms, whether valse, tarantella, or Charleston, to give an associative rhythmic value to works whose mood is hopelessly at variance with that of the original dance forms from which these rhythms derive. Thus, many of the march pieces of Hindemith and Prokofieff owe their stimulus not to any intrinsic vitality but to the left-right left-right, bands-playing, banners-waving, associations of the Sousa rhythms employed. Jazz rhythm entirely detached from jazz

G   193

melody and harmony can become as empty a device as the melodic sequences of the neo-classicists.

The composer of highbrow jazz must obviously extend his harmonic vocabulary beyond the somewhat narrow range of the syncopated kings, but, if his work is to show any sense of style, this development must be on the lines of a broader view of what is desirable as consonance—as in Milhaud— rather than on a narrower view of what constitutes dissonance—as in Hindemith.

The development of jazz is now clearly in the hands of the sophisticated composer. The Negro composer was able to give new life to his music by moving from the harmonies of Dykes to those of Delius, but he cannot execute a similar move today for the simple reason that the post-impressionist harmonic experiments, the austerities and asperities of Stravinsky and Bartók, are hardly of a type to lend themselves to sentimental exploitation. The scoring and execution of jazz reach a far higher level than that of any previous form of dance music, and in Duke Ellington's compositions jazz has produced the most distinguished popular music since Johann Strauss; but having caught up with the high-brow composer in so many ways the jazz composer is now stagnating, bound to a narrow circle of rhythmic and harmonic devices and neglecting the possibilites of form. It is for the highbrow composer to take the next step.

The first-fruits of symphonic jazz have been a little disappointing, it is true, particularly in the land where they have been most common—the United States of America. The Americans seem to live too near Tin Pan Alley to get the beauties of this street in proper perspective; their pictures of it are either too realistic or too romantic. They suffer from the immense disadvantage of being on the spot—are not Rousseau's paintings of tropical landscapes more impressive even than those of Gauguin? The difficulty of making a satisfactory synthesis of jazz is due to the fact that it is not, properly speaking, raw material but half-finished material in which European sophistication has been imposed over coloured crudity. There is always the danger that the highbrow composer may take away the number he first thought of and leave only the sophisticated trappings behind. This indeed is what has happened in that singularly inept albeit popular piece, Gershwin's *Rhapsody in Blue*. The composer, trying to write a Lisztian concerto in jazz style, has used only the non-barbaric elements in dance music, the result being neither good jazz nor good Liszt, and in no sense of the word a good concerto. Although other American composers, and even Gershwin himself, have produced works of greater calibre in this style, the shadow of the *Rhapsody in Blue* hangs over most of them and they remain the hybrid child of a hybrid. A rather knowing and unpleasant child too, ashamed of its parents and boasting of its French lessons.

The French have perhaps too keen a sense of the ridiculous to get the best out of jazz—for jazz is distinguished from earlier forms of dance music by its intense and mumbo-jumbo earnestness. One can be light and frivolous in a valse, but in a foxtrot one can only be either solemn or facetious. Most French symphonic jazz is the latter, and suffers from a rather tiresome consciousness of the Gallic tongue being thrust ever so wittily into the Gallic cheek. Earnestness is a pompous word no doubt, but it is unfortunately necessary to be a little pompous to produce even the slightest of musical achievements. It is boring for the composer, but in the long run less boring for the audience. *Le Boeuf sur le Toit* in which Milhaud guys night-club music is an amusing jeu d'esprit which soon palls; whereas *La Création du Monde*, in which dance idioms are turned to serious use, has remained remarkably undated.

Nationalism and the Exotic

If the French are, for the most part, facetious, the Germans redress the balance with a solemnity of depravity that is at times faintly ridiculous. The jazz idiom is from every point of view so diametrically opposed to the 'echt-Deutsch' tradition that the Germans exploit it with the earnest and thoroughgoing sense of sin that gave such a peculiar flavour to pre-Hitlerite night life. Jannings going to the dogs is not a more melancholy spectacle than some worthy Teutonic fiddler putting a little pep into a 'shimmy-fox'.

This Baudelairian earnestness has, however, given to the best examples of German highbrow jazz an importance which is not to be found in the Parisian school. It has enabled a composer like Kurt Weill, for example, to catch the weariness and nostalgia that is the underlying emotion of present-day dance music. Weill is undoubtedly the most successful and important of the Central European composers who have experimented with the jazz idiom. It is curious that a German should be the first to sum up in musical synthesis certain phases of American life. American jazz is either too Hollywood or too Harlem—it rarely suggests the dusty panorama of American life which gives such strength to even second-rate films. Weill is almost the only composer who can evoke in music the odd, untidy, drably tragic background that is presented to us so forcibly by William Faulkner in *Sanctuary* and *Light in August*.

Unlike so many composers who have taken up jazz as a stunt and dropped it the moment they felt it was no longer the most daring fashion, Weill has gradually evolved from disparate German and American elements a style of highly individual expressiveness. Even in his early and crude *Die Dreigroschenoper* there is a certain Hogarthian quality, a poetic sordidness, which gives a strength to what otherwise might have been a completely worthless work. Just as *Die Drei-groschenoper* in spite of its crude Americanisms catches the ramshackle charm of the poorer quarters of London, so *Mahagonny* in spite of its Teutonic traits sums up the inverted poetry of American 'low life'.

The Seven Deadly Sins marks as great an improvement on *Mahagonny* as *Mahagonny* did on *Die Dreigroschenoper*. Here the American scene is not portrayed realistically, but taken as a convenient background to a cynical morality of unexpectedly profound quality. As presented with décor by Neher and choreography by Balanchine, *The Seven Deadly Sins* is the most important work in ballet form since *Les Noces* and *Parade*. In spite of its superficial air of bustle the music is remarkable for its extraordinary weariness, a neurasthenic fatigue which, though sterile in a way, reaches in the finale a certain grandeur. I am not pretending that *The Seven Deadly Sins* is a work of very great intrinsic or permanent value, but, quite apart from its inevitability of medium—though its swift panorama derives from the screen, there is no moment when we feel that the camera would do the job better—I feel that this work has considerable strength in the way it manages to deal with a modern and emotional subject without chi-chi, false sentiment or mechanical romanticism.

There are remarkably few post-war composers who can get to grips with their audience in the frank and admirable manner of Puccini. This would not matter if it meant they had sufficient strength to rise above the cinematic emotions of *Madam Butterfly*, but it does matter if it means that they have insufficient vitality to rise even so far. No doubt the greatest art is free from this type of emotionalism and free also from any direct reflection of the contemporary scene. We can listen to Sibelius's Seventh Symphony without any evocation of Finland, the twentieth century, or our own personal emotions. But we cannot live permanently in the austere world of Sibelius and Cézanne. It stands to reason that most art is produced at a lower level of concentration and, without being second rate, must belong to the second rank. It is in music of this more genial type that the present age is so conspicuously lacking, and the presence of so many 'renowned impersonations' of great music is no consolation.

Today, everyone with the rudiments of Greek grammar sets out to be a Homer although incapable of even the police-court heroics of an Edgar Wallace. The dreary space of classical titles and classical subjects that floods the music of our time is the symbol not of a classical austerity to be admired but of an antique-fancying aridity to be despised. What a relief to find a writer like Weill who, whatever his merits or demerits, can at least appear in public wrapped neither in cellophane nor a toga but in the clothes of today!

That two works so strikingly different in outlook and texture as *The Seven Deadly Sins* and *La Création du Monde* should both draw their inspiration from the jazz idiom is sufficient answer to those who imagine that this idiom must inevitably produce a flat, monotonous, and restricted style. It is true that in both cases the use of a jazz idiom is justified by the subject matter, in the one case a Negro ritual, in the other the life of an American dancer. There is as yet no purely instrumental and non-pictorial work of any value that is similarly based on the jazz idiom, and it might be thought that the popular associations of this style would prove too strong an element of distraction for a symphony or concerto. I can see no reason, however, why a composer should not be able to rid himself as much from the night-club element in jazz as Haydn did from the ballroom element in the minuet, and produce the modern equivalent of those dance suites of Bach which we treat with as much seriousness as the sonatas of Beethoven.

For reasons I have already stated, the next move in the development of jazz will come, almost inevitably, from the sophisticated or highbrow composers. Although we get an exceptional popular composer like Ellington turning jazz to some use, his skill—as considered apart from that of his executants—is hardly appreciated by any except the high-brow public. To the ordinary public jazz is not even a thing specifically to be danced to, let alone be listened to with any discrimination. It has become a sort of aural tickling, a vague soothing of the nerves giving no more positive pleasure than the mechanically-lit gasper. At its best it provides merely a group emotion for those incapable of more independent sensations.

More than the music of any other period jazz has become a drug for the devitalized. As with all drug habits one dare not stop, for fear of the reaction, and it is no rare experience to meet people whose lives are so surrounded, bolstered up and inflated by jazz that they can hardly get through an hour without its collaboration; with no doubt unconscious logic they make up for the threadbare quality of their own emotions by drawing on the warm capacious .reservoir of group emotion so efficiently provided by the American jazz kings.

The man who plays jazz all day is of course no more a music lover than the man who drinks 'hooch' all day is a connoisseur of wines. The concert-goer who with conscious superiority listens to six Bach concertos in an evening may well think that it is no use wasting tears about the vulgariza-tion of vulgarization. To him it is a matter of indifference whether jazz is a stimulant, a drug, or a piece of mental wallpaper. But he would do well to reflect whether the same process of vulgarization is not taking place in the case of classical works; whether the highbrow as well as the low-brow is not becoming the victim of the appalling popularity of music.

PART FOUR

THE MECHANICAL STIMULUS

(a) The Appalling Popularity of Music

Music has an odd way of reflecting not only the emotional background of an age but also its physical conditions. The present age is one of overproduction. Never has there been so much food and so much starvation, and (as I pointed out before) never has there been so much music-making and so little musical experience of a vital order.

Since the advent of the gramophone, and more particularly the wireless, music of a sort is everywhere and at every time; in the heavens, the lower parts of the earth, the mountains, the forest and every tree therein. It is a Psalmist's nightmare. At one time a cautious glance round the room assured one, through the absence of a piano, that there would at least be no music after dinner. But today the chances are that one's host is a gramophone bore, intent on exhibiting his fifty-seven varieties of soundbox, or a wireless fiend intent on obtaining the obscurest stations irrespective of programme. It is to be noticed that the more people use the wireless the less they listen to it. Some business men actually leave the wireless on all day so that the noise will be heard as they come up the garden path, and they will be spared the ghastly hiatus of silence that elapses between the slam of the front door and the first atmospheric.

The people, and they are legion, who play bridge to the accompaniment of a loud speaker, cannot be put off their game even by *The Amazing Mandarin* of Béla Bartók. Were the Last Trump to be suddenly broadcast from Daventry by special permission of Sir John Reith—and I can think of no event more gratifying to the stern-minded Governors of the BBC—it is doubtful whether it would interfere with the cry of 'No Trumps' from the card table.

What people do in their own homes is fortunately still their own concern, but what takes place in public streets and public-houses concerns us all. The loud speaker is little short of a public menace.

In the neighbourhood where I live, for example, there is a loud speaker every hundred yards or so, and it is only rarely that they are tuned in to different stations. If they are playing the foxtrot I most detest at one corner of the street, I need not think that I can avoid it by walking to the other end. At times there is a certain piquancy in following a tune in two dimensions at once, so to speak—to buy one's cigarettes to the first subject of a symphony, to get scraps of the development as one goes to the newsagent, and to return home to the recapitulation—but the idea of the town as one vast analytical programme, with every pavingstone a barline, soon palls. It would not matter so much were the music bad music, but, as the BBC can boast with some satisfaction, most of it is good. We board buses to the strains of Beethoven and drink our beer to the accompaniment of Bach. And yet we pride ourselves on the popular apprecia-tions of these masters.

Here is yet another example of the gradual fusion of high-brow and lowbrow to which I drew attention before. Instead of the admirable old distinction between classical and popular which used to hold good—classics for the concert hall or home, popular for the street and café—classical music is vulgarized and diffused through every highway and byway, and both highbrow and lowbrow are the losers.

The principal objections to music provided by the now almost universal loud speaker are its monotony and unsuitability. Whereas you can escape from a mechanical piano by going to the next café, you can rarely escape from a BBC gramophone hour by going to the next public-house because they are almost bound to be presenting the same entertainment to their clients. The whole of London, whatever it is doing, and whatever its moods, is made to listen to the choice of a privileged few or even a privileged one.

To take the example of Mr. Christopher Stone whose well-modulated voice has doubtless given pleasure to millions. At certain hours of the day, it is impossible for anyone to escape from his breezy diffidence. That he is a benevolent autocrat I am sure is true, just as I am sure that his choice of records is reasonably intelligent and eclectic. But the fact remains that he enjoys a position of dictatorship as fantastic as anything in Aldous Huxley's *Brave New World*. At one time G. K. Chesterton propounded the amiable and consoling theory that people would cheat the prophets by refusing to do what was laid down in the pseudo-scientific and so-called 'Utopian' books. It would appear, though, that the most jaundiced of imaginative writers can hardly keep pace with the blessings of mechanical progress, that pass in a year or two from a vicious and improbable fancy to a grimly ineluctable fact.

Even worse than the lack of individual choice in loud-speaker music is the almost invariable unsuitability of its style and timbre. Music in the streets, in cafés, and at fairs is an admirable scheme, but a certain gaiety of outline and pungency of timbre is essential. The Catalan coblas are the ideal example of outdoor music, but anything, from a military band playing Sousa to a man playing Carmen on the ocarina, is preferable to having the strains of the Air on the G String, reduced in quality but amplified in quantity, floating out over the noise of traffic. Even the dance music which on stylistic grounds is to be preferred, in the circumstances, to Beethoven or Bach, has a quality of sickening and genteel refinement not to be found in the exhilarating tintinnabulation of the fast-disappearing mechanical piano. It has actually been suggested that the 'inartistic' confusion of fair music, the dizzy and arbitrary counterpoint of roundabouts, with their whistling organs, should be supplanted by the uniform of blaring synchronized loud speakers.

It is clear that we are fast losing even the minor stimulus of genuine healthy vulgarity. In the present age it is impossible to escape from Culture, and the wholesale and whole-time diffusion of musical culture will eventually produce in us, when we hear a Bach concerto, the faint nausea felt towards a piece of toffee by a worker in a sweet factory.

The same phenomenal indifference towards what they listen to can be seen as clearly in those who have loud speakers thrust upon them as in those who deliberately foster their use. One might have thought that the sturdy British working man entering a public-house and being greeted with a talk on the Reclamation of the Zuyder Zee, or a string quartet by Alban Berg, would have requested the proprietor, and not entirely without reason, to 'put a sock in it'; but actually he just sits stolidly there, drinking his synthetic bitter to sounds of synthetic sweetness, not caring whether the loud speaker is tuned in to a jazz band, a talk on wildflowers, a Schönberg opera or a reading from 'The Land' by the authoress. So long as certain waves are set up in the ether to produce a certain reaction on his tympanum he is content. The most severe complaints about the wireless are indeed from people who indignantly discover that for five minutes during the day the machine is not functioning at all.

Far be it from anyone interested in contemporary music to complain that the BBC have the enterprise to put on such works as the operas of Berg and Schönberg. One's complaint is not with the programmes themselves, which through an independence of advertising interests are of an admirably eclectic nature, but with their intolerably wholesale diffusion through portable sets and loud speakers.

In previous ages, listening to music was a matter of personal choice usually involving either individual skill in joining with other people in singing a madrigal, or at least the concentration, and sacrifice of time and money, required by a cycle of *The Ring*. But now no one can avoid listening to music, whether in town or country, in a motor-car, train or restaurant, perched on a hilltop, or immersed in the river. It is even more trying for the musical than for the non-musical; it is impossible for them to escape from their profession or relaxation, as the case may be.

Another symbol of the present age is thus curiously provided. Those who in the eighteenth century felt like killing their fellow creatures were able to exercise their natural faculties with others of the same bent in a comparatively restricted space. The unbellicose were, save in exceptional circumstances, not affected. But today everyone is a potential combatant and will no longer be able to escape mechanized death in the next war than at the present moment he can escape mechanized music.

We have at present no idea of what havoc may be wrought in a few years' time by the combined effect of the noise of city life and the noise of city music—an actual atrophy of the aural nerves would seem to be indicated. Already it is to be observed that people are no longer thrilled or even aggravated by the most powerful of modern tuttis. The explanation is simple. The noise provided by such adjuncts of modern life as the pneumatic drill, the movietone news reel and the war film, leaves the most sadistic and orgiastic of composers at the starting post. When Berlioz wrote the *Symphonie Fantastique* he was providing probably the greatest sonority that anyone, including even those military men present, had ever heard. When George Antheil adds to his score sixteen pianos, an electric buzzer or two, an aeroplane propeller, and a pneumatic drill he is, after all, providing little more than the average background to a telephone conversation.

Although excessive sonority has lost its thrill, we still demand it as an ever-increasing factor in our lives. It is noticeable, indeed, that those whose business lives are the most surrounded by extraneous noises are those who most insist on the continuous support of gramophone and loud speaker during their leisure hours. We live in an age of tonal debauch where the blunting of the finer edge of pleasure leads only to a more hysterical and frenetic attempt to recapture it. It is obvious that second-rate mechanical music is the most suitable fare for those to whom musical experience is no more than a mere aural tickling, just as the prostitute provides the most suitable outlet for those to whom sexual experience is no more than the periodic removal of a recurring itch. The loud speaker is the street walker of music.

(b) Mechanical Romanticism

There is, of course, nothing wrong with street walkers provided people don't get too romantic about them. In the case of mechanical music there is a curious class of people to whom it is not so much a convenient substitute for the concert hall as a thing to be prized in itself for its mechanical qualities. These qualities are even expected to be a stimulus and a guide for the composer.

It is well known that, even in so unintellectual a matter as eating and drinking, people soon acquire a preference for synthetic products. Those who are used to tinned Canadian salmon have little use for fresh Scotch salmon, and those who are used to certain types of London beer would be non-plussed by a drink that was actually brewed from malt and hops. It will, on the same principle, be of the utmost interest to see if the repeal of Prohibition in U.S.A. will lessen the taste for 'hooch' or not.

So it is with canned music. Certain composers, notably Milhaud, make no secret of their preference for the timbres of the tone film. I have heard a woman of some intelligence and musical training actually state that she preferred the magic tone of the oboe over the wireless to the actual sound of it in the concert hall; and I have heard a painter, who prides himself on his modernity, state that the two-dimensional effect of broadcast music was to be preferred because the sound instead of escaping round the hall came straight at you and had 'a frame round it'. These remarks would not be worth quoting were they not typical of a large and increasing class of music-fanciers.

This obsession with the wireless and the gramophone is, however, only a new twist to an old type of mechanical romanticism which goes back to Walt Whitman, with his lists of objects and occupations; to Rudyard Kipling, with his appalling messroom conversations between locomotives; and to writers earlier still, such as T. Baker with his notorious admiration of the power of steam.

The mechanical romanticism of today takes its most familiar forms in stage and interior decoration. How well

Mechanical Romanticism

one knows the reading lamps like X-ray apparatus, the wall cupboards like strong boxes, the cocktail bars like operating theatres, with their daunting array of angular glass and chromium plating. The reaction against the fake antique is no doubt healthy and natural, but that is no reason why a gramophone or wireless set, instead of enjoying the wooden discretion of a commode, should parade itself before us like an electric chair in a gangster film. It is a truism to point out that to the interior decorator of the post-Corbusier period a mechanical aspect is of more importance than the actual pure principles of utility which he professes. A needlessly bare and uninviting mechanical picturesqueness, evocative to Channel-crossings and visits to the dentist, has taken the place of the blue china of the 'nineties and the antimacassars of an earlier period.

As an example of the purely picturesque and non-utilitarian attitude of the mechanical romanticists may be quoted the constructionist scenery of the ballet *La Chatte*, where the stage was cluttered up with a number of objects which, apart from looking as if they might conceivably separate milk from cream, merely served to hinder the movements of the dancers. They were, in fact, obstructionist rather than constructionist and, from the mechanical and utilitarian point of view, were far less justified than the painted canvas of theatrical tradition.

The musical equivalent of this obsession with the mechanical, the *sportif* and the soi-disant contemporary, is provided by the naïvely realistic orchestral pieces of Honegger, such as *Pacific 231* and *Rugby*.

Honegger, with his publicly paraded interest in footplates and supercharging, is a fine example of the new type of sportsman composer as opposed to the old type of poet composer who ruled the roost in the nineteenth century. (We have only to read Berlioz's memoirs or Heine's *Florentine*

Nights to realize the extraordinary impact that the composer had on the public of the time, what, in these days, would vulgarly be called the 'gossip-column value' of musicians.) The glamour of the 'pale and interesting' musican is now supplanted by the glamour of the suntanned and boring athlete, and plus-fours are a more potent symbol than the black hat. This is particularly the case in Paris, which may be described as the fashion centre for minor artists even more than for women. If we see a begoggled leather-coated and plus-foured figure, starting off with a *démarrage formidable* in a rakish racing model, we may be sure that the driver is really more at home in La Rue de la Boëtie than at Brooklands. The old vagabond Don Juan conception of the artist drawn from mingled recollections of *Louise* and *La Bohème* has certainly disappeared, but the new conception is equally a picturesque legend woven by the artists round themselves.

It is doubtful whether the mechanical picturesque is so great an improvement on the romantic picturesque. Honegger's *Pacific 231*, *Skating Rink* and *Rugby*, Mossoloff's *Song of the Machines*, Martinu's *Half-Time* and Prokofieff's *Le Pas d'Acier* are, au fond, as sentimental in conception as the lyric pieces of Grieg. Honegger, indeed, has claimed that *Pacific 231* sets out to capture the lyricism of an express train moving at top speed. Unfortunately this lyricism has been overlaid by the mechanically picturesque onomatopœics of the piece, and the nostalgia of the train journey is lost in a study of escaping steam and jolting points. A little more thought might have told the composer that music, which depends on varying degrees of stylized noise and speed for its expression, is, on the face of it, the last medium in which to attempt an evocation of non-stylized noise and speed (there are few pieces more essentially static than Debussy's *Mouvement*, for example).

The objection to realism in music is not that it makes

things too easy for the listener but that it makes them too difficult. Instead of receiving an immediate and incisive physical impression he receives a vaguely visual one, which has to be related back to early associations and personal experience before it produces the emotional reaction which the music should have evoked directly. It is for the composer, not the listener, to digest the raw material of his inspiration.

There is no reason whatsoever why the composer should not derive inspiration from trains, aeroplanes, moving staircases, penny-in-the-slot machines and other triumphs of mind over matter, provided these sources of inspiration are so absorbed and transformed that the final result produces a directly musical reaction. In a work for the stage this is not necessarily so, for there the eye can implement the oral suggestions. The brilliant realism of *Petrushka* is thoroughly legitimate when performed, as intended, in the theatre. But in the concert hall a work like Debussy's *Fêtes* produces by purely musical means a far greater effect of speed and gaiety than Stravinsky's onomatopœics.

The place for music of the Honegger type is not the concert hall but the cinema. Those who are bored by *Pacific 231* in the concert hall would have been surprised at the brilliant effect it made when used in conjunction with the Soviet film *The Blue Express*.

The present vogue for mechanical realism, being based primarily on the picturesque aspects of machinery, is bound to disappear as the mechanic more and more comes to resemble the bank clerk, and as the Turneresque steam engine gives way to the unphotogenic electric train. It is only comparatively primitive machinery that affords a stimulus, and there is already a faint period touch about *Pacific 231* and *Le Pas d'Acier*. One feels that they should have been written when railways and factories really were beginning to alter our lives; that Prokofieff should have written ballets about the spinning jenny and the Luddite riots; that Honegger should have been there to celebrate the opening of the Stockton and Darlington Railway and the death of Huskisson with a 'Symphonie Triomphale et Funèbre'. Our latter-day mechanical romanticists are indeed only filling in a corner which—save for a few ludicrous exceptions like Marenco's *Excelsior*—was left unexploited by the nineteenth-century aesthetic romanticists.

It may seem contradictory to condemn composers like Honegger for basing their work on the contemporary scene after complaining that the neo-classicists are so out of touch with contemporary life. But works like Honegger's symphonic movements are only in touch with certain purely decorative and ephemeral aspects of contemporary living. They have no spiritual foundation even of a meretricious order. Prokofieff's *Le Pas d'Acier*, for all its realism, tells us less about proletarian Russia than the comparatively stylized and abstract *Les Noces*.

Realistic fantasias have always been a minor part of music, but they lose their savour so rapidly that we are apt to forget they were written in past ages at all, and imagine they are the particular province of the present day. We think of *Rugby* as representing 'the new spirit in music', yet that great critic Roger North writing in the early eighteenth century says: 'But it is very possible that the thoughts of some folks may run upon a dance, ye hurry of football play, ye mad folks at bedlam or mortall Battells at Bear Garden, all wch Bizzarie ye masters of musick will undertake to represent, and many persons that doe not well distinguish between real good and evill, but are hurryed away by caprice, as in a whirlwind, think such musick ye best; & despise those who are not of ye same opinion and (as ye rabble) crye, it is brave sport.' The realistic fancies of which North wrote are now completely forgotten, and it is unlikely that those of Honegger will enjoy an exceptionally long life. They are merely stunts of no intrinsic importance, unlikely to produce any progeny. It would be a pity to treat them too seriously, either in praise or blame, and to do Honegger justice his later works, such as the *Third Symphonic Movement*, suggest that he too is turning back from the decorative cul-de-sac of mechanical romanticism so aptly symbolized by the Rue Mallet-Stevens in Paris.

A far more disastrous example of mechanical romanticism is provided by the works of Hindemith. For whereas Honegger's works only affect the façade of music as we know it, Hindemith's apply a pneumatic drill to its foundations, a pneumatic drill wielded by the most efficient and determined of mechanics.

(c) Craft for Craft's Sake

It would be foolish to underestimate the importance of Hindemith. He is undoubtedly one of the most proficient musicians alive today, and as an influence on modern musical thought is second only to Stravinsky, if not by now the more potent influence of the two. He is everything in fact but an artist, and it is more than likely that he would indignantly repudiate so non-utilitarian a title. To put it vulgarly, Hindemith is the journalist of modern music, the supreme middle brow of our times. Standing in Central European music between the reserved and intellectual Alban Berg on the one hand, and the facile and popular Kurt Weill on the other, he reflects the tempo and colour of modern life in the brisk unpolished manner of the newspaper reporter. His concertos, however varied in content, have the family resemblance of shape and texture that one edition of a newspaper bears to another and, as in journalism, Tuesday's edition irrevocably dates that of Monday.

Lytton Strachey writing of Macaulay says that his style, 'with its metallic exactness and its fatal efficiency was certainly one of the most remarkable products of the Industrial Revolution'. Hindemith bears much the same relation to the German classics as Macaulay did to the English classics, and his style, with its deadness and monotony of rhythm, its atonal jazzing up of Bach's sewing-machine counterpoint, is an equally typical product of the present Mechanical Age. It has the hardness of outline and slightly hollow ring that Strachey finds in Macaulay. To do Hindemith justice his style is lacking in the falsities and incongruities of Stravinsky's; his neo-classicism is not so much a distortion and incongruous harmonization of phrases drawn from the classics as a translation into modern terms of eighteenth-century commonplace.

There is practically no music which does not conjure up a certain type of scene which is at the same time a complement to the music, and the most suitable surroundings in which to hear it—it is in no spirit of preciosity that we prefer to listen to Vittoria in a cathedral and to Ellington in a night club. The social nimbus that surrounds Hindemith's music is of a less colourful order. Listening to his firmly wrought works we seem to see ourselves in a block of hygienic and efficient workmen's flats built in the best modernismus manner, from which emerge troops of healthy uniformed children on their way to the communal gymnasium. Hindemith's technique is indeed a gymnastic technique, and his attitude towards 'expressive' music is reminiscent of an instructor in physical jerks pooh-poohing the poses and affectations of ballet—even though they may demand a higher degree of training than he himself possesses.

A display of gymnastics, though admirable from many

points of view, is boring to watch, and a display of musical gymnastics is not only boring to listen to but hopelessly sterile in aim. The whole problem for the composer is a fusion of emotion and technique, and this is a problem which, up to the present, Hindemith and his numerous followers admittedly refuse or disdain to solve. They have set up, instead of the old doctrine of art for art's sake, the equally 'arty' doctrine of craft for craft's sake. Not only do they refuse to wear their hearts on their sleeves but the sleeves themselves are rolled up in the most approved proletarian fashion.

The obsession with the utilitarian and the mechanical is as much a piece of perverted romanticism as the furnishings of Corbusier houses. The concentration on the specifically new—the cocktail shaker, the movie camera and the typist's office—becomes just as tiresome as the concentration of the older German music on the specifically decaying—withered roses, crumbling ruins and waning loves. It is a kind of proletarian sentimentality that has replaced the individualist sentimentality of the romantic poet.

One can, of course, entirely sympathize with the spirit that has prompted this reaction. When we think of the stranglehold German romanticism had on this country thirty years ago, we can imagine what it must have been like in Germany itself. German romanticism had come to resemble a stuffy and scented drawing-room, overdecorated with silk flounces, and encumbered with vast padded sofas and downy cushions. Hindemith and his followers have thrown open the double windows, torn down the hangings, put sackcloth instead of brocade and replaced the upholstery with glass and chromium plating. But there is still too much furniture about. German music has always been fatally plethoric and the new 'Gebrauchsmusik' is no exception.

As it is felt by some of his followers that Hindemith's

music has been somewhat unduly saddled with the description of Gebrauchsmusik—bread-and-butter music, workaday, or utility music are perhaps the best English equivalents—it is as well to quote the artistic credo of the master himself. Hindemith calls himself a craftsman, never a tone poet, and has said that 'a composer should never write unless he is acquainted with the demand for his work. The times of consistent composing for one's own satisfaction are probably gone for ever.'

This anti-aesthetic no-nonsense-about-me type of argument is so superficially palatable at the present day that few people seem to have given it sufficient attention to realize its patent fallacies. Like most of the decadent movements in modern music, Gebrauchsmusik is based on a misapprehension of the medium in which the composer expresses himself.

In literature, the man who has neither the vision, the imagination, the sense of beauty nor the wit that are popularly supposed to go to the production of a poem, novel or play, can turn his literary skill, such as it is, to the production of advertisements, book reviews and crime reports. He is a utility or workaday writer. In painting, the same type of man, able to use a pencil and brush with some skill without attempting to be a Cézanne or a Picasso, can profitably and pleasantly spend his time in such varied ways as the designing of book jackets, the faking of old masters and the painting of presentation portraits. In the three-dimensional arts one can distinguish even more clearly between art and craft, and the carpenter who makes a chair can claim to be satisfying a universal demand which is not met by the sculptor. A chair is undoubtedly more comfortable to sit on than all save a few examples of the sculptor's art. But in music there can be no such thing as a chair opposed to a painting, or the craftsman opposed to the pure artist.

Craft for Craft's Sake

The whole theory of utility music is based on the misconception that one can distinguish between the aesthetic and the useful in this particular medium. Apart from music for organized and non-aesthetic action such as military marches and foxtrots—which, typically enough, Hindemith has not written—music is only useful if it is good music, whether light or serious. Unless it provides one with some vital experience which no other art can convey it is not only useless but a nuisance. The objective craftsman that Hindemith sets up as an ideal is far more of a sentimental luxury than the despised aesthetic 'tone poet'. His daily covering of music paper is a task as essentially fruitless as those strange tasks assigned to the innocent dupes in the stories of Sherlock Holmes, the man in 'The Red-headed League' who copied out the *Encyclopaedia Britannica* or the stockbroker's clerk who was set to making a list of the pottery firms in Paris.

If we examine Hindemith's second statement we find an even more striking fallacy. With an altogether praiseworthy modesty Hindemith appears to imagine that by ceasing to write for his own satisfaction he is necessarily writing for the satisfaction of others. There is an old and trite saying: 'If you don't believe in yourself, nobody else will', and in music it may with equal truth be said that if a composer is not interested in his own music he can hardly expect others to be. Even the most nauseating of popular tunes, that would appear to be written solely with the desire to satisfy the public taste at its least critical and most mawkish, must mean something to the composer, and be primarily written for his satisfaction, if it is to 'get the public'. Purely 'occasional' music whether deliberately vulgar or deliberately refined always brings boredom and distrust in its wake. Unless the composer has some definite reason for putting pen to paper, he had far better play patience or do a little gardening.

It is this refusal to make music for its own sake that is

responsible for the passionate sincerity and popular success of Puccini's operas, in spite of all their vulgarity. The followers of Hindemith may shudder at this instance, but after all Puccini, as a superb craftsman who certainly satisfied a popular demand, should theoretically speaking be one of their idols; otherwise they are convicted of an antisentimental bias which is the reverse of objective.

Hindemith is equally mistaken when he imagines that the writing of music is governed by the laws of supply and demand. There is no regular demand for musical material as there is for writing material or boxes of matches; there is only a demand for something which creates its own demand —a good piece of music, in fact. By all means let us have as many new piano concertos as possible, provided they are equal to, or superior to, those in the standard repertory. There is no specific demand, however, for a new concerto as such, irrespective of quality. A pianist does not ask for a new piano concerto as he does for a new pair of shoes, giving the old one away to an amateur. Concertos may wear thin in the course of time, but handsewn leather is better than mass-produced cardboard.

As a further example of Hindemith's attitude towards music in general, and to his own compositions in particular, one may quote a few typical passages from the preface to *The Lesson*, a communal entertainment with words by Bert Brecht, who is better known through his collaborations with Kurt Weill: 'As the sole objective of this composition is to employ all present and not primarily to evoke any definite impressions by means of music and poetry, the form of the piece should be adapted as far as possible to the main intention. . . . Omissions, inversions and additions are practicable. Musical portions may be left out . . . passages from other composers may be introduced if necessary, provided they conform to the general style of the original.'

Craft for Craft's Sake

If the composer treats his own music with so little respect, one may well ask why the listener should be expected to show any more. But perhaps Hindemith regards the listener with the lofty contempt with which he regards the artist. He seems to think that some mystic value resides in the mere performance of notes—that the scraping of horsehair over catgut is in itself a health-giving and praiseworthy action, comparable to having a cold bath in the morning or being a Storm Trooper. His view of music would appear to be almost excretory.

There is at the beginning of this work a short quotation from Shakespeare which is symbolical in more ways than one. It will be observed that Cleopatra emphatically preferred billiards to music. This attitude, though somewhat philistine perhaps, is to be praised in that it recognizes that music and billiards represent two different sides of life. Cleopatra neither confused the functions of the two diversions nor suggested that they were better combined. Today, however, she would either have wireless turned on continually in the billiard room, or else she would have to listen to composers like Hindemith, who reduce music to the spiritual level of billiards, pingpong and clock golf.

By resolutely turning his back on 'art' Hindemith has lessened our interest even in his craft. For a problem in craft can only really become a problem when the fusion of emotion and form has to be considered. To confuse the arbitrary counterpoint of Hindemith with the expressive counterpoint of Byrd and Palestrina is to confuse the tightrope itself with the tightrope walker. It need hardly be pointed out that skill in the manipulation of purely academic counterpoint can be acquired in a few months by almost any person of average intelligence, whether musically gifted or not. The galvanic and plethoric counterpoint of Hindemith is only distinguishable from the bustling counterpoint of any nine-

217

teenth-century pedagogue by its slight atonal touches and general air of latterday briskness. Occasionally by sheer quickness of hand Hindemith is able to deceive the ear, but in his slow movements the lack of any genuine motive force or any genuinely lyrical line is pitilessly shown up. Much the same is true of his sense of form which is, in reality, not an intrinsic sense of form but an extrinsic use of formalism.

A musical idea of any real vitality determines, or should determine, its own formal treatment. The orchestral *Images* of Debussy and the later symphonies of Sibelius are not formal in the mechanical post-war sense, but every detail in them is as connected with the main trend of the musical thought as the twig is connected with the trunk of a tree. Having something to say these composers, not unnaturally, also knew how to say it. But a composer like Hindemith appears, on his own admission, to have nothing personal to say, and indeed despises the composer who thus vulgarly thrusts his personality before the public. His musical ideas are consequently lacking in generative power—they are not saplings but dead brushwood. To give them an air of logic he casts them into some pre-established and externally imposed form which, to the non-technical listener, gives a vague impression of solidity and musicianship. His form is an unyielding mould like those hideous porcelain objects into which blancmange and cornflour mixtures are poured, eventually solidifying into a dish known in some circles as 'shape'.

It is true that in one or two works, notably the opera *Cardillac* and the oratorio *Das Unaufhörliche*, Hindemith has clearly made an effort to rise above the uniform drabness of his innumerable pieces of Konzert Musik and Kammermusik. The oratorio, indeed, whose libretto suggests a none too happy collaboration between Nietzsche and James Douglas, almost takes us back to the bad old days of music with a message. Its pessimistic philosophy suggests that Hindemith himself has lost his faith in conscious modernity. But the occasional and praiseworthy attempts in this work to write free, expressive and uninhibited music are not so convincing as the 'echt-Hindemith' baritone solo: 'I'm an Opportunist I'm of the present'. After his utilitarian debauches he evidently finds it difficult to cultivate an aesthetic grande passion. One is reminded of the English poet who after writing political leaders in a jingo paper for a number of years complained that his Muse had deserted him.

(d) Mechanical Music and the Cinema

One is criticizing Hindemith's music, of course, from the point of view of the listener in the concert hall, for in spite of his numerous works for odd and specific occasions the greater part of his music is still designed for performance in the ordinary way. It is often said of this type of music that even if it fails to satisfy us in the concert hall it is eminently suited to mechanical reproduction, or to film or radio work; but this is merely another example of the false thinking engendered by mechanical romanticism. Because a work is mechanically conceived it does not follow that it is suited to mechanical reproduction. It is manifestly ludicrous to eschew all sentiment and pictorialism, and then to claim that your music is the ideal accompaniment for an art like the cinema, which depends to so great a degree on just this type of appeal. The composer has so often been urged to desert the concert hall for the wireless or cinema studio that perhaps it would be as well to examine, without prejudice, the supposed advantages of adapting oneself to contemporary mechanical media.

As regards writing with a view to the limitations of the

gramophone, there is frankly not much to be said for it. Gramophone companies are remarkably chary of taking up any work that has not made its reputation already, and if this is the case then the public want the nearest approximation to what they hear in the concert hall. It is obviously to the advantage of a jazz composer like Ellington to take a ten-inch record as his scale, but in the case of the symphonic writer the man who deliberately designed a work with pauses that coincided with the change-over from one record to another would look faintly silly when the next mechanical improvement obviated the necessity of these pauses. It is said that there have already been patented several forms of mechanical reproduction which abolish the terrible hiatus between one record and another, and that these improvements are deliberately held back by the gramophone companies in view of the wholesale mechanical changes their adoption would enforce. Be that as it may, it is obvious that in a few years' time recording will have improved on the present methods as much as the present methods have improved on the old pre-electric horn recording, with its euphoniums instead of 'cellos, and its handful of Stroh violins.

To write specially with a view to the deficiencies of recording technique is to upset the natural order of things. In the nineteenth century the tremendous improvement in the design and manufacture of wind instruments was directly due to the elaborate demands made on the player's skill by the composer; and the same is true of present-day recording whose advance is due to people demanding from the talking machine the complex subtleties of timbre that they hear in the concert hall. It is not for the composer to play handmaiden to the engineer.

There is only one quality which is the exclusive property of the gramophone, namely, the ability to change the pitch of the music abruptly in the middle of the work. This advice can be put to excellent effect in records of political or patriotic speeches, but it is doubtful whether it is much of a contribution to serious music. Milhaud has made some records of choral works in which, by an adjustment of the speed of the recording machine, the final effect is some two or three tones higher than as actually sung, thus producing a choral climax of peculiar acerbity. The occasional use of this device, however, hardly entitles the gramophone to be considered as a medium in itself.

Works written for the wireless as a medium may be divided into two classes. First there are those which are really concert-hall works orchestrated in a manner specially suited to radio reproduction; and here we are faced by the same arguments that apply to music written especially for the gramophone. The brittle texture of a typical Hindemith work undoubtedly comes over the ether better than the more subtle timbres of works by Delius, Sibelius, or Van Dieren—to take three composers who have only this subtlety in common—but the progress being made in wireless reproduction is so great that it would be waste of time for a composer to deliberately score his works from the microphonic point of view, unless paid to do so. Moreover, while the wireless, unlike the gramophone, offers opportunities for the production of new works, it is necessary to point out that no musical work can make its reputation by radio performance alone. In spite of the wider dissemination of gramophone and radio the composer is still ultimately dependent on the réclame provided by an actual concert-hall performance.

Composing with a view to actual microphone technique is quite another matter. It is clear that the combination of several studios gives scope for a fascinating superimposition of different types of sound particularly in combination with the spoken word. One can easily imagine a wireless drama compounded of speech, stylized realistic sound, synthetically produced music and, possibly, television which would carry to its logical end the expressionism hinted at in the later plays of Strindberg and unobtainable on the legitimate stage. It is equally clear, though, that music qua music must take a subordinate place in such an entertainment. The production of a suitable aural background and the juxtaposition or realistic sound and stylized speech calls for a selective rather than a purely creative artist—a man who will bear the same relation to a composer that the photographer does to a painter. In work of this type a composer of the Hindemith school is obviously to be preferred to the subjective 'tone poet', to use Hindemith's own contemptuous description of the romantic musician. It may well be that wireless entertainment of this type will, in the future, open up to the minor composer the same outlet that the designing of posters open up to the minor painter. In the meanwhile the composer of merit is well advised to regard the wireless as a possible adjunct to his income rather than as a tenth Muse.

The cinema is undoubtedly the most important of the mechanical stimuli offered to the composer of today; and in spite of its ephemeral nature it is the only art whose progress is not at the moment depressing to watch. While the music of today seems either to be a romantic swan song regretting past days, as in Delius, an alembicated and intellectual crossword puzzle, as in Von Webern, or a callow reflection of the drab minutiae of daily life, as in Hindemith, the films with superb insolence have blended old-fashioned naïvety of sentiment with up-to-the-minute sophistication of technique, producing as if by accident the most vigorous art form of today.

Films have the emotional impact for the twentieth century that operas had for the nineteenth. Pudovkin and Eisenstein are the true successors of Mussorgsky, D. W. Griffiths is our Puccini, Cecil B. de Mille our Meyerbeer, and René Clair our Offenbach. It is not exaggerating to say that a film like King Vidor's *Hallelujah* has a far greater aesthetic significance than any opera written since the war, and that the pickaxe spiritual in *I am a Fugitive* is, in its medium, worthy to be compared with the chorus crying for bread in the original version of *Boris*.

The cinema, from being the servant girl of the arts, the butt of every footling dramatic critic who once saw a play by Ibsen, has blossomed out into the one art form of today which while in touch with the public can yet beat the intellectual at his own game. There must be few surrealists and transitionists who do not feel that the Marx Brothers have stolen their thunder and sent it rolling uproariously round the room in Lewis Carroll fashion, and few artists of any kind who do not feel abashed when faced with the phenomenal inventive genius of Walt Disney, the only artist of today who exists triumphantly in a world of his own creation, unhampered by the overshadowing of ancient tradition or the undercutting of contemporary snobbism.

It is little wonder, then, that so many musicians, particularly those who, immediately after the war, toyed with the music-hall aesthetic, should now be attracted by the cinema aesthetic. Unfortunately they are a little too late in the day to achieve anything in the nature of symphonic cinema music. The idea of a film as a musical entity vanished with the first Al Jolson picture. It is true that Pudovkin and Eisenstein are the spiritual successors of Mussorgsky, but unfortunately they found no Mussorgsky to write music for them. The music provided by Meisel for *Potemkin* was a great improvement on the ordinary cinema music of the time, but it would be idle to pretend that it was a worthy counterpart of the film itself.

The Mechanical Stimulus

By the time composers of merit turned their attention to the screen the entire technique of sound accompaniment had been revolutionized. Music as such was banished, except as an invisible and improbable accompaniment to love scenes, and purely realistic synchronized sound took its place.

As far as one can tell, Pudovkin was the first to realize the possibilities latent in purely realistic sound, treated not as an accompaniment but as a counterpoint to the visual image. Sketching out a treatment in sound of a famous sequence in the silent film *Mother*, in which a picture of the mother crying was 'cut in' with a picture of a dripping kichen tap, he remarked that instead of accompanying each with its appropriate aural image he would synchronize the tap with the sound of a woman crying, and vice versa. Modified use of this contrapuntal treatment of sound is by now a commonplace in almost every American film. Its use is limited, however, not only by the fact that the opportunities for pure sound as opposed to human speech are relatively few but by the difference in tempo between our perception of sight and our perception of sound. There are remarkably few sounds whose significance and associations we can immediately perceive without the aid of a visual image; on the other hand a visual image carries with it an immediate association of sound. A photograph of a fire engine carries with it an implication of the sound of its bell greater than the implication of the appearance of a fire engine aroused by its noise.

The specimen counterpoint suggested by Pudovkin is only likely to be successful because both visual images would be shown to the audience as well as both aural images—even though they are shown at different times. The sound of a dripping tap cannot be used as a counterpoint to a visual image unless its own visual image has been previously established, whereas a momentary and unprepared visual image can easily be used as a counterpoint to a continuous aural background. It is impossible, therefore, to achieve in music the equivalent of the 'quick cutting' which is the basis of the Pudovkin-Eisenstein technique. There is no real equivalent in music even of the 'wipe-dissolve' which leads the eye gently but quickly from one scene to another.

The ideal sound counterpoint of Pudovkin has perforce given place to a more flexible and symbolic use of realistic noise blended with, or superimposed upon, a musical background. As an easy example of this type of sound treatment may be quoted a musical effect derived from the sound of riveting which was used in an otherwise completely undistinguished film called *The Half-Naked Truth.* In the scene in question the noises of city life were shown playing on the nerves of an overworked man in an office. First one riveter was heard, combined with its visual image, then another, striking a higher note and gradually assuming a more strictly musical rhythm and tone till, as the shot changed to an office scene, they merged into a neurasthenic blues whose orchestration ingeniously maintained the rapid metallic tremolo of the riveting machine. The example was slight and isolated, but its skill and flexiblity pointed the way to a use of realism and 'actualities' more significant than the undigested concert-hall onomatopœics of *Pacific 231.*

Using the cinema as a medium, composers like Honegger could deal with actualities not only with greater force but with greater artistry. Its strength lies in the fact that it is the only art which can produce significant form out of essentially shoddy material. Sickening sentimentality and revolting brutality can, when treated cinematically, achieve an aesthetic value which would never be theirs in literature or the drama. The reason is that the life of a film lies far more in its texture—understanding by this both the camera work and its montage—than in its theme and outlook. One can conceive a great book being clumsily written, but a film that is clumsily produced automatically loses any possible artistic significance.

The cinema, in fact, not only offers opportunities for the pure craftsmanship which is so meaningless in music but, being mainly a selective rather than a creative art, offers to the minor artist a positive montage instead of a negative pastiche. It is a tenable theory that much of our dissatisfaction with post-war music derives from the fact that the most typical post-war composers are cinema producers manqués. Children of their time, they have yet remained outside the most stimulating medium of their time. Instead of producing null and void concertos, Hindemith should be the camera man, Honegger should be in charge of the sound effects and Stravinsky, with his genius for pastiche, should be entrusted with the cutting. The cinema also offers a more convincing form of expression to artists very different in temperament from the workaday composers. For although in one way the cinema's strength lies in the positive value it can extract from intrinsically negative actualities, in another way its strength lies in its suitability to the 'dream-aesthetic' which can be so irritating in the older arts.

It is fairly clear, I imagine, that films are the only logical medium for the inconsequent dream images of surrealist thought. In literature it is almost impossible to give sufficient visual impact to the conflicting images. If we examine a typical piece of surrealist prose, such as the extract from Soupault's *Death of Nick Carter* quoted by Herbert Read in his *English Prose Style*, we can see that it depends for its effect on its visual content, or suggestions, and not on any verbal rhythm. Rhythm is not even called in to emphasize the visual images which are created by means as direct and as flat as a colour adjective. It reads, as do so many transitional prose pieces, like an elaborate stage direction from some super-Strindbergian play.

In painting, although the visual images can be set before one directly, the absence of any time element is an obvious restriction to the representation of a dream experience. The attempt to overcome this deficiency, rather than any purely formal preoccupation, is probably the cause of the confused and overcrowded design we occasionally find in the pictures of Salvador Dali—in many ways the most important and convincing of the surrealists. His pictures are as hampered by the lack of time element as *The Last Day in the Old Home* of Martineau or the *Belshazzar's Feast* of Martin. The repetition of the same object in two different sizes, that familiar device in surrealist pictures, is also an attempt to represent time experience in spatial form, to capture the sudden and dramatic incongruity of scale which, invented by D. W. Griffiths, has reached its climax in the *Silly Symphonies* of Walt Disney—as for instance the mermaid scene in *King Neptune*.

The best of surrealist literature and surrealist painting seems clumsy and rudimentary when put beside even a minor surrealist film such as Germaine Dulac's *The Sea Shell and the Clergyman*, and there is little doubt that surrealist thought would gravitate entirely round the cinema were it not for the expense involved in the production of a film as compared to the production of a picture or poem.

It has been remarked before that the most striking feature of the art of our time is the way in which the popular, commercial and lowbrow arts have adopted the technical and spiritual sophistication of the highbrow arts. There is not much connection between Maeterlinck and Marie Lloyd, but there is a definite connection between surrealist prose and the Marx Brothers.

This inspired family has achieved in a successful and popular form what the transitional writers labour at in the self-appointed obscurity of an unsuitable medium—the translation into French of the scenario of *Animal Crackers* might have come straight out of *Transition* itself. The outrageous puns and verbal intricacies of the conversations between Groucho and Chico are distinguished from the philological wisecracks of *Work in Progress* by the fact that they invariably come off. Perhaps the most significant of the brothers from a contemporary historian's point of view is not the wisecracking Groucho, magnificent though he is, but the silent and Freudian Harpo. The scene in *Animal Crackers* where he steals the birthmark from the art dealer is surrealist poetry at its most fanciful. The scene where he kicks the hostess, Mrs. Rittenhouse, is surrealist violence at its most practical. How infinitely preferable to Max Ernst is the sculptured group which comes to life, fires a revolver, and then returns to bronze.

The films of the Marx Brothers, though surrealist in content, are, like so many surrealist pictures, realist in method. It is noticeable, though, that more and more American films are introducing, wherever the script allows, dream sequences which, deriving from the early and unappreciated *Beggar on Horseback*, are definitely surrealist in their method. It is only a matter of time before these two lines of thought are linked up and we get the first genuinely surrealist commercial film.

Surrealism is at present connected in most people's minds with cliques and preciosity, but that is no guarantee that it will not, under another name and in cinematic form, become the dominant entertainment of the future. It is a mistake to think that popular taste remains the same or even demands the same sort of thing. Who in the late seventeenth century, straining to hear some trumpery fiddle solo in Banister's public-house Concert Room in Whitefriars, would have foreseen that in the 1930's a popular audience would stand in serried ranks and respectful silence while six 'poderose consorts' were played without interruption?

Music having ousted the other arts in popularity may well sink back again and suffer the same social decline as poetry.

It may be that the break-up of tradition we see in literature, painting, and music is not a transitional disruption paving the way for a new tradition but a definite and final disruption. It may be that specialized experiment in the arts has reached its logical end, and that the only progress lies in a surrealist fantasia that will embrace them all. Selection and superimposition or, if the word be preferred, montage is the key note of such widely differing contemporary manifestations as Eliot's poetry, Diaghileff's ballets, Stravinsky's concertos, Ernst's pictures and Eisenstein's films. It is only natural that these arts, having lost their specifically characteristic background, should merge into the one form which is capable of absorbing them all and producing a significant result—the surrealist film.

Musical montage may not seem the highest form of occupation, but it is the only future for the middlebrow composer of today.

(e) The Disappearing Middlebrow

To return abruptly from the surrealist future to the all too real present, it may be asked in what way Hindemith and his followers are fitted to deal with the mechanical mediums as they stand today. There is nothing impertinent in such a question. If a man announces that he has resigned from his job it is only natural, and indeed sympathetic, to inquire: 'And what do you propose to do now?' Most modern musical criticism is no more than a futile examination of surface texture for the reason that it stops short of the ultimate and inescapable 'and then what?'

Without wishing to set up a hypothetical criterion, it is only reasonable to ask what future lies in store for the composers of Gebrauchsmusik if they are to live up to their declared convictions. Hindemith having turned his back on the composer as poet for the few, we must see if he is in any way fitted for the post of composer as hack for the many. If a man says he is a craftsman we have a right to ask what he can make. We do not judge a mechanic by the cut of his dungarees but by his manual ability, and it would seem that Hindemith is as little suited to lulling the senses of the stupid as he is to arousing the interest of the intelligent.

The surrealist film is of the future, and the symphonic silent film is of the past. At the present moment the only opportunities for the cinema composer—apart from preludial fanfares, short semi-realistic sequences in shots of machinery, etc.—lie in the definite musical film either of the Eddie Cantor revue type or the René Clair operetta type. Hindemith and his followers are patently incapable of tackling such a task, in that they lack all the geniality of melodic invention that is required of composers of this type of music. There is no test so merciless as a 'theme song'— either it is good or it isn't. There is no getting away from failure by describing it as a pregnant thematic fragment. Emotion of some sort is demanded of the least of composers and even synthetic sentiment, the musical equivalent of glycerine tears, is harder to achieve than abstraction. Abstract music is only suited to that dismal and fruitless branch of entertainment, the abstract film.

It is difficult indeed to see what precise function is fulfilled by the composers of Gebrauchsmusik, for all their superficial air of practicality and efficiency. Their technical dexterity is undeniable, but it exists in a vacuum. The poor creatures are all dressed up with nowhere to go.

A composer like Hindemith, although essentially a minor figure, is of considerable importance, however, as a symbol of the modern artist who, having lost or thrown aside the spiritual background of the romantic artist, has signally failed to adapt himself to the physical background of modern life. He is neither a good wife nor an attractive whore—the adjectives are interchangeable. Incapable of the spiritual and technical concentration that has gone to such works as Sibelius's Seventh Symphony, Alban Berg's *Lyric Suite*, or Van Dieren's *Sonetto VII of Edmund Spenser's Amoretti*, to name at random three of the masterpieces of our time, he is equally incapable of the melodic fertility and the ability to synthesize popular sentiment that we find in a work like Kurt Weill's *Seven Deadly Sins*,[1] not to mention such genuinely popular pieces as Duke Ellington's *Mood Indigo* or Cole Porter's *Love for Sale*. There is hardly a work of his which, to use a hackneyed phrase, does not fall spectacularly 'between two stools'. It is permissible to take as a fair example the Philharmonic Concerto that he wrote for the Jubilee of the Berlin Philharmonic Orchestra. It consists of a set of variations on a theme of quite phenomenal dullness, each variation presumably designed to throw into alto relievo a particular section of the orchestra. Not Hindemith's greatest admirer, I imagine, would pretend that this work is to be taken as seriously as, for example, Schönberg's *Variations for orchestra*, yet as a bravura piece it is patently inferior to the glittering *Capriccio Espagnol* of Rimsky-Korsakoff. (Its combination of natural aridity with deliberate virtuosity is

---

[1] Weill has written his utility music and indeed was at one time associated with Hindemith, but it is by his more recent work, as exemplified in *The Seven Deadly Sins*, written since he left Germany, that I am judging him.

indeed most displeasing. Exhibitionism is only to be tolerated in the physically attractive.)

Hindemith having embraced the goddess Practicality must be judged by her own Draconic laws, and there are few works of his that do not lay themselves open to this dual criticism. They fail to satisfy any logical canon of criticism that today offers us, and in criticizing them we must perforce talk in terms of today, for his widespread influence is already on the wane. We need hardly worry ourselves about the verdict of the future, for the journalist who has failed cannot console himself, like the unsuccessful poet, with the possible adoration of posterity. Those who sit in the middle of a joy wheel may seem to move slowly, but their permanence is more assured than those who for the sake of a momentary exhilaration try to pin themselves to its smooth and shining periphery.

By rejecting the individualist attitude towards art Hindemith has bound himself to the law of social change, and although it is rash to prophesy these changes I think we may say that Gebrauchsmusik, as we at present understand it, will find no place in the social life of the future. As far as we can discern any general social trend in the music of today it would appear that the middlebrow composer is disappearing. Music in this way is following much the same course as poetry.

In the early nineteenth century one could be a great poet and yet a popular figure. It was possible by poetry alone, and good poetry at that, to achieve the popular success now vouchsafed only to the prose of Arlen and Priestley. But now poetry of any merit has become the specialized enjoyment of the few and there is no great poet of our time who is genuinely in touch with the public as a whole. While the highbrow poet, through his no doubt sincere complexity, has lost all save a small section of the old middlebrow public, the lowbrow poet—the type of writer who in the nineteenth century produced 'Champagne Charlie' and now produces revue lyrics—has, through his social and technical sophistication, gained the greater part of it. The middlebrow poet, as represented by the present Poet Laureate and the old volumes of Georgian verse, has been left stranded.

The poetic atmosphere of our time may be likened to a severe winter that kills off all animals except those sufficiently sophisticated to live indoors and those sufficiently primitive to have tough hides. The sensitive nature-poet now presents the pathetic yet suitable spectacle of a frozen robin. Although middlebrow poetry drags on a kind of half-sentient existence, it is clear that poetry is now divided up between the unpopular and sophisticated highbrow, like Sacheverell Sitwell, and the popular and sophisticated low-brow like Cole Porter or Noel Coward. Anything between the two is a *terrain vague*—a deserted kitchen garden littered with rusty rakes and empty birdcages.

Much the same process of splitting up is taking place in music. Elgar was the last serious composer to be in touch with the great public. Sophisticated composers are either becoming more sophisticated, like Alban Berg, or they are deliberately turning their sophistication to popular account, like Kurt Weill.

As far as I can see it, music written by composers whose individualism links them with the great composers of the past and whose work, being the result of a spiritual concentration, requires at least a modicum of this concentration from the listener, will become a specialized art like poetry, appreciated with the same intensity by an equally small public. Apart from this, music will be a definitely popular form of art, not revolving round the concert hall but adapting itself to wireless and the films. An easy-going, pleasant and exhilarating noise which will form a kind of *musique d'ameublement*. There may be writers in both camps, just as there are poets who turn their hand to journalism, but their two professions will be recognized as being completely different.

In this process of splitting up, any music which does not belong specifically to either type will be ruthlessly disregarded. The middlebrow composer will disappear in the same way as the middlebrow poet, and the mechanically conceived Gebrauchsmusik of Hindemith and his followers will suffer the same swift oblivion as yesterday's newspaper.

PART FIVE

ESCAPE OR SUBMISSION

(a) A Psychological Cul-de-sac

I f by now the reader is left with a somewhat confused impression of post-war music then I have, if only negatively, succeeded; for a clear impression of post-war music would of necessity be false. The New Music of today displays no such recognizable and direct tendency as the New Music of the early seventeenth century. We cannot speak of any contemporary composer as Roger North spoke of Purcell—'Mr. H. Purcell who unhappily began to show his great skill before ye reforme of musick al Italiana'— because we are none of us agreed as to what constitutes present-day reform or present-day revolution. Yet apart from the one or two isolated and exceptional figures who constitute all that ultimately counts in contemporary music there are few composers who are not attached, either officially or unwittingly, to some one or other revolutionary 'movement'. Just as the various coloured-shirt political parties that have sprung up in Europe having nothing in common save their faith in the shirt as a symbol, so these various musical parties have nothing in common save their faith in the label 'revolutionary' or 'avant-garde'.

The unsophisticated listener may well be puzzled as to what constitutes revolution in music when he is successfully asked to regard atonality, polytonality, highbrow jazz and neo-classicism as the dernier cri. He may, though, on closer acquaintance, detect two common threads which, however twisted and coloured, run through all contemporary musical movements. One is revolution, the other classicism; and their confused proximity is sufficient indication of their shallow spiritual foundation. The post-war composer is lacking in the genuine spirit of revolt that we find in a composer like Mussorgsky, or the genuine spirit of conservatism that we find in a composer like Cherubini; for to him revolution has become merely a mechanical reaction and classicism merely a receptacle, a roll-top desk into which he can thrust incongruous scraps of paper.

The label 'modern' is already become a stale joke, as one can see by the dreary comedy that is being played in advanced musical circles in Central Europe. Whereas before the war we had the familiar spectacle of old conservatives chiding youth for its earsplitting cacophony and bad manners, we now have the delicious spectacle of old revolutionaries chiding youth for its consonance and its good manners.

A particularly happy instance of this new development was provided by the reception accorded Walton's latest work at that officially revolutionary meeting the Festival of the International Society for Contemporary Music. Some ten years ago an immature quartet of Walton's, written in the then fashionable revolutionary manner of Central Europe, earned for him the title of 'International Pioneer'. In 1933 his mature but regrettably consonant *Belshazzar's Feast* was dismissed, particularly by the older critics, as 'routinier', conventional, and unworthy of its place in so selectly revolutionary a festival. The rest of the works were still in the style that Walton himself had used ten years before, but it so happened that Walton's development had led him away from official revolt to personal revolt. It would be a tenable hypothesis that Walton himself was the real revolutionary and the others the conservatives. In fact, if A accuses B of being reactionary, B can always reply: 'On the contrary, I am merely reacting against your reaction against reaction.' Whatever else we may blame the post-war composer for, we can only be grateful to him for having deprived of any conceivable meaning the epithet 'revolutionary'.

In the present age the word classicism has become not so much deprived of meaning as degraded in meaning. The classic spirit should be something as positive as the revolutionary spirit, it should represent not a rejection, or even curbing, of the imagination, but the direction of it through interlinked channels—neither a flood nor a dam but an aqueduct. The neo-classicism of today, as we have seen in examining different aspects of it in Stravinsky and Hindemith, is a bare framework, a stereotyped scaffolding designed to give to the inconsequent and devitalized ideas of the post-war composers a superficial air of logic and construction. It is a conscious revival of formulas that were the unconscious inessentials of the age that originally produced them—as who should confuse archaic spelling or the use of the long 's' with the content of the writers in whom these devices are to be found.

The moment we realize that the revolutionary spirit and the classical spirit, which would appear to form such odd bedfellows in the work of the average post-war composer, are in fact not revolution and classicism at all but reaction and formalism, then we see that there is no real conflict between the two, that they are both expressions of the same underlying weakness—lack of faith, or, if that phrase be considered too sentimental, soft and yellow for this tough, red-blooded, poker-faced, he-man age, shall we say, no sense of direction. The feverish fashionable reactions of post-war Paris, the mathematical revolutionary formulas of post-war Vienna, indicate that the average post-war composer has either nothing to say or does not know how to say it—possibly both. That so many works written today depend to such an unparalleled extent on the modern adaptation of academic device is a sign not of formal strength but of emotional weakness. We have almost no composer who has sufficient faith in himself to get to grips with his medium directly, in the fashion of Mussorgsky or Debussy, and create a personal yet intelligible idiom. We bolster up our lack of faith with party cries, and pour out bootleg gin into cracked leather bottles with olde-worlde labels.

The spiritual background of the eighteenth-century classics and the nineteenth-century romantics has gone, and it now seems that even the spiritual background of the pre-war revolutionaries has gone also. The composer finds himself in a spiritual waste land with only the cold and uncertain glimmer of intellectual theorizing to guide and console him. It is, of course, in his spiritual and social background that we must seek the reasons of his decline, of which technical mannerisms are only the outward expression. There is, I imagine, no critic who still thinks that the contemporary composer adopts any particular style through sheer lack of ability or through a desire to leg-pull. Technical craftsmanship is at as high a level as ever, and indeed is apt to intrude itself too much—not too little.

'The spirit of the age' is a vulgar and easily misapplied phrase, like 'the will of the people', but after all some peoples show a common will and some ages a common spirit. To say that the spirit of the romantic age found fuller and more successful expression in music than in painting may be a crude generalization, but it is undoubtedly a true one. Similarly we may say that the spirit of the present age finds its best expression not so much in music as in abstract painting and satire, whether literary or cinematic.

Abstraction and satire are not so opposed in impulse as might at first appear. The one is an escape from reality, the other an attack on it.

There is very little Whitmanesque acceptance of life about the artist of today. He is not a 'yea-sayer'. Faced with life, he either turns away from it or debunks it. Joyce's *Work in Progress*, abstract films, and Disney's *Silly Symphonies*, represent the escape attitude, Lewis's *Apes of God* and the James Cagney, Lee Tracy type of tough Hollywood film represent the debunking attitude. Both attitudes, though perhaps negative in impulse, have in certain media produced results that are positive in their excellence. But neither abstraction nor satire is suited to the medium of music, and consequently the typical composition of today is either a swan song echoing from another period or else a present-day echo from another art.

This state of affairs may only be a temporary lull due to present-day social conditions or, as I have suggested in a previous chapter, it may be that the various arts are going to merge into the all-embracing medium of the surrealist film. In any case it can hardly be denied that the composer of today is out of joint with both his medium and his period. He is too intellectualized or too commercialized and, unable to cope with life and music on equal terms, he becomes either an aesthete or a whoremonger. Stravinsky's intellectual pastiches represent an escape and Hindemith's 'work for the day' represents a submission. Neither represents a satisfactory and positive solution.

To give the problem that local touch that so endears, let us take the case of a composer in present-day England—patriotically assuming that a great composer is as likely to be produced here as anywhere else. The England that formed the background to Byrd, Purcell, and even Boyce is completely gone, only a dismal echo of it remaining in the imaginations of the folk-song school. The collapse of English music during the nineteenth century might seem almost an advantage from the purely contemporary point of view, in that the modern English composer is not so hampered by the bulky shadows of the recent past as his rivals in Berlin and Vienna. But the English church-music tradition—the only branch of English music that in any way flourished during the Victorian age—provides on a smaller scale the positive influence of a tradition that is in our blood, and the negative stimulus of something that has deliberately to be fought against. (Thus the complete absence of anything approaching Dykes-like harmonies in Holst's music points to a deliberate discarding which is in itself a proof of negative influence.) The lack, however, of any important English composer in the nineteenth century simplifies the problem to some extent. The classical tradition that slowly declined in other countries was in England abruptly broken off, and any attempt to revive it is therefore revealed in its full artificiality.

In Elgar, the first figure of importance since Boyce, we get an example of a composer, in touch both with his audience and his period, expressing himself nationally in an international language. It is more than probable that, but for the social and spiritual changes brought about by the war, Elgar would have been a more potent influence on English music than Vaughan Williams; but the aggressive Edwardian prosperity that lends so comfortable a background to Elgar's finales is now as strange to us as the England that produced *Greensleeves* and *The Woodes so wilde*. Stranger, in fact, and less sympathetic. In consequence much of Elgar's music, through no fault of its own, has for the present generation an almost intolerable air of smugness, self-assurance and autocratic benevolence.

Owing to the late sprouting of nationalism in this country

the inevitable post-war reaction to the spirit of Elgar took advantage of the world of escape provided by the folk-song revival, and there is thus no genuinely Georgian music to oppose to the Edwardian symphonies of Elgar. This rustic arbour is now showing signs of imminent collapse, and since the Shropshire Lad himself published his last poems some ten years ago it may without impertinence be suggested that it is high time his musical followers published their last songs. The ground might then be left clear for something less nostalgically consoling but more vital.

It is difficult to see what is genuinely vital in English civilization at the moment, a civilization that is summed up by the buildings, with neither the elegance of the Old World nor the efficiency of the New, that are now being set up in London. One does not so much bemoan the passing of picturesque old London as deplore the absence of any-thing stimulating in the newly built London. One would not mind the Dickens streets disappearing to give way to the Babylonian beauty of the New York skyscrapers, but one does object to their giving way to such appalling examples of modern degeneracy as, for example, Regent Street.

What is true of London is true of the country as a whole. We have concentrated on a prosperous industrial civiliza-tion to the exclusion of everything else, and now that our material supremacy is passing we have no other form of life to console us. To the English artist that is the great difficulty. It is no use his sentimentalizing about the old England, yet what is there to inspire him in our present state, which is lacking even the stimulus of the mechanical hysteria of America? To be honest he must accept a work like Eliot's *Waste Land* as symbolizing the essentially negative and bleak spirit of post-war intellectual England. Yet what a rejection of lyrical impulse this acceptation involves!

It is typical of the hiatus that exists between music and

the other arts today that in England, the country where poetry and music have, in the past, been almost indissolubly linked, there are no musical settings of the more important poems of our time. I say 'of our time' advisedly, for although there are magnificent settings of early Yeats—notably Peter Warlock's *The Curlew*—there are none of later Yeats, let alone of poets more closely in touch with the contemporary *Zeitgeist*. (Walton's settings of Edith Sitwell's *Façade*, being for spoken voice, hardly constitute a fair exception.)

The position in England has, of course, its local vagaries and peculiarities, but it represents roughly the position in which the composer finds himself in every country today. Unable to progress any further in the way of modernity he has not a sufficiently sympathetic or stimulating background to enable him to start afresh or to consolidate his experiments. The stupider composers—to whom, regrettably enough, most of this book has been devoted—escape from the situation either by an empty and wilful pastiche of an older tradition or by an equally fruitless concentration on the purely mechanical and objective sides of their arts. The more intelligent composer is forced in on himself and made to overconcentrate on his own musical personality, a process which is inclined to be dangerous and sterilizing.

The premature senility of so many modern composers can mainly be ascribed to this concentration on purely personal mannerisms. Most of the great figures of the past have been content to leave their personal imprint on the *materia musica* of the day without remodelling it entirely. It is only the minor figure whose every bar is recognizable, just as it is only the minor painter, like Marie Laurencin, whose handiwork can be detected at a hundred yards. The number of musical devices, turns of phrase and tricks of rhythm that a composer can appropriate to himself alone, is surprisingly few, and a refusal to lose caste by vulgarly moving outside these self-imposed barriers results in a similarly narrow and restricted content.

This can clearly be seen in the case of Béla Bartók. Though one respects the spiritual integrity that has led to his self-concentration, one cannot help feeling that his later works are a warning of the dangers of too great subjectivity on the part of the composer. The austere but impressive line which gave such strength to the opera *Bluebeard's Castle* has by now been fined down to a barbaric minimum of inflection, while the stark harmonies that supported it have been concentrated into a percussive cluster of notes. So much so that in certain works the limit of intelligibility and concentration is reached, if not passed.

A composer must, through the very nature of his art, externalize his emotions to some slight degree. He cannot demand collaboration from his audience while deliberately turning his back on them. The obsession with a narrowly personal world of sound that is to be noticed in some of the later works of Bartók—his fourth quartet, for instance—is the musical equivalent of navel gazing on the part of a philosopher.

What we require from the composer is neither a contemplation of his own navel, nor a frenzied dashing about in sports cars, but an expression of musical personality free from deliberate pastiche—which is escape—or from mechanical revolution—which is submission. The composers, such as Sibelius, Busoni, and Van Dieren, who in different ways represent this spiritual freedom rarely, if ever, form a school and are not usually the most outwardly advanced in style. They are free from the vulgarity of the label, above all the official 'revolutionary' label with which so great a figure as Schönberg has unfortunately been associated.

(b) Schönberg and Official Revolution

An intelligent musician who, for some reason or other, had been kept completely out of touch with the movements of the last thirty years, would think on examining for the first time a score by Schönberg that here was one of the great isolated figures in the history of music, an 'original' like Gesualdo, Berlioz or Busoni. It would come as a shock to him to find that Schönberg was a leader of a school, and that a style at first sight so peculiarly personal had been aped with moderate success by ever other student in Central Europe. Schönberg at one time was indeed the great isolated figure of Europe, but he has gradually become the official leader of the official revolutionaries, and is in many ways the most pedantic of modern composers. He has escaped from an academic set of rules only to be shackled by his own set of rules, and this self-imposed tyranny is taken over *en bloc* by his pupils.

The similarity of method shared by the atonal composers is, on the face of it, as suspect as the similarity of method shared by the abstract and surrealist painters. The desire to escape from the tyranny of the key system in music is as understandable as the desire to escape from academic realism in painting; but, whether we like it or not, tonality in music and realism in painting are a norm that is in our blood—departure from them, however successful and however praiseworthy, is technically speaking an abnormality. While a school of normality is a logical and harmless affair, a school of abnormality is a psychological contradiction. Those who wish to overthrow the formulas of convention have everyone's sympathy but, unlike political revolutionaries, they must revolt alone. Every man his own surrealist and every man his own atonalist should be the slogan for today.

If we can rid the word abnormal of any outside associations of taboo, or even glamour, then we must admit that the atonal movement is by far the most abnormal movement music has ever known. It cannot be compared with the gradual breaking down of accepted harmonic formulas that we find in Debussy, Stravinsky or Bartók, the slow destruction of the key system that we find in Milhaud's polytonality or Vaughan Williams's polymodality. It is a radical and intellectual revolution whose origins are not to be found in any primitive school of music, and which has no instinctive physical basis.

The unco, a species of Malayan ape noted for its singing in quarter-tones, is, as far as one can tell, the only living creature, capable of vocal production, that posesses no sense of tonality. Although the scales of folk music may vary from the simple pentatonic scales of the Hebridean to the complicated ragas of the Hindu, the same outlook on tonality is implied; and without this tonal sense not only our sense of concord and discord—without which counterpoint is meaningless—but our sense of form, even, becomes mechanical and arbitrary.

To the child who has not been trained to expect certain harmonic formulas there is nothing intrinsically strange or shocking in *Le Sacre du Printemps*, for example; and he finds no more difficulty in accepting it as sound than he does in the case of Wagner. But atonalism is often a stumbling block to the most sympathetically inclined of listeners. It is not that the sound shocks in itself, for by totally abandoning tonality Schönberg also destroys all sense of discord. Passively speaking, his music is easy to listen to, or rather to accept as sound; but actively speaking the listener finds it difficult to think clearly or convincingly in an idiom so

245

essentially unvocal, so remote from primitive song—which is the ultimate foundation of our musical sense. It is to be noticed also that the best interpreters of atonal music confine themselves to this school alone, as though it were only by shutting out all other idioms from their consciousness that they could think naturally in this particular one.

While the listener finds that most aural stumbling blocks disappear with repeated experience, it is rarely that he overcomes the initial strangeness of atonalism, even when sufficiently familiar with the idiom to detect immediately the difference between its few masters and the many fumbling secondraters. It is true that there are more practising atonalists in Europe today than there were ten years ago. This may mean that as an idiom it has become acclimatized, or it may mean that Schönberg's peculiar methods of approach have degenerated into a mechanical and easily applied formula.

Except for a few isolated figures, however, I think it in the highest degree unlikely that atonalism will ever become an instinctive and natural idiom, part of our mental background, in the way that Debussy's idiom has become so—his mannerisms now being the property of every jazz hack. 'So much the better', may think the followers of Schönberg, Berg and Von Webern, but, after all, the vulgarization of Debussy, like the vulgarization of Wagner, is a proof of the essentially solid basis on which these one-time revolutionaries built.

There is one objection to atonalism so simple and childish that no one seems to have had the courage to make it. Although atonalism has produced complicated and objective fugal structures that can with justice be compared with the *Kunst der Fuge* of Bach, subjective and neurasthenic opera that can be compared with *Tristan and Isolde* or *Parsifal*, it has produced nothing that we can set beside Chabrier and Offenbach, let alone the comic operas of Mozart. The dance movements in the *Serenade* and the *Op. 25 Piano Suite*, which are Schönberg's nearest approach to this genre, are sufficient proof of the essential solemnity of atonalism. An atonal comic opera is a chimerical thought, and though it is unlikely that either Schönberg or Berg would in any case wish to attempt such a genre, the mere fact that the task would be impossible is a proof of the narrow emotional range offered by their idiom.

Atonalism, though plastic in minor details of texture, is in fact the least flexible and most monotonous of media, and for that reason alone it is unlikely to play much part in the music of the future. It will always remain a thing apart, having something of the hieratical solemnity and exclusiveness of a hereditary religious order; and the more we free ourselves from tonal prejudice and from the tyranny of text-book harmony the less appeal atonalism will have, because it is based on a direct reversal of academic method. Like blasphemy, it requires a background of belief for its full effect. Composers like Bartók or Vaughan Williams could no more become atonalists than a freethinker could take part in a Black Mass.

There is a strong flavour of the Black Mass about Schönberg. He has the complete lack of humour of the diabolist, while a glance at his earlier work indicates how devout a believer he once was. His later eccentricities are in direct ratio to his early conventionalities, just as the excesses of a revolution are in direct ratio to the previous oppression.

There is no composer whose early work, superficially examined, displays so great a contrast to his later development. Debussy's early piano pieces and Bartók's early orchestral suites may seem conventional enough when compared to their more mature work, but they contain the seeds of their later efflorescence. But in Schönberg's early works such individuality as he had was completely stifled by the over-bearing influence of German romanticism. There is always a temptation to be wise after the event and to detect in some innocent early work the flavour of a later masterpiece, but in Schönberg's case the smell that detaches itself from his early *Lieder* is the familiar Teutonic aroma of stale pot-pourri prevented from leaving the room by the heavy curtains and double windows. These songs belong essentially to the 'nineties and in that, rather than in any intrinsic merit, lies their interest for the student of Schönberg. The fin-de-siècle quality of these works is a constant factor in all Schönberg's music—at least up to the war—and the more advanced and revolutionary his methods become, the greater is our sense of the spiritual conflict between his subjective and sentimental vision and his objective and mathematical technique.

If, while admitting the superficial contrast between Schönberg's earlier and later works, we examine their technique in more detail, we find that Schönberg, although sabotaging the conventional tonal sense of German romanticism, has in many ways retained its general texture and rhythm. Although it may seem a far cry from Schumann's *Frauenliebe und Leben* to Schönberg's nightmare *Herzgewachse*, there is no denying a certain resemblance in shape between Schönberg's melodies and those of the romanticists. The rhythm is the same and the placing of the wider intervals is the same. A typical Schönberg phrase bears far more re-semblance to the preludes to the first act of *Tristan* or the third act of *Parsifal* than it does to the work of any more recent composer. It is this that makes so much of his music disturbing to listen to, and gives it a curious flavour of morbidity that reaches its climax in the operas.

Music does not strike us as abnormal unless at the same time it recalls the normal—as in Strauss's *Salome* and

Elektra. We can listen to Bartók's *Amazing Mandarin* without a qualm, for we accept the composer's statements directly without referring them back to conventional experience. We do not feel that we are listening to Liszt or Dvořák 'gone wrong'. But in many of Schönberg's transitional works we do emphatically feel that we are listening to Schumann and Wagner 'gone wrong'. To hear a performance of the *Kammer Symphonie*, for example, is as disquieting an experience as meeting a respected family friend in a state of half-maudlin, half-truculent intoxication. Even in *Pierrot Lunaire*, one of the masterpieces of our time, there is a slight touch of a *Lieder* recital that has taken the wrong turning. Yet *Pierrot Lunaire* undoubtedly owes its force to the curious conflict of outlook and method. It is like an explosive formed out of two elements that in themselves are anodyne, and only develop their disruptive power when mixed in precisely the right proportions. In many of the earlier works the emotional force has not received the definition given by the technique, while in too many of the later works the technique is unleavened by any emotional force.

To find a parallel to Schönberg's amazing technical virtuosity, his exasperated sensibility and his strange half-mathematical, half-sentimental outlook, we have to turn to literature, where James Joyce provides an example of a remarkably similar mentality proceeding through much the same phases of thought and technique. The work of each, taken up to date, divides itself into the usual textbook 'three periods'. Joyce's weakly sentimental *Chamber Music* and dully realistic *Dubliners* are a parallel to the stodgy and academic imagination of *Verklärte Nacht*, and Schönberg's early work in general. In the *Portrait of the Artist as a Young Man* Joyce is beinning to find himself in much the way that Schönberg develops his personality in his settings of Stefan George. The revolutionary and monumental *Ulysses* may be compared to *Pierrot Lunaire* and the other works of Schönberg's middle period, while the intellectual juggling of *Work in Progress* is the equivalent of the cerebral counter-point of Schönberg's post-war compositions.

The quality which is most obviously common to both writers is the faded romanticism of their early work. With Schönberg it takes the form of a rather stuffy Teutonic nostalgia; with Joyce a mild and watery variation on themes from the 'nineties seen through Celtic eyes. Both writers are in fact born sentimentalists—however much their technical harshness, Schönberg's 'daring' discords or Joyce's 'daring' frankness, may seem to deny this. The ex-treme feminine emotional sensibility shown by their first works combined with their inquiring, mathematical and de-tached intellect is partly responsible for the violence of their subsequent revolution. Their intellect almost seems to have dragged them where their emotions alone would have turned away in disgust.

There is no Rabelaisian enjoyment about the obscenities in *Ulysses* and no primitive delight in noise and harshness about the operas of Schönberg—which provide a parallel to the nightmare fantasia in *Ulysses*. There runs through the work of both a curious neurasthenic horror which is partly a relic of the old Edgar Allan Poe cum Aubrey Beardsley spirit but mainly, one feels, the horror of an oversensitive artistic mind disgusted with life, yet too intellectually honest to turn away from it into a sentimental dream world of its own. Both writers express their warped romanticism in forms of the utmost complexity, but here again one may detect a sense of withdrawal as of a man so shy that he is unable to write a love letter except in the form of a cross-word puzzle.

In their later work, such as Joyce's *Anna Livia Plurabelle* and Schönberg's post-war piano pieces, the crossword-puzzle technique gains the upper hand of the romanticism it once expressed. What, however, may be acceptable as a vehicle of expression may not be so as a purely detached essay in technique. Both Schönberg and Joyce, unable to achieve anything of importance with the accepted vocabulary, forged for themselves a highly revolutionary technique in an obviously sincere attempt to express their own particular cast of mind. But to the reader and listener the interest lay not so much in their method itself as in its power to convey new meanings and sensations. The Schönberg method unaccompanied by the morbid fire of his best works is frankly dull and pedantic, as his followers have only too convincingly shown. Its monotonous inversions and mathematical contortions of ordinary procedure are as academic as the worst Kapellmeister music of the old school. (Most imitators of Schönberg belong to the type who, in an earlier generation, would have been followers of Max Reger.)

Atonalism as a school of thought and as a formulated set of principles has, as might be expected, centred round those works of Schönberg where the musical interest is at its lowest and the mathematical complexity at its most acute— namely, those works which come in between *Pierrot Lunaire* and his recent *Orchestral Variations*. In this period the devices which were occasionally present in *Pierrot Lunaire* as a means to an end are now treated as the be-all and end-all of music. Schönberg's innate romanticism is suppressed as far as possible and mechanically applied contrapuntal conceits are multiplied in number to an extent that is frankly ludicrous. It need hardly be pointed out that a contrapuntal device has no more intrinsic value than an unsuccessful pun if it is not recognizable by the ear alone. It may be a convenient method of filling in a blank patch, but it can hardly claim to have, prima facie, any real significance as sound. The ear must be the final judge—not the eye.

Escape or Submission

People are apt to forget that the score of a work is not the work itself, but a convenient visual representation of it that enables the band parts to be copied and the conductor to study it. The widespread publication of scores as an aid to the student has led to visual conception being confused with aural execution. A piece of music is not like a poem which can be listened to as a whole, or read word by word; it has no real existence save in actual performance at the proper speed. A man trained in reading scores can gain an excellent idea of the resultant effect from the printed page, just as a chef can see from looking at a recipe whether a dish will be palatable or not—but the actual process of listening or eating is what really matters.

Music consists not of symbols in space, but of definite vibrations in time. The innumerable inversions, augmentations, diminutions and crabwise canons of Schönberg's later works can, for the most part, be detected only by the visual analyst with time to spare. That a work is capable of elaborate analysis proves nothing, for a bad work may be just as interesting from the analyst's point of view as a good one. It is quite amusing, for example, to discover in the introduction to Schönberg's *Variations* that one instrument is playing the notes B-A-C-H very slowly while another is playing them backwards at four time the speed, but such tricks in no way effect the ultimate value of the work. They are *au fond* as childish as the hidden rivers and prep school puns that adorn Joyce's *Anna Livia Plurabelle*.

There is, of course, no reason why these devices should not be used, provided they are not allowed to usurp the place of genuinely significant material. Schönberg's contrapuntal writing varies in quality as much as Bach's fugues: at times it is worthy to be set beside the more introspective of the '48', while at others it sinks below the level of the Mirror fugues in the *Kunst der Fuge*—which, being visually conceived, are, apart from their more agreeable consonance, open to precisely the same objections as Schönberg's crabwise canons. We must distinguish between the occasional and expressive counterpoint in *Pierrot Lunaire* and the contrapuntal obsessions of the wind quintet.

Because since his Op. 10, or thereabouts, Schönberg's work has been consistently atonal, we are apt to think of it as a consistent and logical development, forgetting that his post-war works represent almost as great a reaction from his pre-war works as do Stravinsky's post-war concertos from his pre-war ballets. In Stravinsky's case the reaction was spectacular because, his pre-war technique being based in barbaric impressionism, he had to adopt an entirely new paraphernalia of sound to achieve a neo-classical result. Schönberg's pre-war works were, as I have pointed out in the opening chapter, impressionist, also, but they were impressionist in spite of themselves. Their technique, viewed on paper at least, was often cold and scientific; and therefore by lowering, if not eliminating, the subjective content of his works and by emphasizing their contrapuntal construction, Schönberg achieved the objective and anti-romantic ideal of the post-war movement without the dislocation of outward style that Stravinsky found necessary.

Had Schönberg not written his *Orchestral Variations* one would be tempted to look upon him as yet another modern composer who, through self-conscious theorizing and over-concentration on the objective side of technique, had reached a premature and desiccated senility. But his *Variations* represent a return, if not to the freedom of method of his earlier work, at least to its freedom of outlook. It is significant that it is Schönberg's first work for full orchestra since the works of his middle period; its scoring is more contrapuntal, but still has a definite pointillism which—particularly in variations 6 and 7—emphasizes its connection with his early works. Though it would be absurd to describe it as being either popular or eclectic, it marks a definite break away from the narrow range of ideas and mathematical self-concentration of Schönberg's post-war period. In spite of the acrostics on the name Bach, the introduction is definitely atmospheric in colour; while in spite of its mathematical inversions, the theme itself is purely romantic in feeling.

Just as Joyce in order to bring *Anna Livia Plurabelle* to a climax has to drop his philological wisecracks and relapse into the frank Negro-spiritual sentimentality of 'Beside the rivering waters of, hither and thithering waters of', so Schönberg, in order to achieve a work of importance, has to return—though in a less neurasthenic and more solidly constructive spirit—to the romanticism of *Pierrot Lunaire*. It is interesting to compare the *Variations* with Schönberg's only other purely orchestral work, the *Five Pieces for Orchestra*. In both cases the final section is the least convincing, and it would seem that Schönberg, in spite of his technical dexterity, is unable to build up a symphonic structure that will satisfy not only our appreciation of incidental formalism but our sense of organic form. The romantic nature of his art is emphasized by the fact that his two most satisfactory finales, those of *Pierrot Lunaire* and the second string quartet, are both of them settings of poems.

One likes to think that just as the *Five Pieces* paved the way for *Pierrot Lunaire* so the *Variations* are paving the way for a second masterpiece of similar calibre. Even if this be not the case, the *Variations* remain among the most outstanding works written since the war and are undoubtedly the most important music Schönberg has written for twenty years. For whereas the post-war piano suites might have been written by any of Schönberg's followers, the *Variations* could only have been written by the master himself.

Of Schönberg's pupils and followers by far the most significant is Alban Berg. With the others one feels that they have taken over Schönberg's methods without in any way sharing the spiritual experience that produced them—but with Berg we feel we are dealing with a very similar type of romantic mentality to whom atonalism has become a natural background. It would not be too much to say that Berg's recent works are far more worthy and genuine successors to Schönberg's pre-war works than Schönberg's later works themselves; for we find in them the same sombre imagination, the same nervous feeling for orchestral colour, the same paradoxical combination of intellectual method and physical result. Thus, in the *allegro-misterioso* movement of the *Lyric Suite* an examination on paper reveals a mathematical series of inversions, but in performance these inversions pass for nothing and what chiefly impresses us is the nervous and impressionistic physical effect—an effect which cannot be imagined from a visual examination alone. Similarly, the opera *Wozzeck* is on paper a soberly planned symphony, but in performance a 'thriller' of the most theatrical order.

Although in some of his works, notably the uninviting but undeniably impressive Double Concerto for violin, piano, and wind instruments, Berg is *plus royaliste que le roi* —he cannot be described as a wholehogging atonalist. Much of *Wozzeck* is definitely tonal, and although the greater part of the *Lyric Suite* is technically speaking atonal, the compromise Berg effects with *pur-sang* atonalism may be judged by the fact that he introduces two bars from the prelude to *Tristan* without any real dislocation of style. The whole work, as its title suggests, is no typical post-war piece of warped romanticism but an example of genuine lyricism which, though in no way derivative, is worthy to be put beside the work of Wagner from which it quotes. Of all atonal works it is the most readily acceptable to those who find initial difficulty in appreciating this idiom, and its reception by the amateur public has, on the whole, been far more friendly than its reception by the professional critics. Although written after the Double Concerto, the distance between the two, one year only, is not sufficient for us to draw deductions as to future tendencies. It may be noticed, though, that the relapse from strict atonalism which we find in Berg's *Lyric Suite* is partially echoed in Schönberg's recent *Variations*. Berg may now be almost considered the spiritual leader of the two, and the direction his work takes in the next few years cannot fail to be indicative of far-reaching future developments.

A typical individualist and romantic, making no compromise with his audience, writing at rare intervals works for his own satisfaction, Berg is yet the only atonal composer who is in any way in touch with the general public, having achieved with his opera *Wozzeck* a far greater success than is usually vouchsafed to the musical 'extremists'. Unfortunately the great part of his public was confined to Germany, where the atonal school was favourably received for two reasons: consciously, because technically speaking it sabotaged the moribund romantic tradition; and unconsciously, because it was emotionally linked to it. In Vienna, its own home town, atonalism is a small and detested cult; in Paris its appreciation is restricted to a few; and though in London Schönberg's works have had since pre-war days a sympathetic following, the sympathy has, on the whole, been more respectful than enthusiastic.

However much one may have disliked the almost political prejudice in favour of a revolutionary idiom that marked pre-Hitlerite Germany, in consequence of which many thirdrate figures achieved a momentary notoriety due to their idiom only, there is no doubt that this revolutionary atmosphere enabled a few composers of genuine merit to obtain that actual hearing without which a composer may be compared to an airman flying blind. Since the advent of Hitlerism, however, music of the Alban Berg type has been completely banished. Even in the case of an atonal composer who was neither a Jew nor a Communist, his music would be banned on the grounds of idiom alone, such sounds being officially classed as 'intellectual Bolshevism'.

Were there to be a Communist counter-revolution in Germany—and more unlikely things have happened—no doubt atonalism, though hardly a popular idiom, would be encouraged on the grounds of its 'revolutionary' label, much as Prokofieff, that completely bourgeois figure, received the official blessing of the Soviet; but until that day Schönberg and Berg are cut off from the greater part of their already small audience, with only a precarious chance of obtaining a foothold in England or America. However much we may deplore the writing-to-order Gebrauchsmusik attitude of Hindemith, it is difficult to imagine how any but the most exceptional figure can go on writing for a non-existent audience. It will be interesting to see whether Berg in face of this situation will proudly concentrate on the most extreme aspects of his style, eventually becoming a remote and romantic legend—Berg, or the last of the Atonalists—or whether he will adopt a more eclectic and less outré manner, establishing that contact with his audience which, in spite of initial prejudice, all the great composers of the past have eventually established and which a composer like Sibelius appears to be establishing today.

(c) Sibelius and the Integration of Form

Sibelius differs from all the other composers in this study in that it is impossible to attach any 'label' to him. He is the only composer of today who enjoys both a popular and an intellectual esteem. His *Valse Triste* is as widely known and as vulgarized as anything by Puccini, yet his Fourth Symphony is as little known and as little comprehended as the work of Schönberg. Although already established as an important figure by the end of the nineteenth century, he does not strike us as belonging to the older generation of Elgar and Strauss. On the contrary, he is the only modern composer who has maintained a steady and logical progress, being forced neither into a mechanical repetition of his own mannerisms nor into an equally mechanical reaction against them. It is only recently indeed that he has been estimated at anything like his true worth.

The reasons for this tardy appreciation are of two kinds. To begin with, though Sibelius's popular works have kept his name before the general public they have created a prejudice amongst the 'snob' public which has so regrettably powerful an influence. It is still necessary when talking to a certain type of person to explain that when you refer to Sibelius as a great composer you are not thinking of *Valse Triste*—which is as though when praising Beethoven you had to say 'but not of course the *Minuet in G*, or the March from *The Ruins of Athens*'. *Finlandia*, though a better work than *Valse Triste*, has had an even more regrettable effect on the public. The pleasantly Nordic nationalism of this work has led many people into believing Sibelius to be no more than a local petit maître, a Finnish Grieg. As late as 1933 we find Mr. W. J. Turner actually describing *Tapiola* as 'neo-Grieg', although this work, even to those who may dislike its poetic atmosphere, gives clear evidence of a constructive ability and continuity which is unparalleled within the last fifty years.

There is no conceivable reason from the artistic point of view why a great composer should not write works like

Sibelius and the Integration of Form

Finlandia, the *Karelia March* and even *Valse Triste*—which are all excellent examples of their genre. The great composers of the past have never been afraid to come down to earth, and their ability to do so on occasion is a certain negative tribute to their integrity and spiritual force, which is of too solid a nature to be shattered by a brush with the man in the street. It is better for the commonplace to be definitely segregated into a separate genre, as in the case of Sibelius, than for it to be a subtle but all-pervading aroma, as in the case of Richard Strauss.

But from the outside point of view the result in Sibelius's case has been peculiarly unfortunate—I am speaking now of the years before the recent and gratifying interest in his music. On the rare occasions when an important work of his was performed, the highbrow public stayed away and the lowbrow public, drawn there through memories of *Finlandia* and *Valse Triste*, were frankly nonplussed. Confusion was still worse confounded by a certain number of works that were neither potboilers nor works of individual genius, but honest Kapellmeister achievement, and when we consider that these three types of work do not represent any chronological development, but are found existing side by side from his earliest period up to the present day, it is scarcely surprising that until recently critics have been inclined to sit on the fence, particularly those who have been propagandists of the more revolutionary schools of writing.

Even if Sibelius, instead of being an all-embracing and protean figure, had concentrated only on the production of his greatest and most personal works—namely, the seven symphonies, and the symphonic poems, *A Saga, The Bard, The Oceanides,* and *Tapiola*—it is doubtful if opinion among the more advanced critics would have been more decided.

Let us take, for example, the case of Sibelius's Fourth Symphony in A Minor Op. 63 which, written in 1912, may be considered the highest point reached by Sibelius before the war. This Symphony, although in every way as remarkable and challenging a work as the famous 'spot' pieces of Debussy, Stravinsky and Schönberg that were studied in the first chapter of this book, seems to have made singularly little impact on the consciousness of the time, and even today it remains among the least comprehended and most neglected of his works. The reason is that it obstinately refuses to be fitted into any category, ancient or modern.

To start with it is a symphony written at the time when all revolutionary composers were turning their backs on any title that smacked of the conservatoire. Yet it in no way satisfies the conservatives by carrying on the older tradition of the Brahms or Tchaikovsky school of symphonic writing. The harmonic idiom, with its occasional touches of polytonality, is at times sufficiently disturbing to frighten off the academic critic without being sufficiently outré, or specialized in manner, to attract the attention of the revolutionary propagandist. The restrained and economical orchestration, though of the utmost originality, is lacking entirely in the refined sensuality of Debussy and Ravel, the opulent vulgarity of Strauss and Scriabin, or the barbaric glitter of Stravinsky. The work as a whole is notable for its tragic intensity of mood, its grim austerity of colour and its elliptical compactness of form, qualities at no time very popular with the multitude, and in 1912, the period when it was written, definitely out of fashion with the so-called advanced composers.

Like all great works, it does not lend itself to superficial analysis or specialized comment. It is a sign of weakness in a composer's make-up when our attention is inevitably directed towards one particular facet of his music—Delius's harmony, Stravinsky's rhythm, etc. We do not say of Mozart's *Prague Symphony*: 'What interesting rhythm, what delightful scoring, what sense of counterpoint', although, of course, we should be right in saying so. We say simply and dully: 'What a great symphony'. So it is with Sibelius; his music is three-dimensional and, as with a good piece of sculpture, although we may choose to focus our attention on one particular silhouette, the work is equally satisfactory when viewed from any angle.

The only quality which stands out with such distinctness that it can be used as a handle by the superficial commentator is Sibelius's sense of orchestration. Unlike so much modern scoring, which is directed mainly towards the exploitation of the most acute and acidulated timbres of the wind instruments to the detriment of string writing, Sibelius's scoring is marked by an intense realization of the un-explored possibilities of string colour, while the neglected lower registers of the orchestra are treated with great virtu-osity, his use of independent harmonic parts on double-basses and tympani being particularly striking.

His orchestral requirements rarely exceed those of the Tchaikovsky orchestra, and even this orchestra is used in his later works with unwonted restraint. But though his use of the brass is sparing, concentrating far more on its sos-tenuto than on its percussive qualities, and making no use of the fashionable muted effects, there is no one who can build up a more overwhelming climax when he so desires. The last five minutes of *Tapiola* is a revelation of the effect that can be obtained by essentially normal and legi-timate means. The climaxes of Scriabin's *Poème de l'Extase* are angry waves beating vainly at the breakwater of our intelligence—the climaxes of *Tapiola* and *The Oceanides* are a rising flood that carries all before it. Sibelius for all his restraint is the greatest orchestral innovator of our time. The scoring of almost all other modern composers can be traced back to one or other of those two great innovators,

Berlioz and Glinka. Strauss, making allowances for a certain Teutonic thickness of texture, may be considered the successor of Berlioz, while Stravinsky is the successor of Glinka; the scoring of Stravinsky's ballets, admittedly of the utmost brilliance, is a direct continuation of the tradition begun by Chernomor's March and the Caucasian Leszginka in *Russlan*. In his search for ever more brilliant and pungent tones, Stravinsky was led away from the clear colours of Rimsky-Korsakoff's orchestration to a gradual distortion of the natural timbres of each instrument, so that it is rarely that a player is given a passage to be played in the ordinary manner in the ordinary register. This persistent use of extreme colouring eventually becomes as monotonous in its way as the drab shades and muddy impasto of Brahms. The principal objection to Stravinsky's scoring lies not so much in its monotonous eccentricity as in the fact that it is essentially applied scoring; it is quite possible to conceive several different and equally effective ways of orchestrating any given passage in Stravinsky, just as it is possible to detach Stravinsky's methods from their contents and apply Stravinsky's scoring to any piece of music. Like everything else in his music, it is two-dimensional, and bears much the same relation to Sibelius's scoring as Gauguin's colour does to that of Cézanne.

Like the colour in a Cézanne landscape, Sibelius's orchestration is an integral part of the form. One might almost describe it as having a kind of aural perspective, supplying a contrapuntal element that is sometimes lacking in the music itself. Just as in the polyphonic period a vertical section taken through the counterpoint often reveals harmonic combinations more remarkable than any to be found in the Monteverdi school of writers, so in Sibelius's symphonies a vertical section taken through the orchestration often reveals a spacing of instruments more remarkable than anything to be found in the impressionist school. But, as in the case of the polyphonic writers, this point of colour is the result of a logical development of independent lines. It cannot be detached from its context, and for this reason Sibelius's scoring does not lend itself to plagiarism as do Delius's harmony or Stravinsky's rhythm.

If I have concentrated on what may seem a superficial aspect of Sibelius's genius, it is to show that even in the case of an often purely external quality like orchestration his technique is always a means to an end, and is never deployed for its own sake. Whatever aspect of his music we may look at, our attention is finally drawn towards his astonishing sense of form. The word form has been so degraded by the 'pure music' school of critics that perhaps it would be better to say power of sustained musical thinking.

Whereas most modern music is concerned mainly with vocabulary, Sibelius is concerned with content; he has not, like so many contemporary composers, been forced to adopt an outré manner in a vain attempt to disguise the commonplace character of his thought. The quarter-tone quartets of Aloys Haba, for example, differ from the quartets of Brahms only through being written in the quarter-tone scale. Once we have assimilated their somewhat uninviting sounds, we find ourselves back in the old world of thought and form. Sibelius's symphonies rarely contain any chords which, examined by themselves, cannot be found in the works of Grieg or Tchaikovsky. Yet through the manner of their presentation these chords are made to take on an entirely new meaning. Their importance is due, not to their momentary sound in space, but to their placing in time.

This power of sustained concentrated thought over a long period of time gives to Sibelius's works a spaciousness which is in striking contrast to the shortwindedness of even the best 'revolutionary music', and for a parallel to which we must go back beyond even Wagner to the first movements of the *Eroica* and *Choral* Symphonies. One is so used to being told that some trifling and shortwinded neo-classical pastiche represents a return to the spirit of Bach, that one is a little chary of evoking the shade of Beethoven where Sibelius is concerned; but the comparison is inevitable, for not only is Sibelius the most important symphonic writer since Beethoven, but he may even be described as the only writer since Beethoven who has definitely advanced what, after all, is the most complete formal expression of the musical spirit.

(d) The Symphonic Problem

However perfect we may consider the symphonies of Mozart to be, we must admit that the first movements of the third and ninth symphonies of Beethoven—to mention only two instances—represent a new scale of thought. Mozart may be more temperamentally sympathetic to us, but it is by the standard set by the greatest creations of Beethoven that any succeeding symphony must be judged. Standing at the threshold of the romantic movement, yet imbued with all the tradition of a classical upbringing, Beethoven gave to the symphony a new richness of expression and yet achieved a balance between expression and form that has, except in one instance, never been equalled since. But his symphonies carry with them the seeds of destruction. By giving to his themes a greater emotional content and a more contrasted individuality than we find in the symphonies of the eighteenth century he raised the problem—always present in the symphony but never stated so acutely before—of the clash between emotional and formal balance.

The element of formal balance provided by the recapitulation that is an integral part of sonata form is one of the greatest stumbling blocks to a sensitive composer—for although he is dealing with time in the abstract he has to express himself with time in the concrete. We know from his letters that Mozart conceived his symphonies in a moment of time, that is to say from his point of view the recapitulation did not necessarily come after the development, but that does not alter the fact that the audience will have to hear them in that order. The composer's mind must to some extent resemble that of the scientist who can conceive time according to the theories of Einstein and Dunne, whereas the listener probably shares the mentality of those who conceive time as symbolized by the clock face. The composer may see the whole design at once, as in a framed picture, but the listener can only appreciate it as if being shown a long Chinese picture on rollers, of which only a fragment is visible at one moment. He will be conscious of the repetitions as such, and whether these repetitions— admittedly necessary in one form or another for reasons of balance—strike him as being redundant and tautological depends not only on the quality but on the nature of the music.

Repetitions that are charming in Haydn become wearisome in Tchaikovsky, but we should not jump to the conclusion that the cause lies only in Tchaikovsky's inferiority as a composer. The repetitions in Tchaikovsky are wearisome because a definite emotional reaction is attached to the different themes as they occur, whereas in Haydn or Mozart our emotional reaction is derived from the movement as a whole. The nineteenth century added to sonata form the element of dramatic contrast, or surprise.

Mr. Milestone, in Peacock's *Headlong Hall*, when told that the principal quality in a landscape garden was that of *unexpectedness* said: 'Pray sir, by what name do you distinguish this character when a person walks round the grounds for a second time?' His remark admirably sums up the difficulty of writing a romantic work in classical form, for in the sonata we are willy nilly taken round or led up the garden for a second time.

In a formal Italian garden (to which we may compare the eighteenth-century symphony) it is not only excusable but desirable that one grove of trees should balance another, that the beds should be placed symmetrically; but in an English landscape garden—to which we may compare the nineteenth-century romantic movement—the sinister effect of an overshadowed ruin is completely spoiled if it occurs every hundred yards.

Beethoven marks the transition from formal to landscape gardening. It is to the influence of the C Minor Symphony that we owe the 'masculine' first subject, the 'feminine' second subject, and also the deplorable school of romantic analysts from Sir George Grove to Dr. Hugo Leichtentritt. And it is to Beethoven also—or rather to his commentators —that we owe the conception of the artist as being alternately bludgeoned by Fate and consoled by Platonic Love, the Beauties of Nature and Ultimate Faith in a Beneficent Providence. This atmosphere of storm and stress is excellent material for music, provided it is not poured into the wrong mould. Unfortunately, the balanced repetitions of sonata form are a poor medium for emotional narrative—however suited they may be to emotional statement or summing up, as in the symphonies of Mozart. The nineteenth-century composers gave to their symphonic subjects a dramatic significance which was reduced to anticlimax by their adherence to a formal construction only suited to music of a totally different order of conception. Tchaikovsky's symphonies are wearing thin not so much because we are losing faith in his dramatic conception of Fate, as because he himself destroys this faith by bringing in Fate at such fixed and mechanical intervals.

The *Lamento e Trionfo*, the idea of the artist as hero winning through adversity to a glorious apotheosis, that lies behind so much of nineteenth-century romanticism, is a conception wholly suited to musical expression, but not to that branch of it known as symphonic writing. Liszt, with his unerring though unrecognized instinct for form, was the first to realize this and evolved the symphonic poem, the nineteenth-century form par excellence, and the logical development of the programme symphonies of Berlioz. The ascription of actual individuality to a recurrent or 'motto theme' and the attaching of symbolical significance to its later transformations, devices wholly at variance with the classic principles of symphonic form, are here perfectly justified, and in his thirteen symphonic poems Liszt achieves a unity of expression and form which may be sought for in vain in the symphonies of the period.

Although chronologically speaking one might have expected the symphony to develop during the nineteenth century, we have only to look at the spiritual foundations of the period to realize why it did not. The two fertilizing sources of inspiration during the nineteenth century were romanticism and nationalism. Nationalism, as we have seen, is antagonistic to formal construction—*Thamar*, the one formal masterpiece of the Russian school, is romantic rather than nationalist—and while romanticism is not specifically anti-formal it is specifically anti-symphonic. For that reason the formal progress of nineteenth-century music is to be judged not by the pale repetitions of classic form to be found in the symphonies of Mendelssohn, Schumann, and Brahms, but by the symphonic poems of Liszt and the operas of Wagner which, as Mr. Newman has rightly pointed out, may be considered symphonic poems on a vast scale.

Escape or Submission

One might almost say that the only good romantic symphonies are not, strictly speaking, symphonies at all, for the *Fantastique* of Berlioz, in spite of its classical first movement, marks a transition towards the symphonic poem established in Liszt's great *Faust* symphony, which in reality is three interlinked symphonic poems of which the first happens to be based on sonata form. Even in Tchaikovsky's case the *Manfred* symphony, which belongs to the Berlioz-Liszt school, shows more organic unity than his pseudo-classical symphonies.

The classical symphony in the nineteenth century, far from marking a development of the Beethoven tradition, marks a definite decline. On the credit side there are Borodin's symphonies, genial works which continue the Haydn rather than the Beethoven tradition, and the symphonies of Brahms, which, though entirely lacking in the germinating vitality of Beethoven, command at least our respect. But for the typical nineteenth-century symphony as represented by Tchaikovsky *No. 5*, Dvořák's *From the New World*, and César Franck in D Minor, there is frankly nothing to be said; their mingling of academic procedure with undigested nationalism or maudlin sentiment, or both, produces a chimerical monster, a musical Minotaur that fortunately has had no progeny.

The decline of the symphony from 1820 to 1900 is more spectacular than its advance from 1800 to 1820. By the opening of this century the symphony as a form was completely moribund. So also was the romantic movement, and it might have been thought that the decline of romanticism would have marked a return to the principles of the classical symphony; but the advent of impressionism with its disintegrating and anti-formal bias completed the process of corruption. (It is true that the English took to writing symphonies at a time when other nations were ceasing to do so;

but in view of the peculiar hiatus in English musical history this may be looked on as a making up for lost time rather than as a contemporary gesture. The symphonies of Bax, though technically speaking of our day, belong spiritually to the nineteenth century and suffer from the same inherent disadvantages as the romantic symphonies. It is doubtful whether future critics will consider them as important as his symphonic poems, any more than they will place Elgar *No. I* beside *Falstaff* and the *Enigma Variations* or Vaughan Williams's *London Symphony* beside *Flos Campi* and *Job*.)

The great revolutionary figures of before the war, Debussy, Stravinsky, Schönberg and Bartók, turned their back on the symphony and all that it stood for, and a pre-war critic, ignorant of Sibelius's work, might pardonably have thought that the symphony was as outmoded and antediluvian as the horse bus.

In Sibelius, however, we have the first great composer since Beethoven whose mind thinks naturally in terms of symphonic form. Coming at the end of the romantic movement, he is as far removed from the apex of the romantic past as Beethoven was from its future. His symphonies, then, though subjective in mood, are free from the tautological emotional repetitions of romantic music cast in the classic mould. Though their grim colouring clearly owes much to the composer's nationality and surrounding there is nothing in them that can be considered a folk song. Therefore, without being eclectic they address an international audience and are free from the conflict between local colour and construction which is to be observed in the Russian school. Finally, Sibelius is the one important figure of our times who has been uninfluenced by the Impressionist revolution —even *The Oceanides* though pointillist in orchestration and superficially Impressionist in form reveals on close analysis a construction as firmly knit as any of the symphonies. He has concentrated on the integration of form and has not wasted his energies on the disintegration of colour.

This formal strength explains why, unlike all other composers who belong equally to the pre-war and post-war periods of modern music, Sibelius's work does not split itself into two periods, and shows no sign of the definite reaction that we associate with the last ten years. One soon reaches the end to the possible dissection of technique and elaboration of vocabulary. This end was reached for all practical purposes in 1913, and since then the revolutionary composers having pulled the cloth to pieces and being mentally incapable of putting it together again have taken to arranging the wheels and levers in neat little patterns.

Formalism is only the complementary reaction to formlessness, and montage follows naturally enough on disruption. But a sense of musical form, the power not only to arrange sounds tastefully but to think in them vitally, is a living and generative force which reaches no such dead end, and Sibelius's symphonies in consequence show a steady and logical process both formally and emotionally. The Olympian calm of *No. 7* may seem in contrast to the bitter and tragic quality of *No. 4*, but technically speaking it is the logical result of the process of concentration and integration that is to be observed from the second symphony onwards.

The first symphony hardly comes into a book on contemporary music. This opulently scored and virile work is the final flowering of the later nineteenth-century symphony, and though an excellent example of its genre it is constructed for the most part on recognized lines. Not until the second symphony are we faced with Sibelius's highly individual method of formal construction. The first movement of Sibelius's *No. 2* differs from any previous symphonic movement in that its undoubted continuity and formal balance are not established until the last bars. The exposition of a

Beethoven symphony is by no means a complete statement, but it is logical enough as far as it goes. The exposition of this particular movement, a string of apparently loosely knit episodes, is completely incomprehensible at a first hearing, and it is only towards the end of the development and in the curiously telescoped recapitulation that the full significance of the opening begins to be apparent. Instead of being presented with a fait accompli of a theme that is then analysed and developed in fragments, we are presented with several enigmatic fragments that only become a fait accompli on the final page. It is like watching a sculptured head being built up from the armature with little pellets of clay or, to put it more vulgarly, it is like a detective story in which the reader does not know until the final chapter whether the blotting paper or the ashtray throws more light on the discovery of the corpse in the library.

This individual formal outlook is not to be found in the rest of the symphony. The second movement is finely and broadly planned, but apart from the sinister outbursts in the bass, which convey a curious sense of frustration, it offers us no problem; the last two movements though full of vigorous material are disappointingly conventional in form and hark back to the outlook of the first symphony.

The third symphony, though enjoyable, is a rather transitional work. The first movement, clearly analysable according to the accepted principles of sonata form, is, though more compact, less individual in method than the similar movement in *No. 2*. The second movement foreshadows and in some respect excels that of *No. 5*, in the way a seemingly monotonous repetition of a monotonous theme is made to yield an astonishing variety of feeling and colour. It is in the third movement that we find the continuation of the formal integration begun in the first movement of *No. 2*. A distorted wisp of melody from the slow movement leads to a sombrelycoloured but capricious scherzo in which short thematic fragments are swept aside by the obstinate rhythmic figures on the strings. It is only gradually that these fragments resolve themselves into the broad chorale-like tune, so typical of Sibelius in its apparent commonplace and actual distinction, which dominates the symphony with increasing power until the final bars. All the elements of the last two movements in a Beethoven symphony are here, but instead of these elements being marshalled into opposed and regular military formation they proceed naturally one from the other and, once formulated, are thrown aside. We seem to have been unseen spectators of the artist at work rather than guests at a private view.

The formal concentration of the last movement of the third symphony prepares us for the astonishing conciseness of the great A Minor Symphony, even if its comparatively cheerful mood is in the utmost contrast to the bitter and gloomy note that is apparent in every bar of its successor. In the fourth symphony the classical four-movement form is reduced to its bare bones. Conventional repetition and development are reduced to a minimum, but the evocative significance of the themes is so great that in some instances, notably at the end of the scherzo, the most fragmentary reference to a previous theme is sufficient to restore our sense of formal balance. For grave beauty of sound the slow movement is unsurpassed in modern music, even by Sibelius himself, and the deceptively carefree opening of the finale is evidently planned as a temporary relief from its weight of introspection. The comparatively spacious lines of the last movement faintly recall Sibelius's earlier symphonies, but the astounding coda recalls nothing that has been written before or since, even if its almost unbearable spiritual and technical concentration may be held to form a modern parallel to the posthumous quartets of Beethoven.

The Symphonic Problem

It is curious how certain critics, more noteworthy for geographical knowledge than for nervous sensibility, have ascribed the undoubted coldness of this work to the inclement climatic conditions that prevail in Sibelius's home country. The chilly atmosphere of the fourth symphony is something more than a Christmas-card nip in the air: it is a bitter and heroic resignation of the spirit with nothing in it of external theatricality or maudlin emotionalism. The fourth symphony is the crowning work of Sibelius's middle period—it is to Sibelius what *Pierrot Lunaire* is to Schönberg, and like *Pierrot Lunaire* it only yields up all its secrets after close study. To maintain this standard is hardly to be expected of any man, and it cannot be held that the more popular *No. 5* is a work of equal significance. To develop in each individual movement the fining-down process to be observed in the fourth symphony was clearly impossible— if only for the reason that further compactness would have eliminated not only the inessentials but also the essentials.

The fifth symphony, with its imposing finale and heroic proportions, might at first sight seem to be a mature reversion to an earlier mood, and it may be described as the most obviously great of Sibelius's symphonies. Actually, though, it is not a backward step but a gradual approach to the one monumental movement of *No. 7*. The first movement consists of two interlinked sections of which the second, in the nature of a scherzo, is based to a large extent on the material of the sombre first section. The relation between the two sections is much closer than is the case in the finale of *No. 3*, and this fusion of the customary first movement and scherzo prepares us for the fusion of all four movements in the seventh symphony.

If *No. 5* is a technical foreshadowing of *No. 7*, the sixth symphony is a spiritual foreshadowing. In its four-movement form it may superficially be compared to the A Minor Symphony, but the different movements have none of the dramatic contrast we find in the earlier work, and are indeed less differentiated then the two interlinked sections of *No. 5*. In their continuity of mood and texture they do not look back to the tragic abruptness of *No. 4*, but to the spiritual calm and serene continuity of *No. 7*. Although at present this fascinating study in half-tones, emotional and orchestral, is overshadowed by the grandeur of *No. 5*, I feel that future commentators may find its intimate quality more indicative of the true Sibelius, just as many of us feel that Beethoven's fourth and eighth symphonies are more 'echt-Beethoven' than the popular odd-number symphonies.

The one-movement Symphony in C Major, *No. 7*, is a continuation—an elliptical summing up—of the intellectual and emotional content of the two preceding symphonies, combining the austere grandeur of the fifth with the subtle and elusive methods of the sixth, and in it Sibelius's art reaches its second great apex. It is impossible to convey on paper the magnificent formal sweep and emotional logic of this work, and only repeated hearings—fortunately the work is recorded—enable us to appreciate the perfection of its structure. Just as in the second symphony the group of contrasted themes at the opening is gradually resolved into one integral idea, so in this symphony the traditional group of contrasted movements is resolved into one continuous web of sound. This work seems not only to contain all the elements of the old type of four-movement symphony, but also to create a satisfactory synthesis of the various 'warring' forms of the last two centuries—the fugue, with its continuous development, the symphony, with its balanced sections, the symphonic poem, with its imaginative freedom.

Mr. Cecil Gray in his book on Sibelius—to which every subsequent writer must needs be indebted—has rightly pointed out its 'lofty grandeur and dignity, a truly Olympian serenity and repose which are unique in modern music'. One might qualify this statement by saying that is the only modern work whose repose has in it no hint of any lack of vitality, and whose classicism has in it no hint of pastiche. We should not confuse its Olympian serenity with the cold detachment of Stravinsky's *Apollo Musagetes* and its many neo-classical imitations. There is a repose which marks a final victory and a repose which marks an early defeat. Not everyone who renounces the world is a Buddha.

The symphonic poem *Tapiola* marks a totally different aspect of Sibelius's formal mastery. Unlike the symphonies, which reduce a contrasting series of fragment to one simple statement, *Tapiola* is an example of the wealth of variation and colour that can be obtained from a handful of notes. The work is entirely monothematic, and—although less rhetorical and more closely knit—should be regarded as a continuation of the formal principles first evolved by Liszt. More immediately attractive and picturesque than the later symphonies, it is a fine example of Sibelius's ability to propound the most complex statement in terms of absolute intelligibility. There is nothing in it to perplex the ordinary listener, yet to the technician it is a never-ending source of wonder.

The climax of this remarkable work is an apt symbol of Sibelius's art as a whole. Though in performance the effect is overwhelming, suggesting an orchestra of vast dimensions treated with the utmost elaboration, an examination on paper reveals nothing more than a chromatic tremolo on the strings and simple placing of a moderate-sized group of brass. Sibelius has not found it necessary to distort his medium; in a sudden moment of intense vision he has, like a Newton or an Einstein, revealed the electrifying possibilities that are latent in the apparently commonplace.

(e) Sibelius and the Music of the Future

If, in a book that for the most part has purposely avoided a point-to-point analysis of individual works, I have devoted so much space to Sibelius's symphonies, it is not only that I consider the fourth and seventh symphonies to be two of the most astonishing creative efforts of our time, but also because I feel that Sibelius's music contains the answer to so many of the questions, both direct and implied, that have been raised in this study.

Sibelius has always been a figure apart from the rest of modern music. The lack of revolutionary vocabulary in his music has in the past led superficial critics to believe that he was apart through being behind the times. Now that the smoke of bombs and gunfire has cleared away we can see that his solitary position is really due to his having been in advance of the anarchists. Although, chronologically speaking, of the same generation as Strauss and Elgar, he is of all living composers the most interesting and stimulating to the post-war generation. The pre-war revolutionaries have become victims to their own mannerisms, and any attempt to imitate them produces a pastiche of a pastiche. The succeeding generation, in spite of individually good works such as Milhaud's *Protée* and *La Création du Monde*, Prokofieff's third piano concerto and *L'Enfant Prodigue*, is curiously lacking in any sense of direction, oscillating disturbingly between the pretty-pretty and the ugly-ugly. Though technically mature, both Milhaud and Prokofieff seem to suffer from a permanent spiritual adolescence; one does not feel that their undoubted talent will ever reach a convincing fruition. The composers of a still younger generation are even less decided in outlook, ranging feverishly through the many movements and 'isms' that to some extent have been tabulated in this book.

Of all contemporary music that of Sibelius seems to point forward most surely to the future. Since the death of Debussy, Sibelius and Schönberg are the most significant figures in European music, and Sibelius is undoubtedly the more complete artist of the two. However much one may admire Schönberg's powerful imagination and unique genius, it is difficult not to feel that the world of sound and thought that he opens up—though apparently iconoclastic —is *au fond* as restricted as the academicism it has supplanted. Sibelius's music suffers from no such restriction, and it indicates not a particular avenue of escape but a world of thought which is free from the paralysing alternatives of escape or submission. It offers no material for the plagiarist, and is to be considered more as a spiritual example than as a technical influence. We are not likely to find any imitations of Sibelius's *No. 7*, such as we find of Stravinsky's *Symphonie des Psaumes*, because the spiritual calm of this work is the climax of the spiritual experience of a lifetime and cannot be achieved by any aping of external mannerisms.

Sibelius has had no direct influence on his generation, but if we compare the recent work of the revolutionary composers—Bartók's second Piano Concerto and Schönberg's *Orchestral Variations* for example—with that of ten years ago we can see that it represents an approach to the spirit of integration and artistic completeness that has always characterized his music. There are signs, too, that the most vital minds of the present generation are turning their back on both the disruption of the Impressionists and the montage or pastiche of the Neo-Classicists. Walton's Viola Concerto, one of the most thoughtful and sincerely conceived works of recent years, refuses to be put into any specific category from

277

the point of view either of technique or tendency. It is neither English nor cosmopolitan, neo-classic nor neo-romantic—it is that least sensational yet most satisfying of all things, a finished and well-balanced work of art.

No composer can surprise us now with sensational technical discoveries, nor are we content with self-expression that takes the form of a personal alembication of a family joke. The glamour of the anarchist and the mystery of the sphinx have begun to pall, and we are faced with the unenviable task of making constructive effort and plain statement appear interesting. The modern composer has now to consolidate the reckless and fascinating experiments of the pre-war pioneers while avoiding the dog-Latin classicism of the post-war pasticheurs. He must make a synthesis of the present varied elements with an emphasis on the one that has been most neglected, namely, form.

The task after all is not so impossible. While one soon reaches the physical limits of harmonic or rhythmic experiment, per se, there is no limit to the development of a complete musical statement in which every element is duly considered. To take the isolated case of harmonic experiment: it might seem that after Schönberg the only possible progress lay in the further subdivision of the scale. But the music of Bernard Van Dieren indicates other lines of development less sensational but no less far reaching. His earlier works, it is true—such as the piano sketches and the still unperformed *Chinese Symphony*—show signs of a Schönbergian ruthlessness, and it is surprising to see in his later work—such as the *Spenser Sonnet*—hardly any chord which, taken by itself, cannot be found in Wagner. In his later work, however, the chords are not used specifically as such, but are the result of a melodic counterpoint of fascinating complexity. The approach to each chord is so unusual that the most familiar combinations of notes take on an entirely new meaning. Van

Dieren's attitude towards harmony is more indicative of future developments than the 'note clusters' of Henry Cowell or the quarter-tones of Aloys Haba; it represents one facet of the general consolidation of technique with which the modern composer is faced.

There is nothing in music which has really lost its meaning, no device of rhythm, no harmonic combination which the composer of vision cannot reanimate.

The music of the future, if it is to avoid the many psychological cul-de-sacs which have been examined in this volume, must inevitably be directed towards a new angle of vision rather than to the exploitation of a new vocabulary. This music will not be outwardly sensational, and though at times it may seem extremely unusual it will not be of the type that can be labelled 'the new This' or 'the new That'. It will not truckle to topicality by pretending to be inspired by sporting events or by the opening of a wireless station, nor will it lose itself in a dream world of forgotten loves and vanished days. It is highly unlikely that it will be popular. But then we cannot pretend that the best music of any time was at all popular in the genuine sense of the word. Sibelius, it is true, has a popular following today but, like that of Beethoven, it is mainly a tribute to his worst works. His fourth symphony is as unappreciated now as were the later sonatas and quartets of Beethoven in their day. Nevertheless, just as the later quartets of Beethoven have influenced modern thought far more than the fashionable works of Hummel and Czerny, so will the symphonies of Sibelius have a more profound influence on future generations that the pièces d'occasion of his contemporaries— the composers like Stravinsky and Hindemith who have made their compromise with vogue.

I am not suggesting for a moment that the important composers of the future will imitate Sibelius's form, any more than they will imitate Van Dieren's harmony, but I am convinced that they will draw more inspiration from the solitary figures of present-day music than from the various petty movements which spring up every five years—and disappear as rapidly. For if their work is to have any but ephemeral value they will be solitary figures themselves.

The artist who is one of a group writes for that group alone, whereas the artist who expresses personal experience may in the end reach universal experience. He must not mind if for the moment he appears to be without an audience. He has no right to complain if Cleopatra prefers billiards. There is always the chance that she may become bored with billiards also, and when she returns to the musician his song will be all the more moving for having been written to please not her but himself.

INDEX

Index

Index

Index

Index

Index

Index